Supremacy and Subordination of Labour

Supremacy and Subordination of Labour

The Hierarchy of Work in the Early Labour Movement

Mike Holbrook-Jones

HEINEMANN EDUCATIONAL BOOKS · London

For my dad, for Gill, and in memory of my mother

Heinemann Educational Books Ltd
22 Bedford Square, London, WC1B 3HH
LONDON   EDINBURGH   MELBOURNE   AUCKLAND
HONG KONG   SINGAPORE   KUALA LUMPUR   NEW DELHI
IBADAN   NAIROBI   JOHANNESBURG
EXETER (NH)   KINGSTON   PORT OF SPAIN

British Library Cataloguing in Publication Data

Holbrook-Jones, Mike
   Supremacy and subordination of labour.
   1. Labor and laboring classes – Great Britain
   – History
   I. Title
   305.5'6   HD8390

   ISBN 0-435-82417-1

Typeset by Inforum Ltd, Portsmouth
Printed in Great Britain by Biddles Ltd,
Guildford, Surrey

Contents

Introduction

Industrial society, whatever its nomenclature, creates the historically unique problem of *control* at *work*. Whether this is resolved democratically or by fiat, it is, nonetheless, specific to a form of social organisation based upon the separation of labour from the home and the worker from legal obligations. Whilst the most obvious and spectacular manifestations catch the attention of the historian, that fiercest wrench from the past – the creation of labour discipline – receives much less consideration. Despite its importance it is, of course, less tangible than population growth, capital accumulation, inventions, parties, trade organisation and the other usual indices of industrial change. Theoretical pioneers in this area have examined the question in the reflection of another more 'factual' one: Hobsbawm in the effects of wage differentials and incentives (1976: 344–63), Thompson through the learning of the ritual of 'time' (1967: 55–97) and Pollard in the course of study of the rise of management as a conscious 'practice' (1968). Crucially all these investigations, worthy as they are, consider the historical period of enquiry as 1750 to 1850 or thereabouts. In its wake this assumption tends to focus the debate over the working-class response to industrialisation towards ideology (in the form of the printed historical legacy) or organisational structure (the lack, or corporate activity of, associations). From the formation of the first 'modern' trade union, the Amalgamated Society of Engineers, in 1851, its pronouncements and internal administration becomes a barometer of the degree of accommodation and acceptance by the labour movement as a whole.

Then comes the revision of the conclusions of this method: perhaps the Webbs' *History of Trade Unionism* overestimated the degree of passivity amongst Victorian workers? (Cole, 1962; Allen 1962; Clements, 1961.) One of the main implications of *this* book is that labour historiography needs a new set of *questions* before really significant strides can be taken in our understanding. Primarily this means a re-evaluation of the importance of the activity of work, the discipline it imposes, and the graduations of status and position engendered; in short the role of work as the prime mediator of the impact of capitalism.

With the publication of John Foster's *Class Struggle and the Industrial Revolution* in 1977 the debate over these 'new' questions has quickened. Foster presents his case as a development of classical Leninism, but in fact his use of the labour aristocracy thesis is poignantly 'revisionist'. Avoiding the crude equation of imperialism with bribery and betrayal, he firmly identifies the labour aristocracy with the use of sub-contracting and piecework, following the elimination of craft control, thereby the creation of a new form of capitalist social control, *now operating in the place of work itself rather than externally upon the labour community as a whole*. However, whilst his analysis of the decline of mass consciousness and activity, and the absorption of the leadership is meticulous, the account of the actual processes in work are cursory and localised (*ibid.*, 1976: 224–38). Furthermore, his attempt to link 'liberalisation' with capital export requires this shift in the economy to be dated to the 1840s – 30 years before Lenin.

Foster is quite right to insist upon both the connection of reformism with a wider overall change in the nature of English capitalism, and a restabilisation of the labour process on a new basis. But the central weakness of his case lies in the refusal to admit that the *location* of reformist is in the internal manufacturing relationships of capitalist industry. In the quest for the reconstruction of the experience of work and its role in the formation of consciousness, 'which comes first' is *not* crucial, that is, whether external forces of industrial change produced particular types of work organisation or, alternatively, whether these latter facilitated shifts in the economy. What has to be established is the actual progress of work in particular industries, the genealogy of types of industrial discipline and the aetiology of the consequent organisational form.

This book therefore intends to go beyond the questions discussed in the labour aristocracy debate, to the wider issues that the dispute has raised: the role of craft unionism, the internal hierarchies of work and the consequences that they may have for the ideology and structure of unionism in general. This emphasis is consistent with a view of the relationship between sociology and history which, whilst not new, is certainly not the orthodoxy. Put at its crudest, history is not conceived as 'fact-grubbing', nor sociology as 'fact-relating'. The quest for casuality is not, however, abandoned.

For example, I hope to show in the following pages that the social sub-division of the labour movement is as contradictory and uneven as is the development of the system of which it is part. The demonstration of this is *primarily* an empirical task, a validation of the theoretical concerns of the first three chapters. Another task of the early part of this book is the redefinition of the role and significance of craft unionism. I suggest that a 'craft' union is best thought of as an organisation employing a particular brand of social action to defend its interests, rather than embodying any 'certain' degree of skill. Again I hope to show empirically, in the actual history of work, the value of this perspective. Finally, an abiding concern of this book is the permeation of the incentive principle within the capitalist enterprise – the practical realisation of the 'Protestant work ethic'.

To do this I have chosen to examine three occupational groups – engineers, miners and spinners – from around 1830 to 1914. This is prefaced by a collation of the available material on the size, ownership and structure of each industry. They were chosen for two reasons: the first was purely practical – they are occupations of relatively clear boundaries with, for varying reasons, a reasonable amount of primary information surviving. The second rationale was quite conjectural – it seemed to me that they represented a spectrum of work experience in nineteenth-century Britain: the spinners, semi-skilled machine-minders dominated by factory mass production; the engineers, craft-workers, in greatly varying work situations constantly resisting the downgrading of their vocation; the miners, working in a community-based occupation where the work remained basically unchanged throughout the period. I do not claim they were typical, or a 'sample'; to begin with nearly all were male. But I do claim they were crucial to the formation of the labour movement, and to what we label, 'labourism' (Saville, 1973). I will leave the reader to assess the worth of this judgment.

I use the phrase 'work experience' to indicate my perspective, and it is best explained at the outset. Ordinary people leave behind them organisations, formal and informal, in history (from the horticultural society to the trade union), and it is only to be expected that labour history tends to concentrate on these institutional legacies: minutes survive better than memories. In order to reconstruct the experience of work in these industries I have, where possible, let the subject speak for him or herself – even if it was in the intimidating ritualistic atmosphere of a Royal Commission. How people worked, in what organisational format, under which informal relations of authority – all these real issues of history are largely well buried beneath a plethora of statistics, official documentation and plain propaganda.

For example, during the early years of this century *The Engineer* (an employers' trade paper) ran a series called 'Factory Visits'. It is the best source I know of the workings of an average engineering firm in that era, containing details from the manager's style of dress to the number of tea-breaks. But would a contemporary researcher trust a trade paper's description of factory conditions? I think not. Yet the historian is sorely tempted by the paucity of reportage of mundane detail. Of course, using such sources to write an anti-institutional account only reverses (rather than abolishes) the inherent bias of the text. As Raphael Samuel has observed (1981: xlvii):

A large part of the historian's work consists in subverting – or escaping from – the categories of thought in which documents are conceived.

I think I'll leave the excuses there.

The Sociological Connection

Within the sub-discipline known as industrial sociology there has, in the last decade, been a flowering of debate concerned with the authority relations and labour process of the capitalist enterprise (Hill 1981). Theoretically this was one of the many off-shoots of the declining hold of Stalinism in Marxist theory, which equated change in the ownership of the means of production as a necessary and sufficient pre-condition for the liberation of the worker from the tyranny of 'machino-facture'. Harry Braverman's *Labour and Monopoly Capitalism* (1974) extended and systematised an alternative which set out to restore to centrality 'the critique of the capitalist mode of production, originally the most trenchant weapon of Marxism' (1974: 13). In mainstream sociology non-Marxist radicals, such as Alvin Gouldner (1971) and C. Wright Mills (1959), began to analyse the trajectory of Western and Eastern social science: a convergence towards an institutional theory of spontaneous and self-maintaining mechanisms of social control and stability.

These developments were paralleled 'from below', as it were, by the emergence of anthropologically influenced studies of work (largely in America) concerned with ethnographic accounts of working lives. Donald Roy's pioneering participant observation of work-groups and payment systems (1952; 1960; 1961), and Studs Terkel's many biographies (1975), established and merged with this revival of interest amongst Marxists in the labour process. In Britain this tradition was represented by Ronald Fraser (1969), Tom Lupton (1963) and, in a more sophisticated manner, by Huw Beynon (1973). Although studying different industries in differing ways, a common theme was the degrading 'non-human' character of much work, and the competitive atomised spirit it engendered. The fundamentally revolutionary kernel of this critique of industrial life was confirmed by Miklos Haraszti's brilliant book, *A Worker in a Worker's State* (1977), which proved, if proof were needed, that the formal socialisation of the factories is no solution to the alienation of the worker from work and from his fellow human beings.

Meanwhile in America, France and Britain, theorists of the awkwardly labelled 'neo-Marxist' school, were extending this debate back to Marx and Marxist history. Publication in 1976 of a previously little known appendix to *Capital* Volume I, 'Results of the Immediate Process of Production', seemed to endorse its latent importance in the original texts. From the Conference of Socialist Economists came an integration of the labour process into the totality of Marx's thought (1977); from Stephen Marglin, a novel critique of technological determinism in the structure of capitalist hierarchy and a return to the determining role of accumulation (1974); from André Gorz, the implication for the class structure and struggle (1978); and from Raphael Samuel, a truly original application of the often used but little examined phrase, the 'combined and uneven development' of capitalism (1977).

Retrospectively, I would now place the following pages within this debate. They reveal how the concerns of the itinerant engineer of the 1890s were remarkably similar to those of his counterpart in Longbridge or Fiat's in the 1980s – the 'nibbling' at prices or speed, the subtle erosion of apprenticeships and skill (now under the guise of 'job rotation' or 'job enrichment'), and the covert or overt threat to trade unionism. But I would also say that the forms under which the working class is involved in its own subordination to capital have fundamentally changed. Speaking solely of the realm of work, this principally implies the vast panoply of managerial theory (founded on studies in sociology and psychology) now employed to ensure the co-operation of the labour force. Even here, however, events are undermining orthodoxy. As the capitalist escapes more and more from the limitations of the *physical* effort of the worker, he delves increasingly into his or her psychological profile. Moreover, this involves not just a change of strategy, but also of strata. 'Appraisal' techniques are now mainly aimed at the managerial and white-collar sector, as the distribution of knowledge (and thus of power) shifts inexorably up the occupational hierarchy (Anthony, 1977: 239). Thus the old debate about the 'incorporation' of the working class becomes increasingly removed from the sphere of work into the sphere of politics. And, in its wake, the foundations upon which a generation of sociological enquiry (and careers) were built are threatened as it struggles to comprehend its revolutionary object of study – late capitalism.

With the customary disclaimers I would like to thank the following for their help and support in writing this book: Gill Holbrook, Chris Phillipson, Huw Beynon, Chris Jones, Tony Novak, Richard Brown, Alan Anderson, Pete Rushton, David Hill, Esther Eisenthal, and Heinemann's anonymous reviewer.

August 1981

1 Class Action in Emergent Industrialism

Marxist theory has traditionally been accused of an over-formal *dichotomous* representation of the class structure. Whilst many sociologists implicitly accept Marx's fundamental starting point (the relation between property and non-property, productive and unproductive, wage and interest receivers, and so on), just as many have rejected his actual usage of the concept as outdated. A major factor in their rejection of this is the so-called 'rise of the middle class', said to accompany modern industrialisation, and the consequent reduction in class differentials created by this 'social bridge' between the working class and the upper class. More recently, sociologists have emphasised that even if the wide discrepancies of wealth remain, and therefore the 'middle class' as such is economically unimportant, the *political* impetus towards radical developments in the working class has been ended by the institutionalisation or mediation of overt conflict.

It is commonplace to note that Marx did not give a satisfactory account of how a class 'in itself' becomes a class 'for itself' (Wolpe, 1970). But this is just one part of wider theoretical lacunae concerning the nature and implications of class action in pursuit of its immediate interests. This dispute has turned, at least in Marxist theory, around the related questions of spontaneity and consciousness, and the role of the mass party.

For our purposes I wish to concentrate on the somewhat surprising contention that Marxist theory needs a 'dichotomous' theory of class *action*. By this I mean an understanding of the relationship between the *emergence of class interests in the process of the actual struggle for immediate goals*. As has been mentioned Marx only dealt intermittently with the conditions facilitating the growth of the class consciousness of the proletariat. This was partly as a consequence of his failure to fully identify the centrifugal forces in the process of class formation.

Obviously this process is neither linear nor uniform, that is there is no 'objectification' of the class structure or consequently a 'subjectivisation' of consciousness. In one sense this book is concerned with both these problems; but by focusing on the question of work experience it is hoped in fact to direct attention to the really crucial problem of the *relationship* between the two.

> Class consciousness, as all consciousness, is determined by existence; existence, however, is not limited to the existence of one class, but also embraces inter-action of classes.
>
> (Rothstein, 1929: 267)

In the writings of Marx and Engels on the probable developments inside the labour movement as capitalism became established, a gradual retreat from the 'polarisation thesis' of *The Communist Manifesto* can be identified, culminating in Engels's *England in 1845* and *1885*. The early theoretical optimism, based as it was on a determinist relation between the mode of production and ideology, forecast a rapid politicisation of the workers' movement, where capitalist contradictions were present in their most acute form. It was in this vein that Engels wrote in 1844:

> The English Chartists will rise up first because it is precisely here that the struggle between bourgeoisie and proletariat is at its most fierce . . . thus the struggle has been simplified, thus the struggle will be resolved at one decisive blow.
>
> (1950: 229)

Hence the concentration in *The Communist Manifesto* on the role of the bourgeoisie clearing the debris of pre-capitalist social relations and with it the mystification of custom, duties, rights, that constituted the dense ideological order of feudalism. The separation of the mass of the population from the means of production and the creation of wage labourers concentrated together (both in an urban and economic sense), reduced the relation between the two classes to the 'cash nexus'. This simplification of all social relations meant that the proletarian movement could develop in a straight line from economic combination to socialist revolution; hence the passive role of Communists, who were merely the conscious agents of an inevitable process underway amongst the, as yet unaware, mass of the working class (Marx, 1970: 60–64).

Nonetheless, this incorrect view of ideological progress was accompanied by a crucial insight into the *nature* of the labour-capital relation. The extraction of surplus value from the labour process is separated from the use of physical coercion by the employer. This permits an increasing separation of the *organisation of production* from the *organisation of violence*, or, to put it in other terms, of *economics* from *politics*. Capitalism has an internal motivator (the majority have no other recourse than to sell their labour power) at the level of the productive unit, whilst the element of coercion is removed to politics, in the form of the 'public' state – the 'committee of the whole bourgeoisie' (*ibid*.: 44).

Within the urban working class the emphasis of Marx's consideration begins to move away from equating proletarianisation (the separation from the means of production) with class consciousness (an ideological reflection of their objective circumstance). This occurred at two levels: firstly, the role of the state and political parties as agencies of 'public' coercion and 'private' socialisation and accommodation of the workers. Marx's writings on France and his later polemics against the policies of the German Social Democratic Party, reflected this concern, as did Engels's rather laconic assessments of the English labour movement (Blackburn, 1976: 23–32). Second, Marx began, in theory at least, to consider consequences of the uneven and contradictory progress of the capitalist form of organisation of the labour process. As we shall see, it was from these considerations that *in abstract* a much more complex account of the structuration and gradations of the working class was constructed. From this would flow a much more cautious prognosis of the development of a 'class-in-itself' to a 'class-for-itself' and, by implication, of the morphology of the trade union movement.

Class Action and the Craft Union

At one level a theory of craft unionism is a specific statement of a theory of class consciousness *in toto*. But here we are primarily concerned to show the connections between our interpretation of Marx's account of class action and the organisational context of exclusive behaviour — the craft union. First the Leninist formulation on the relation between imperialism and the labour aristocracy, to which Lenin ascribes the material basis of reformism must be confronted:

The bourgeoisie of a 'Great' Imperialist Power is *economically in a position* to bribe the upper sections of 'its' workers by devoting for this purpose one or two hundred million francs a year since its *super*-profits amount to perhaps a billion.

Before the imperialist epoch this was only possible within one nation: however, with the ending of British monopoly this became a feature of all rival powers. Whilst the upper strata of the workers enjoy the benefits of imperialism, the masses are more oppressed than formerly, and thus provide the basic foundation of the anti-capitalist movement (1969: 146–7).

If this were the case we would expect to see working-class reformism closely correlated to the strength of British capital, in so far as this would provide the economic room for manoeuvre and 'bribery'. However, applying this approach in the British context we come across a fundamental difficulty. Precisely as a consequence of being the first industrialised nation, the process of capital accumulation did not proceed on the basis of large-scale factory production – a phenomenon to be examined in detail later. Out-working, family businesses, and the 'cottage-industry' structure remained important into the second half of the nineteenth century (Samuel, 1977). Dobb noted that this meant that 'not until the last quarter of the century did the working class begin to assume the homogeneous character of a factory proletariat' (1972: 265). The notion of a labour aristocracy implies a stratum differentiated by prestige, wages, skill or whatever, but nonetheless a layer within an objectively definable wider entity, that is, 'the working class'.

In his pre-*Imperialism* writings Lenin refers to the

results of the preceding period in the development of the labour movement . . . [which] taught the working class to utilise such important means of struggle as parliamentarianism and all legal opportunities, create a mass economic and political organisations, a widespread labour press, etc.

(1964: 161)

This approach, which anticipates the writing of Gramsci on reformism is, as Hobsbawm points out, far more fruitful than the later and more well-known thesis advanced in *Imperialism*. The outstanding Communist writer on this period, Andrew Rothstein, put it in a nutshell:

Hitherto it has been customary to explain the opportunist mentality and sentiments of the English proletariat as chiefly due to one fact – British predominance in the industrial world, which has enabled the English capitalist to dole out more or less considerable crumbs to the working class. This explanation is obviously inadequate, since the opportunist psychology of the English worker became particularly noticeable at the very period when English industrial monopoly had come to an end . . .

(1929: 263)

It has been shown that in the 'classic period' of the labour aristocracy (1850–70) this layer was not suppressing a mass movement – there was none (Foster, 1976; Burgess, 1975 and 1980).

It is precisely in the last quarter of the century as general political militancy once more appeared, that is, when the *material* foundation of reformism was on the ebb, that the role of the labour aristocracy as a 'buffer', slowing down the political development of the working class, was most effective (Hobsbawm, 1976).

In this light Lenin's earlier formulations stressing the importance of the *ideological* formation of the labour aristocracy assume a new importance. For if, as has been suggested, the period 1870–1900 constitutes *the* era of the labour aristocracy, that is, three decades of absolute economic decline, we should expect to find the validity of this concept not merely in the 'bribes' of the capitalist, but in the historical structuration of working-class activity created by the legacy of economic dominance. In this sense imperialism had a vital ideological role in the creation of supra-class images and myths which could both confuse and distort nascent proletarian consciousness, and, perhaps more crucially, mould and crystallise petit bourgeois and ruling-class solidarity – whose distinguishing feature may be the denial of the concept of class itself.

Thus, we should not be looking for an *absence* of strikes or political activity in the labour movement but rather the *limitation of this activity to a particular layer*, and a change in its character. It is in this period we see two processes at work on the nature of labour activity. Firstly, there is a significant move towards the extension of 'citizenship', both in the national electoral arena and in local government politics. Second, there is the gradual and uneven process of the creation of class through the 'factorisation' of trades and skills, and from this the development of the social expression of wage-labour, the trade union.

The former has been well documented (Blewett, 1972; Clarke, 1971; Rothstein, 1929; Semmel, 1960), so it is the latter question that is now considered. What were the consequences for the working class of the emergence of the large scale organisations of their own making, and what were the decisive factors in the creation of the form and ideology of such organisations? The problem with all explanations at the level of ideology is to give them a 'material' or 'real' basis. Lenin attempted to do this in considering the distribution of rewards from imperialism, but, as has been seen, the argument becomes circular. Why do the ruling class wish to 'buy off' a section of the workers? Because, it is said, this will frustrate the emergence of a wider class consciousness. But the generator of this consciousness, the class struggle, was by all accounts, including Engels's and the Webbs', notably absent within the very period it was supposedly being 'frustrated'.

One important attempt to solve this problem is *Class Struggle and the Industrial Revolution* by John Foster. In this book he traces, in the 1850s and 1860s in Oldham, the actual formation of a labour aristocracy from the ruins of an earlier period of collective labour solidarity. In his account of the two preceding decades Foster shows how the working-class movement, led in the main by the cotton spinners, used their techniques of struggle in the work place to influence and control the *political* structure of the town from which they were disenfranchised. In particular the tactics of boycotting unfriendly shopkeepers ('exclusive dealing') to ensure the election of sympathetic local representatives, the control of poor relief and the expenses of the police, all relied on the fostering of *mass discipline* and allegiance. It was this utilisation of the lessons of the factory and trade union struggle in the affairs of the local state authority which allows Foster to claim that this constituted the 'first' class consciousness (1977: 51–69). The erosion of working-class unity, it is argued, occurred primarily through the creation of a spinner *industrial* élite in the factory hierarchy. This mediated the authority of the employer, and thus the capitalist class over the community (Jones, 1975).

It is at this point that the argument turns to the decisive factors influencing the creation of a labour aristocracy, and its relation to changes in the method and hierarchy of the work situation, and thus rejoins the main thread of this analysis. For, as stressed earlier, this discussion is not *primarily* concerned with the theory of the labour aristocracy, but with the questions it raises in the understanding of its impact on industrial life in the last quarter of the nineteenth century. Foster's contention is that the new authority 'internal' to the workforce was the product of the *elimination* of craft autonomy and the creation of a new privileged layer 'policing' the layer below (*ibid*. 224–30). In his fixation with 'defending' Leninist orthodoxy Foster presents a universalistic answer to a question, which, by his own premises, is an essentially disparate problem. For if the new source of capitalist social control now operates at the place of work rather than externally upon the labour community as a whole, it follows from the dictum of the 'combined and uneven development' thesis that this could not result in a *corporate* ideological legacy.

The great strength of Lenin's approach is, however, that it forces the labour historian to consider the *relationships* between objects of study which are otherwise so often categorised and pigeon-holed: trade unionism, the industrial economy, party politics, strikes and conciliation. Of course, it is easy to err in the other direction and rely on sweeping generalisations, as undoubtedly did Lenin, whose main task was polemical.

Perhaps the main contribution Lenin made was to direct attention to the fact that because of the diversity of conditions in, for example, different industries and regions of the same economy, a purely 'economist' labour movement must emerge segmented into its own concerns, which are defined by the circumstances of the trade. This point is made most forcefully (again for polemical reasons) in the famous pamphlet *What is to be Done?* (1970, I: 162–171). From this he deduced the need for a particular type of organisation, politics and programme, the details of which are not relevant here. The significant point is that the relationship proposed is not between 'economics' and 'politics' but between class *action* and class *ideology* (Mandel, 1977).

In a somewhat more orthodox application of this approach Hobsbawm has, with great skill and accuracy, proposed several ways in which the labour aristocracy might be 'defined', that is, differentials, sub-contraction, the degree of de-skilling, security of employment and life. Of these, for theoretical and practical reasons, he suggests the first is the 'main criterion' (1976: 273). In one sense this is obviously correct: in a society now based on the accumulation of money, a central feature of any relatively privileged layer would be income or wealth (depending on their relation to the means of production). However, the dangers of determinism are obvious. Once established as existing 'objectively' its effects can be assumed (reformism) and its decline implying its antinomy (class consciousness). Hence the search for explanations at the level of ideas, and the totally false debate about the pronunciations of trade union and working-class leaders in the Victorian era (Clements 1961; Harrison 1965; Musson 1976: 49–56). Realising this problem, recent writers have introduced the writings of Gramsci into the debate (Gray, 1975: 181–6; Hobsbawm, 1976: 302).

The danger inherent in all explanations based on defining a 'membership card' for the labour aristocracy is the tendency to portray the group as passive and manipulated from above – either by conscious political strategy or 'naturally' through the evolution of imperialism. The use of the concept of 'social closure', originally evolved by Weber, and recently modified and expanded by Frank Parkin, can begin to answer these problems (1974: 1–19). Parkin uses this concept in a manner largely ignored by Weber. Weber defined 'social closure' as a process by which a 'social collectivity maximised rewards by restricting access to a limited circle of eligibles', achieved by singling out one attribute in order that the group may then create a monopoly of it. In his use of the concept Weber specifically detaches it from the notion of class: 'community closure' may occur at varying levels of the stratification hierarchy and is not the prerogative of dominant groups. However, the 'attribute' which becomes monopolised is often concomitant with a rational pursuance of economic and political interests, which Weber calls 'associative relationships'. These are contrasted with 'ethnic communities' which rely on criteria 'outside' the opportunity structure to create symbolic racial or religious communities which in general *reflect* the existing pattern of reward, and thus are used as pretexts for excluding competition in those groups which are so labelled. Weber did not envisage relationships within such communities as harmonious – but on the contrary considered that a condition of their continued unity was a vigorous internal struggle between subgroups for the forceful subjection of the weaker by the stronger. It is out of this process that ethnic and racial stereotypes arise via the disparity of communicative symbols. He also notes that the response of excluded 'negatively privileged groups' is effectively controlled; resistance cannot normally take the form of retaliation along a similar line of action, that is, exclusion (Neuwirth, 1970: 56).

This point is restated by Parkin, as a distinction between 'two general strategies for staking claims to resources: those based upon the power of *exclusion* and those based upon the power of *solidarism*', of which the latter is the predominant 'mode of closure' in all stratification systems. Solidarism 'may be regarded as collective responses to excluded groups which are themselves unable to maximise resources by exclusion practices'. Parkin, unlike Weber, wishes to relate this to the division between the bourgeoisie and the proletariat, but also unlike Marx,

not specifically in relation to their place in the productive process, but in relation to their prevalent modes of closure: exclusion and solidarism. From this angle it is possible to visualise the fundamental cleavage in the stratification order as that point where one set of closure strategies gives way to a radically different set.

(Parkin, 1974: 5)

Parkin goes on to contrast bourgeois forms of exclusion with those of solidarism. The former rest in the modern world on the rhetoric of individualism and 'classes of nomination', behind which is a *de facto* collectivist exclusion and a 'class of reproduction'. The latter, however are largely dependent upon social mobilisation and organisation rather than the maintenance of the juridical and ideological *status quo*. Solidarism is always aimed at usurpation of the resources of existing groups and thus involves convincing members to act contrary to the distributive justices of the 'excluding' or dominant group. Further, it follows that the extent to which the dominant group successfully convinces the excluded group of the merits of individual aspiration would divide the latter, weakening the totalising character of communal status.

The use to which Parkin puts Weber's notion clearly fits into his general theoretical understanding of the *occupational* order as the dominant distributive focus of the reward structure, via the interchange of skills and expertise in the labour market (Parkin, 1972: 18). The interpretation he offers has some weaknesses which will subsequently become clearer, but first let us examine what it has to offer. Obviously and primarily the exposition links the nature of social action to the 'structure of rewards', and the *limitations* placed on disadvantaged groups in challenging that structure. This reveals how dominant groups, by virtue of their privileged position, not only create institutions to defend their interests, but, in the process, define and direct the strategies of groups attempting to usurp them. In other words, the *definitions of what constitutes an élite is in part a definition and explanation of how that élite is maintained*. Hence the possibility of a theoretic bridge between production relations and class domination is created by elucidating the dialectical framework of action 'imposed' upon the contending classes by their mutual interdependence. In this way the familiar dichotomy of 'base v. superstructure' (often conceived of in 'zero-sum' terms) can be subsumed within a more general problematic of the role of class action, in that the former is determinate only insofar as it limits the *modes of action possible*, not the 'forms' and 'types' of consciousness. In other words, the debate can be removed 'from heaven to earth', from speculative attempts to determine what goes on in people's heads to a practical theoretic conception of man – as Gramsci puts it, a

> series of active relationships (a process) . . . these relations are not mechanical. They are active and conscious . . . one's own individuality is the ensemble of these relations . . .
>
> (1973: 352)

This articulation of this model requires a break with the Weberian framework within which Parkin operates. His ideas are used only insofar as they are reminders of what is a central thread in this section, namely, that the action undertaken by classes to defend and extend their interests is a prime factor in the manner by which they are maintained in a dominant or subordinate role, and thereby in the formation of ideological views which confirm this relation. Insofar as his approach conjures a particular 'picture' of the class structure based on the differing forms of collective defence of opposing interests, then it is an important element of a theory of class *action*. In fact, it can be argued that the *method* of Parkin's model intimates a conclusion fundamentally at odds with his basic contention that the modes of closure adopted by collectivities are a function of their place in the occupational order. Rather, it is that the types of action adopted are a product of the *structural* resources open to collectivities in the social order, in which the adoption of a predominant mode of closure indicates the form of action and the dynamics of the class struggle, rather than the agency of the conflict itself. Parkin seems to assume that an adoption of a predominant 'mode of closure' is a signal of an automatic access to a particular form of power and is *ipso facto* a defined position in the social structure. In reality the process is exactly the reverse; the 'ability' of collectivities to adopt differing strategies is primarily determined by their relation to the mode of production.

However, in as much as the categories of solidarism and exclusion are fundamentally modes of *action*, this is a forceful reminder that the class structure is a process rather than a state, and as such is inseparable from the evocation of collective action by groups within it – institutionalised, crystallised, reified, naturalised or whatever – but not a phenomenon of a separate order from the action that constitutes it. In this context it is argued that Parkin's categories of exclusion and solidarism, revised to be included in Marxist theory, could provide an introductory re-evaluation of the relation between class *action* and class *domination* which remains only implicit in Marx's writings.

A craft union may be viewed, in this light, as an organisational form of exclusive class action, but whose 'resources' are dictated by the objective position of its members as wage labourers. Investigation of this role as an independent force within the boundaries of capitalism allows the construction of a theory of the variegated nature of working-class activity: dichotomous class action within a dichotomous class structure.

If the proposition is correct, therefore, that the fundamental line of enquiry is an examination of the context of class action, and that this is inseparable from the organisational form it takes, it must follow that the study of an élite of the *working* class has to be based on its role *within* the process of production. The structure of this élite will therefore also be an expression of the conditions by which it is maintained, and thereby the tactics adopted to achieve this. But since the development of capitalist social and economic organisation takes the 'combined and uneven' form, there will not be *one* strategy, or *one* ideology typical of this élite, but a whole series of them corresponding to the special conditions of each sector.

From this can be concluded, firstly, that the impact of British capitalism on the labour movement was, because of its pioneer characteristics, primarily the articulation of class interests in the form of the sum total of occupational interests. Second, that as a consequence of this, the locus of the labour élite lies in an analysis of the internal manufacturing relationships. And third and finally, that the character of this élite will be defined by its *own* activity in the maintenance of its position in the occupational order. In this specific sense the relationship of the labour aristocracy to imperialism is an empirical question: a demonstration of a relation sustained over time, embodied in an organisational form and sanctified by an ideological order. It is to be found in an historical reconstruction of the daily life of 'working-class work'.

Labour Discipline and the Labour Process

This section is intended to consider some of the implications of the argument with reference to the labour process. In the discussion of the coal, cotton and engineering industrial organisation an assumption will be the prime importance of the accumulation of (rather than competition between) capital in each sector (Yaffe, 1972; Rowthorn, 1980). Consequently, the progress of 'machino-facture' will be shown neither as an internal unfolding of technical systems, nor as a series of economic paradigms. As a recent writer has argued, in Marx's discussion of the factory system,

machinery seems less and less essential to its hegemony . . . Mechanisation comes to appear more a result of modern industry than a cause – the capitalist way of escaping from worker resistance.

(Samuel, 1977: 12)

This is an important insight, but one which could well be placed in a slightly different context. The interpretation of Marx's theory of the labour process utilised here links the creation of labour discipline to the creation of capital – this is the fulcrum of the capitalist enterprise (Marglin, 1974; Johnson, 1980). This view flows from the analysis of working-class action in hierarchical work situations. The exclusiveness of craft unions, for example, becomes a product of the distribution of social power – a refraction of the way work is organised *which itself* structures the labour market. This formulation might appear at first to be both economically and technologically determinist: the labour process defines the resources workers can use to defend their interests. (The distortion stems from the concentration on the 'micro' aspects of the functions of capital in the firm.) In fact the argument, taken as a whole, suggests the reverse. The distribution of 'social power' ensures that 'technology, instead of simply *producing* social relations, is *produced by* the social relations represented by capital'. (Braverman, 1974: 20). To progress any further it is necessary to integrate the varying stages of the factory regimes to the production process, and this in turn with the relation between labour and capital.

Marx's argument in *Capital* Volume I is remarkably simple to summarise, expressed as it is at this stage at a purely abstract or formal level. Integral to the capitalist system is the need to replace 'living' with 'dead' labour, in other words, to increase the component of mechanisation in the production process. This stems not just from a desire by the capitalist to escape from reliance on 'real' workers, but is crucial for the accumulation (as opposed to the mere circulation) of capital. The technicalities of this are discussed and debated in Fine and Lawrence (1976), Yaffe (1972) and Rowthorn (1980).

In the early stages of capitalism the rate of surplus value (that part of labour power not recompensed by wages) can only be extended 'absolutely', that is, by extending the length and number of working days (Mandel, 1971: 135–40; Thompson, 1967). This was achieved initially by the centralisation of work under one roof, rather than improving the work process – for example, the 'factories' of individual weavers who no longer owned their own handlooms (Pollard, 1968: 42–50). In Marx's terminology this corresponds to the stage where the capitalist controls the *objective* factors of production: the quality of raw material, consumption of power, attentiveness and regularity of labour, and so on. At this point the rate of surplus value is determined by the 'surplus part of the working day' (Marx, 1976: 326). This is limited by two factors: the physical endurance of labour and the increasing organisation of workers to resist further extensions. Because of these 'natural' limitations Marx calls this the period of 'formal subsumption' of labour to capital.

The tendency so far has been to *increase* the proportion of 'living' labour in each unit produced (extensive exploitation); once the boundaries of this are reached, however, the reverse process begins (intensive exploitation). To do this the labour process itself (the way things are made) has to be revolutionised, and thus the degree of control of the worker over the rhythm, pace and character of work lessened. This has the consequence of reducing the 'counter-vailing' power of labour within the enterprise, but it is not the motive. The intensification of work by mechanisation results in a change in the exploitative relation between capital and labour – no longer is capital dependent on absolute extensions of surplus value.

The production of absolute surplus value turns exclusively on the length of the working day, whereas the production of relative surplus value completely revolutionises the technical processes of labour and the groupings into which society is divided.

(ibid: 645)

Relative surplus value vastly increases the rate of capital accumulation, first in one sector, then, by the 'domino effect', 'becomes the universal, socially predominant form of the production process' *(ibid: 646)*.

Constant changes in working methods are not only the foundation of cumulative capital, but also of the different stages of the factory regime (Pollard, 1968: 213–25). Once the labour process is 'freed' from dependence on *individual* labour power the capitalist in effect controls the objective *and* subjective factors of production. Only at this stage, argues Marx, can one speak of a capitalist *mode of production* (Marx, 1976: 1034–6). Because of the absence of 'natural' limitations on the productivity of labour Marx labels this the period of 'real subsumption' of labour to capital *(ibid: 1025)*.

In purely descriptive and schematic terms the argument so far is represented in Table 1 i.

TABLE 1 i

Form of exploitation	Forms of control of the factors of production	
	Objective	*Objective and subjective*
Absolute surplus value	'Formal subsumption' (1) ——————▶	Transitional stage (2)
Relative surplus value	Transitional stage (3) ——————▶	'Real subsumption' (4)

Anticipating the later chapters, each stage is illustrated by examples from the cotton textile industry, distilled into caricatures in order to draw the boundaries sharply:

1   1780–1830: unregulated hours, hand mules, water power, punishment-based rules, seasonal working.
2   1840–50: long but regular hours, hand mules with a prime mover (because of fine spinning), punishment/incentive rules for attendance.
3   1860s onwards: hours limited by law, self-actor mules, spinners (male) in closed union, pay by piecework and subcontraction, overtime worked during high demand.
4   1900s onwards: limited hours, ring-frame mules, spinners (female) in open union, decreasing piecework and overtime.

An important conceptual caveat is required here. This model does not imply that the transition from 1 to 4 occurs in a unilinear fashion, within either an economy or an industrial sector – although it is true that Marx thought it probably would (because of the increasing interdependent or 'social' nature of capital) (*ibid*.: 1036). A recent critique by Elbaum *et al*. (1979) accuses Marx of just this, *viz*, an uncritical acceptance of capitalist ideology that technology and the division of labour destroyed workers' job control. Certain occupations, such as the spinners, were bypassed by the rationalising wave, primarily because of severe inter-capitalist competition. Consequently traditional forms of labour management persisted in the face of this artificial organisational inertia. This process, writ large, explains why the predicted homogenization of the working class failed to materialise. Differentiation along skill and status lines not only continued, but flourished where capital and labour's interests temporarily converged.

One consequence of the neglect of the hierarchical division of labour and the fragmentation of both capital and labour in shaping capital-labour relations is that the 'terrain of compromise' upon which capitalist and workers can find room to co-operate in the development of the productive forces and the distribution of the social product has not been systematically explored by Marxists.

(*ibid*: 229)

Earlier, the possibility of integrating the impact of variegated class action into Marxist theory was shown. There is much, however, in Marx's speculations in *Capital* Volume I to support Elbaum *et al*., in the classic case of the spinners, where technical innovation did not drive them into the ranks of the unskilled. The approach adopted here (seen as consistent with Marx's *method*) views the survival of craft and 'plebeian' occupations as *functional to, and a product of, the 'real subsumption' of labour to capital*, understood in the context of the prior definition of the labour process. This contrasts with Elbaum *et al*. who essentially view it as an anachronism created by abnormal competition. At this juncture it is simply argued that the hidden assumption of logicality behind this analysis is not warranted. As will be seen, the survival of all forms of indirect and haphazard relationships between capital and labour are a result of the need to mediate authority. In this sense capitalist hegemony is superordinate to technological consistency, and thus irrational forms of labour process are an expected feature of this mode of production.

Finally some more general and explanatory comments can be made on the thesis that the process of accumulation does not overthrow, in a uniform manner, the established modes of labour, but rather in a manner corresponding to its contradictory socialisation of labour. The progress toward the 'real subsumption' of capital to labour is marked not just by a developing relation of economic supremacy, but also in a redefinition of the social roles of each and the crystallisation into a *class* structure. For example, the capitalist is no longer a co-producer (journeyman or artisan) or co-ordinator (merchant) but a supervisor and director of the process. Thus the formation of the classes also reflects, in an uneven manner, the changes in the organisation of production, and the 'social distance' between the two groups. Furthermore, 'formal subsumption' establishes the 'cash nexus' as the form of relation between the classes: the worker experiences this as a free exchange involving money, as an abstract social form of wealth. Within the limitations of the structural differentials of income this puts the worker on an equal footing with any other buyer: 'he is responsible to himself for the way he spends his wages. *He learns to control himself in contrast to the slave,* who needs a master' (Marx, 1976: 1033). This obviously has limited applicability to England, but Marx is suggesting the general notion that the stage of 'formal subsumption' is in part a process of the ideological preparation of the proletariat.

What then are the consequences of the 'real subsumption' of labour to capital? Firstly, and most importantly, it establishes *relative* surplus value as the dominant form of exploitation via the creation of a capitalist labour process. Expressed in terms of our earlier discussion the capitalist now controls the objective *and* subjective factors of production, which in turn facilitates the necessary increasing magnitude of capital that enters the production process. In this stage (sometimes referred to by Marx as the progress from 'manufacture' to 'machino-facture') the labourer serves the machine and not the machine, labour. The natural co-operation of manufacture with its complex traditional modes of labour is replaced by a scientifically organised system which is solely geared towards the creation of surplus value and involves a reorganisation of the instruments of labour employed and the form of social combination that is imposed upon labour (*ibid.*: 1034–5).

Second, the labour process is *objectified*, and the workforce *collectivised* from above, or from without, by the productive process. The organisation of work no longer corresponds to the 'natural' mode of labour necessary for co-operative effort:

> The entire development of productive forces of *socialised labour* (in contrast to the more or less isolated labour of individuals) and together with the *use of science* . . . in the *immediate processes of production*, takes the form of the *productive power of capital*. It does not appear as the productive power of labour . . .
>
> (*ibid.*: 1024)

Thus there is a third consequence: the ideological strengthening of capital resulting from the actual separation of labour from the means, instruments and techniques of production, save that fraction in which the worker is involved.

> The mystification implicit in the relations of capital as a whole is greatly intensified here, far beyond the point it had reached, or could have reached in the merely formal subsumption of labour under capital.
>
> (*ibid.*)

In other words, the complexity of 'machino-facture' necessitates *some* agency to assemble the disparate elements of production; 'fetishism' results from the conflation of this to equal *capital*.

> Capital thus becomes a very mystic being since all of labour's social productive forces appear to be due to capital, rather than labour as such, and seem to issue from the womb of capital itself.
>
> (Marx, 1972: 827)

The 'real subsumption' stage would initially suggest a clear dichotomous organisation of production of 'supremacy and subordination' by capital over labour, and hence provide at the level of the factory a confirmation of the wider 'polarisation' thesis. However, whilst suggesting an *objectification* and *separation* of tasks in a 'real' sense – involving the minute specialisation for the labourer, the monopoly of knowledge of production techniques, and the 'freeing' of the capitalist from direct work – in fact, when considered jointly they do not imply a simplistic dichotomous organisational structure.

Firstly, implicit in the idea of a *capitalist* labour process is the division between 'intellectual' and 'manual' labour, insofar as the former now have a monopoly over *technique* and the latter over *execution*. In order for this to be fully exploited a specialised department is created, firstly within the larger factories, and then centrally through, for example, universities and institutes. Pollard has shown how this process was related to mechanisation, mass production and the division of labour, and did not become general until the mid-nineteenth century, and even then only in large-scale factories (1968: 188). The majority attitude towards labour was that

> they were dealing with a recalcitrant, hostile workforce whose morale, whose

habits of work and whose culture had to be broken in order to fit them for a form of employment in which they had to become obedient servants of the machine, of its owners and of crude monetary incentives.

(ibid.: 297)

Or in the words of a contemporary they had: 'to renounce their desultory habits of work and identify themselves with the unvarying regularity of the complex automaton' (Ure, 1834: 15). Thus, an ideological order for this stratum emerged as a consequence of this objective position in the labour process. Furthermore, the 'de-skilling' effect of 'real subsumption' facilitated the emergence of a clear differential of payment and status of the manager/supervisor above that of the clerical staff (Pollard, 1968: 165–172).

Second, Marx concludes that the antagonism of capital and labour expressed in the instrumentalist mentality of the proletariat creates another category, the 'labour of supervision and management'. Hierarchical authority relations interfere with the natural co-operation created by the complexity of work and administration in modern industrialism. As Hill has noted:

This internal control function directly inflates salary costs by the number of supervisory and managerial staff needed for the purpose, diverts the attention of all levels of management away from other aspects of the business, and distorts the evolution of production technology.

(1981: 260)

Thus the stage of the 'real subsumption' of labour to capital, the *capitalist* labour process, simultaneously creates objective relations of capital which requires the unification of the means of production and the producers, whilst in reality creating an ideological and organisational hierarchic order, based on their complete and actual separation. The insights of *Capital* on this allow the examination of the actual history of the organisation of work in three industries of British capitalism as a totality. The first part of this equation is thus an account of the 'objective' circumstances of accumulation in the three examples.

2 Pioneer Capitalism and Industrial Organisation

If it is important to understand theoretically the relationship between accumulation and the character of labour discipline, an empirical description of the varying circumstances in which this takes place is also crucial. In this chapter, therefore, the available statistics on the size and structure of the three chosen industries will be collated in order to present the best possible picture to the reader of the context of work experience.

The Introduction mentioned some of the questions which inspired this book. One such was the simple, if not naive, inquiry: how large were the industrial enterprises of early capitalism? Investigating this proved inordinately time-consuming – nowhere in secondary material, it seemed, was this considered important. The official primary sources before the 1907 Census of Production, made no centralised account of size, with one exception – those industries subject to the provisions of the Factory and Workshop Acts. However, since these were mainly in textiles and not started until the 1850s, no complete reconstruction was possible.

Before this period there is one compilation of figures: H.D. Fong's *The Rise of the Factory System*, published in 1930. Despite his meticulous work on Government documents, he felt unable to claim to have presented a complete picture of the factory system as it appeared in 1840. The bias and paucity of statistics reflects the character of the industrial revolution itself. The breakthrough of the 1780s and 1790s was based on one industry – cotton – with weaving remaining unmechanised for the next 40 years. This, and other sporadic technological refinements over the next 50 years, created typically in its wake a series of semi-skilled or unskilled tertiary jobs. 'The industrial revolution far from abridging human labour created a whole new world of labour intensive jobs . . .' (Samuel, 1977: 8). The bedrock of British entrepreneurs remained the small-scale 'Gradgrinds' of popular contemporary fiction up to the 1870s (Clapham, 1932: 124). Furthermore the rapid rate of return of capital investment, both domestically and in international trading which applied up to this period, also favoured the continuance of an informal capital market, and in turn hindered the emergence of monopolist or oligarchical industrial enterprises. The absence of tariffs, or a natural monopoly of minerals was also a factor (Levy, 1927: 298).

Another relevant feature of the economy was that the main consumers of capital were those industries orientated towards export and not the home domestic market. In cotton, wool, iron and coal the percentage exported had, by the third quarter of the century, risen to 60, 30, 40 and 55 per cent, respectively (Deane and Cole, 1969: 187, 196, 225, 216). It was here that the first moves were made to end the traditional complex partnership system of British entrepreneurship, and towards the corporate firm based upon institutional financing and controlled by a board of directors (Jeffries, 1938: 105). The lack of a large-scale domestic consumer sector reflected both the logic of capital accumulation, 'the priority of profits', and the consequent lack of demand from the home market. This in turn facilitated the continuance of large numbers of small concerns (often based on out-working with little fixed capital) to provide for the limited consumer spending, over and above food and housing. The generous labour supply placed no incentive (from that angle) on employers to economise and thereby to develop a clear hierarchy of differentials.

Given the elasticity of the labour market in Britain up to the 1890s, this suggests that innovation would tend towards the replacement of skill by semi-skilled or unskilled tasks rather than the drastic reduction of labour itself. First in the cotton, then the paper industry, engineering, weaving, iron, and then in the pre-industrial sectors such as carpentry, the boot and shoe industry and printing, technology tended towards de-skilling rather than depopulating the industry *as a whole*. Technological displacement was, as we shall see, the major concern of organised workers throughout the second half of the century (until 'new unionism'), the classic example being the 1851 engineers' lockout. This economic pressure reinforced the sectoral outlook of the trade societies as they struggled to accommodate themselves to mechanisation, rather than resist it *in toto*.

The combination of labour-intensive factory production with considerable out-working and domestic production, inevitably meant a high proportion of working to fixed capital within the economy as a whole. Clapham has described how the former came mainly from the London market or the discountable bill procedure, and thus in consequence relied on internal profits for *fixed* capital investment (1932: 355–6). This retarded the structuration on any *significant* scale of the working class into high, medium and low paid until the last quarter of the century – or, to put it in economic terms, severely limited the emergence of a mass consumer home market. This is not the same as arguing that there were little differentials. On the contrary, the wage system reflected strongly the pre-industrial stratification of craftsmen, helper, labourer and apprentice, male and female. What is significant is the degree to which the staple industries of the economy relied on overseas requirements; if mass production of consumer durables and services implied concentration, so the absence of this type of production implied both limited demand and limited concentration. There are examples of the delay in the application of innovations due to the limited mass demand: an example being the self-actor mule which was unsuitable for fine spinning of luxury articles (*ibid.*: 69–79). The other side of this coin is, of course, a low wage economy, strengthening the attraction of labour-intensive work organisation and thereby satisfying small-scale domestic techniques. This process, which Habakkuk has called a 'widening rather than a deepening of capital' (1962: 141), explains (in harness with the other factors) the continued survival of the small-scale manufacturer and merchant even when the *supply* of capital was objectively sufficient to enable a technologically more advanced, and organisationally more concentrated, industrial structure.

Engineering: Size, Structure and Ownership

The purpose of this section is, as already mentioned, to explain the basic parameters of the work experience of the three groups via an examination of the structure of their respective industries. The engineers pose a problem. The location of both cotton and mine workers is obvious: overwhelmingly within one industry. However, the engineers and their union, the Amalgamated Society of Engineers' (ASE) membership, was spread widely throughout the whole industrial structure, often in small specialist groups within a wider generic labour force: a position reinforcing their traditional craft exclusiveness. The engineering firm and indeed the term 'engineer' were comparatively late arrivals, the census returns still referring to 'machine, engine-boiler maker, wheelwright' up to 1861. Consequently the fragmentary statistical returns have to be treated with caution, and the impressions they give taken only as indicative.

With these caveats, the evidence suggests a consistent tendency, throughout the century up to the last two decades, towards a relatively small unit size. According to the Select Committee of 1824 there existed in London around 500 engineering works, employing a total of only 10,000 workers, although there was one example of a northern firm of 150 (1824 V: 156, 357). The reason for the uneven development of the industry lay with the narrow base of technology.

The relatively small scale of most machine-using industries other than cotton is sufficient to account for the smallness of the young engineering firms.

(Clapham, 1926: 155)

Given the character of engineering as an occupation, when interpreting the Census returns the researcher has to make educated assumptions in amalgamating several categories to reach a figure for the industry as a whole. According to the 1892 *Rules* of the ASE the following occupations qualified for membership:

Smiths, ship smiths, Angle iron smiths, Fitters, Turners, Patternmakers, Millwrights, Mechanical draughtsmen, Planers, Borers, Slotters, Brass finishers, Coppersmiths, Machine joiners, Die sinkers, Press tool makers, Stampers or drop hammer forgers.

(Weekes, 1970: 35 fn)

Official figures use a different, less specific, nomenclature: the category 'engineer and engine worker' almost certainly constituted two distinct trades, namely, engine and machine maker, and engine tender, that is, railway workers (Day, 1927: 142). Thus in order to arrive at a figure for 'engineers' we are forced to halve the Census return for this category, and add in those for (1) general machinery and machine working, (2) steam engine construction, (3) hydraulic machinery, and (4) machine tools The composite total in 1851 was 32,667 persons (1851 XIV: Table cclxxvii).

But what of size? In evidence to the Committee on the Export of Machinery in 1841 a witness gave a number of estimates of 'mechanical establishments' in Lancashire. Unfortunately, whilst the number of firms and the capital employed is given, the number of workers at each factory is an estimate of the *optimum* capacity of the firm at its present position. This was to illustrate the results of doubling production on employment. Reducing therefore these figures by 40 per cent, we have an average factory size of 91 employees, the largest apparently being in Bolton at around 193 (1841 VII: 100–2). This is confirmed by Fong's analysis of the Factory Inspectorate returns for 1838, which produced an average of 92 workers per factory in the North West (1930: 29).

However, it would be misleading not to give an indication of the size of the larger (and more famous) concerns, who nonetheless, as we have seen, were the exception rather than the rule. Fong found seven enterprises employing over 1,000 including such names as T. Ashton of Hyde (1149), M'Connell and Company of Manchester (1545), and, the largest of all, Birley and Kirk of Duckenfield (1692) (*ibid.*: 33).

The 1851 Census, for the first and last time that century, asked employers to record their size. The results, for what they are worth, showed only five per cent of engine and machine-making firms with over 100 workers (Clapham, 1932: 35). This is undoubtedly an underestimate since ten years earlier 47 per cent of Lancashire factories employed over a hundred (Fong, 1930: 31). Although, of course, this was the centre of industry, it is likely the real figure is midway between these two.

From an analysis of trade directories in the years 1877 to 1907, a picture of the stability of firms in engineering is obtained. During those years there was a 50 per cent increase in the number of enterprises – a growth that was accompanied by a substantial turnover – so that in both 1892 and 1907 a majority of concerns had been founded in the previous year (Floud, 1976: 9–10). Size was not indicated in this study, but the average number employed by firms before the 1892 Labour Commission was 453, and 375 for those investigated by Booth in 1903 in London (1892 VII: 178–88; Booth, 1903 V: 357–63).

The basic boundaries of the engineering industry which ultimately determined its structure in the last half of the nineteenth century can be summarised as follows: The market for engineering products was dominated by capital goods requirements largely for export, with little output directed towards the home consumer demand (Habakkuk, 1962: 207–8). As a result production runs were short and distinct, orders differed widely and the firms to which they went worked from the necessities of each requirement rather than universal guidelines (the slow introduction of Whitworth's plane surface and gauges is indicative). With the exception of bicycles the industry was very slow in turning towards the items of the 'second industrial revolution' – for example, electrical goods, typewriters, cars, sewing machines (Clapham, 1938: 123). Thus the lack of standardisation corresponded to the character of production, which itself flowed from the limitations of the market.

This factor is clearly related to early crystallisation of the industry into specialised sectors around the concerns of the 'first industrial revolution'. The basic distribution was established by the 1850s, and by 1877, 72 per cent of engineering firms produced only one product (Floud, 1976: 10). Textiles, the major innovatory industry of this period, both expanded and contained its ancillary services. Whilst dramatically increasing the demand for machinery and power, the high element of raw material in the unit cost and the inelastic demand both combined to limit the overspill into the economy as a whole (Habakkuk, 1962: 181; Saul, 1967: 112–4). This process was reinforced by the geographical concentration in Lancashire. It was not market opportunities that were lacking, particularly abroad, but the static nature of this market and its slow *rate* of growth in relation to other areas that was the problem. As far as the end of the century textile machinery came to about a quarter of total machinery exports (which, of course, strengthened overseas competition to home textiles) (Clapham, 1938: 65).

As the market stabilised so did the rate of domestic technological advance, insofar as the latter depended on the *availability* of capital (*ibid.*: 233–5). Innovation did not cease after the 1850s, but in terms of major changes in labour utilisation no significant advances were implemented for 40 years, as will be demonstrated in detail later. This is significant in explaining the relatively trouble-free advance of skilled trade unionism, up to the 1880s, a progress facilitated by the stability of the capital:labour ratio. This is best reflected in the federal structure of the ASE, where local bargaining strength in some areas produced regional wage differences of 30 to 40 per cent (Burgess, 1975: 27).

By the turn of the century the industry could be divided into three broad categories:

1 General engineering: machine-making, shipbuilding, armaments and munitions, locomotives, engines, tools and implements.
2 Electrical engineering.
3 Vehicle building, motor cars, bicycles, etc.

Each area had its own special characteristics: higher capitalisation in armaments and munitions, but a stable market; rapid technological change in electrical engineering, weak trade unionism, but fierce domestic competition, and so on. Altogether around 2,000,000 found employment by the 1900s – one-sixth of insured workers, and one-eighth of all wage-earners (Labour Research Department, 1922: 6). The 1907 Census of Production estimated that from one-half to two-thirds of the total product of engineering was exported, with only the electrical sector producing mainly for domestic consumption.

These figures in their own way demonstrate an often made criticism of economic historians: the industry's commitment to the past. Exports were weakest in the fastest-growing area of electrical engineering, and greatest in the relatively declining market for steam power (*ibid.*). It is to be expected, therefore, that differing degrees of pressure upon trade union customs and tradition in these varying sectors are found. Chapter 3 discusses the consequences of this.

The structure of ownership in engineering is very difficult to assess. Not only are there the wide differences in product, markets, techniques, and so on, but also the large number of firms in which engineers were employed but whose output could not be considered part of the industry. The Engineering Employers Federation itself was not formed until 1896, from an amalgamation of regional associations in the Clyde, the North East, Barrow, Belfast and, in 1897, London; not until after the war did the Birmingham employers complete the Federation. This history of regionalism is significant and reflects the relative insularity, even of this industry, from the pressure of national economic considerations. Indeed the timing of Federation suggests unity was fostered primarily by the need to organise a concerted drive against craft restrictions culminating in the 1897 lock-out. The Federation had, by 1918, 2,500 members, and the issued capital of 200 of the largest firms amounted to £300 million. Given a total capital estimate of £500 million for industry as a whole this means the average capital of the remaining 2,300 enterprises was under £90,000 (*ibid.*: 10; 1918 XIII: 345).

However, what is perhaps as important as the actual size of concerns is the extent to which, in engineering, growth meant the accretion of fresh layers of clerical, supervisory and managerial staff as a consequence of the 'upward drift' of knowledge and power from the shop floor. Pollard's study of the origins of management shows clearly how their proliferation was linked to the question of control. It was not the arrival of technology *per se*, but its *application* in the capitalist form of organisation that demanded the creation of a group of industrial NCOs. It is significant here that it is in the factory industries, that is, those in which the techniques of work were most altered, that the position of a non-manual supervisor first appeared (Pollard, 1968: 185–8). Engineering is an example of the class basis of this process, for the chronology of control within the trade clearly shows that the movement away from the discipline of the task and the work group was related to the elimination of skill.

To summarise: the conditions of the market and the 'innate industrial Toryism' of the engineering worker combined to allow the small family firm to remain the dominant form of business organisation up to the 1900s. Standardisation, specialisation and repetition were thus limited to few sectors, principally the new light industries. In this sense the federalism of the ASE was reflected by their employers' parochialism, and both were living off the legacy of the lost industrial supremacy of the 1850s.

The Coal Industry: a Revolution of Scale

The character and structure of the coal industry is an example of a revolution of scale rather than method: capitalism 'above ground' penetrated little into the work experience of miners until the early years of the twentieth century. Given the privatised character of work the central problem of management has always been to ensure its continuity and regularity. In this sense the system of yearly 'bonding' and complex piecework arrangements are two answers to the same problem – *labour discipline* – an issue not eradicated by the emergence of a mature capitalist economy.

Industrialisation in mining did not imply a radical change in the capital:labour ratio. Whilst pits became deeper, transport more organised and markets internationalised, the *instruments* of production remained largely unchanged. Both miner and employer existed in an essentially unstable industrial environment, the former working with the changing quality and accessibility of the coal face, the latter unable to directly intervene in the character of production or (in the nineteenth century) have any long term confidence in the price of coal. A corollary of the low capital ratio was, of course, the disproportional effect on profits caused by price fluctuations. Whilst all capitalists faced this to a degree, in the coal industry the market determined far more directly and immediately the entry and exit of capital and labour.

At different periods both employers and employees have used the same tactic: namely, the restriction of output. The workers' side will be discussed later; here concentration will be on the capitalists' attempts to control market forces. It is this disproportionate influence on both sides of the effect of price changes which explains why the coal owners are obsessed with the selling market, and, concomitantly, why miners' unions, in accepting this doctrine, have not applied their efforts to influencing the *labour* market.

It has been noted by economic historians that, comparatively speaking, English industrial development was characterised by remarkably little monopolisation and integration (Dobb, 1972: 25; Foster, 1976:7). A classic analysis of this phenomenon gave the reasons for it:

In England there is no protective tariff, freights from abroad are insignificant, and minerals which can be easily monopolised and which command a monopoly in the home market are very few.

(Levy, 1927: 298)

One exception to this, at least up to the mid-nineteenth century, was coal. However, this was not simply a 'natural' monopoly: certainly up to the 1750s the North East was the only significant coal producing region – a trade that went almost exclusively to London. The coal producers, or 'Hostmen' as they were known, were not petty sub-contractors. Their Guild, formed in 1600 of 44 partnerships or concerns, paid one shilling per chaldron (roughly 53 hundredweight) to the Monarchy for the sole trading prerogatives of sea-borne coal from the Tyne to the Thames (Sweezy, 1938: 9). In 1689 the power of the Crown to grant such advantages was removed and control over mineral deposits passed to landowners, so that during the 1720s coal traders switched attention to the securing of land and wayleave leases. This period also saw the entry of large landowners into the trade, which in turn gave it closer ties to the House of Commons than any other industry, thereby enabling it to avoid punitive legislation (Rogers, 1866: 360–84; Sweezy, 1938: 52). From the 1700s competition appeared from Sunderland and the Wear which the Hostmen could not suppress. Intense competition leads to one of two alternatives, an agreement between the parties, or the suppression or absorption of one by the other. Since the latter was not possible, the monopolists of the Tyne joined with those of the Wear in 1771 to formulate an agreement –

the 'Limitation of the Vend' – which, with a few minor interruptions, continued until 1844. It was remarkably successful: in 1780, of the 866,627 tons of coal imported to London, 98.5 per cent came from the 'Vend' (Williams, 1924: 29).

The operations of this monopoly were described in this way in 1830:

a representative is named for each of the collieries . . . from amongst them a committee is elected of nine for the Tyne and seven for the Wear; this being [done] the proprietors of the best coals are called upon to name the price at which they intend to sell their coal for the succeeding twelve months . . .

(1830 VIII: 10–12)

This became the 'fixed' price for collieries of the Vend; next, each sent a statement showing the quantity they *could* raise in that year, and using these proportions the Committee once a month issued an 'allowance' to each 'whatever quantity the markets may demand' (*ibid.*). Thus a monthly balance was achieved, neither causing a glut nor a shortage, and thereby maintaining actual prices as close as possible to the 'fixed' price.

The stability of all this rested upon the sea trade; once this transportation prerogative was challenged by the railways the system as a whole was undermined. Sweezy, however, has pointed out that the underlying contradiction was the inherent drive to increase productive capacity: once profit could best be achieved by this rather than by rigging the market the Vend became obsolete. Unlike Clapham who saw its demise in terms of emergent 'pure' competition, Sweezy demonstrates how the Vend was essentially at odds with rational *capital accumulation* (Clapham, 1926: 202; Sweezy, 1938: 112).

The main significance of this early monopoly was its central contribution to the uneven development of the coal industry: whilst the North Eastern pits in the 1840s were often steam-aided integrated units, Scotland, Staffordshire and South Wales remained technologically primitive. In the latter district a pit employing over 200 was very unusual, whereas on the Tyne it was considered small (Morris and Williams, 1958: 12; Clapham, 1926: 186). In turn, there was a great difference in the amount, and social origins of capital. In South Wales the cost of opening a pit could be as low as £3–4,000, a sum that, with good fortune, could be returned in the first year. Small capitalists could therefore play a central role: grocers, farmers, solicitors and clergymen were amongst the subscribers to mining partnerships (Morris and Williams, 1958: 141). In the Tyne area the typical investment per mine was £30,000, with the main source of capital being the landed aristocracy (A.J. Taylor, 1960: 221).

The effect of rail transport in the second half of the century was two-fold: on the one hand it created a truly nationally competitive industry, as opposed to the previous regional insularity, whilst on the other hand linking coal as a prime mover to the foundation of the economy. But this occurred unevenly and gradually. Up to 1851 rail traffic had no major part in supplying London; the first North Eastern lines were designed to deliver to existing markets more efficiently, and, up to the late 1820s, were short in length and 'curiously localised' (Clapham, 1926: 87). In short, it was urbanisation and the worker's fireside, rather than industry and the steam engine, that initiated the break-up of the monopolistic trading system, and thereby laid the foundations for the expansion of the second half of the century. The type of coal and coal mine needed for industry is different from that supplied to consumers: namely, larger nuts, cut from 'hard', that is, older, seams, for a market less seasonal in its demand and geometrical rather than arithmetic in its growth. At a later stage the export trade reintroduced significant fluctuations into the industry, particularly in certain coalfields.

The rate of growth in output reflects this. Between 1800 and 1830 average yearly tonnage increased by 3 per cent; from 1830 to 1850 by 4.4 per cent; from 1850 to 1870 by 3.5 per cent; and from 1870 to 1890 by 2.5 per cent (after Deane and Cole, 1969: 216). The most rapid expansion took place before 1850, while of course its *significance* to the economy was greater later on. It is clear that most of this expansion

TABLE 2 i

Year	Area Averages		National Average
1830[1]	Tyneside	300	–
1846	Tyneside, Blyth and Wear	164	–
1869	South Durham	188	
	Northumberland & North Durham	124	107
	Staffs. and Worcs.	72	
1878	South Durham	241	
	Northumberland & North Durham	219	119
	Staffs. and Worcs.	60	
1888	–		148
1897	Durham	404	
	Derbyshire	229	
	Northumberland	283	216
	Staffs.	145	
1914	–		373
1924	Durham	628	
	South Wales & Monmouthshire	415	488
	Derbyshire & Notts.	806	

Note: 1 Clapham, 1926: 186; other figures from the relevant year of *Mining Statistics* (see *Sources*).

came from the multiplication of units rather than from the enlargement of existing ones. Taking the year 1878 as a fulcrum (when the number of collieries was highest, at 3,968), in the 20 years previously the increase was 39 per cent, whilst in the 20 years following it fell by 20 per cent, and by 1924 by another 17 per cent, to 2,481 units (Holbrook-Jones, 1979: 74). It is interesting to note that it was not until the 1880s that increased production did not rest on a growing number of collieries. Average yearly increases for 1870 to 1890 were 2.5 per cent whilst the number of workings fell by around 20 per cent. This is of course only a crude guide to efficiency in an extractive industry, and the size of pits had been rising since the mid-century; but it is indicative of the fact that the highest percentage growth rates were achieved during the period of expanding units.

This trend is also revealed in the numbers of persons employed in pits. The national average grew only very slowly until the 1880s, although of course in certain areas the larger unit was already established (Table 2 i). These figures illustrate not only the leisurely development of the large unit, but also the slow differentiation and domination of the main coalfields. Not until the 1880s does the national average begin to rise significantly. Despite a rush of iron firms opening or amalgamating with collieries in the 1870s, up to this period the typical mining concern had about two workings and a small proportion of fixed working capital.

Price fluctuations directly affected profits and labour's bargaining power, so that capital was likely to be available at times when the work force was best able to resist its introduction into the labour process. On the other hand, the traditional response of employers to increased demand – hiring more labour or opening new pits – continued to be viable. Between 1883 and 1913 the number of miners rose by 125 per cent, whilst the growth in the national labour force was only 40 per cent.

The disparate structure of this industry and its regional peculiarities make the structure of ownership particularly important, as was reflected in the Royal Commissions of 1907, 1919 and 1925. Originally it was the tremendous differences between the type of operation required to raise the coal in, for example, the 10-yard seam in Staffordshire compared with the deeper pits of the Tyne, that led to the wide range of capital and class background amongst the owners. The typical Northern coal-owner had, by the 1830s, £30–50,000 involved, 300 to 600 men employed, and possibly came from, or was connected with, the landed aristocracy. Working on the Midlands 10-yard seam it was possible to launch a colliery with only £2–3,000, employing perhaps 50 to 75 men (Taylor, 1960: 221). In South Wales, whilst small scale operations were possible, the iron trade led to a predominance of middling sized collieries whose production and organisation was directed towards the needs of the furnaces.

By the 1850s the railways had opened up the era of fierce competition for domestic and external trade. This did not lead, however, to a rapid concentration of ownership; what did follow was the *polarisation* of the industrial structure in certain areas. The Midlands and the North seem to have developed the highest proportion of larger pits – but in no way was the small man eradicated (Appendix: Table II). Right into the present century the numbers of mines was responsive to the price of coal. The clearest indication of this can be seen during the price boom of 1865–75. The number of mines peaked in 1867 with 3,258 undertakings, falling to 2,810 in 1872, as the price increases were less dramatic (1873 X: 313). The commission enquiring into the situation reported the emergence of concerns employing as few as 30 men in places as different as South Staffordshire and Durham (*ibid.*: 41, 57). The quixotic state of the industry meant labour was more casual and seasonal. William Brown, a North Staffordshire miner, said that he, like many, made their attendance at work dependent on the price of coal, summer being spent almost entirely at the harvest. Accordingly his local union's policy was to press for the 'best wages the state of the market will allow' (*ibid.*: 230). In Lancashire, 38 concerns had begun in 1872: 'every manufacturer who has any chance of opening out a piece of coal upon the outcrop has opened it' (*ibid.*: 147). The Inspector for South Staffordshire reported that 'collieries spring up like mushrooms, working in some cases a few weeks or months at most' (*ibid.*: 221).

The organisation of the commercial side of the industry was also somewhat unstable. On the one hand, there were the London coal merchants who bought from the factors of the owners and controlled large distributive operations to domestic and industrial consumers. But also there remained a large class of petty coal-dealers who bought from the wharves or railyards (sometimes as little as 140 lbs) and sold it door to door (*ibid.*: 120). Out in the provinces many small pits sold direct to the consumer, particularly in the inland fields such as Derbyshire and Yorkshire (Clapham, 1932: 302).

The next national survey of the industry can be derived from the evidence and appendices of the 1892 Labour Commission. In the expanding South Wales field there continued a rush of 'thousands of immigrants, absolutely unskilled, from agricultural districts' (1892–4 VII:79), whilst in Scotland Keir Hardie attributed the failure of trade unionism in the mines to the fluctuations in agriculture: 'when trade is very bad men flock into the pits. They are always open to all-comers . . .' (1892 XXXIV: 192). The squeezing of the crofters and the exodus from Ireland added to the flow of labour at various times, and since the system of work was 'share and share alike', wages as a whole fell until either the new arrivals returned to their former occupations or the coal trade demand improved. The chaotic state of labour in such areas may have been an advantage to the owners in one sense, but the turnover of miners and the consequent general lack of experience led to costly errors in working the coal, and a higher accident rate (*ibid.*: 187–8; 125).

The major owners had combined to form the Mining Association of Great Britain, but its 121 members employing on average 958 men obviously excluded small collieries. However, the questionnaire sent by the Labour Commission seems to have covered a slightly more representative group. In South Lancashire and Cheshire there were 66 firms owning 130 collieries; in Durham, 48 firms and 149 collieries; in Northumberland, 21 firms and 50 collieries; in Fife, Clackmannon and Kinross, 22 firms and 40 collieries; and in Lanarkshire, 21 firms and 43 collieries. The more systematic enquiry of 1925 demonstrates that the average here of two collieries per firm was (given the intervening period of contraction) still biased towards the larger enterprise (1892 XXXVI Pt. III: 374–82; Appendix: Table II).

Joint stock enterprises arose from the 1860s, but were not really important until the turn of the century. Generally, the greater the regional concentration, the more likely was capital concentration. In South Wales by the 1900s, 80 per cent of the steam coal output was produced by 20 firms. In Scotland the Fife Coal Company was responsible in 1907 for well over half the output of the district (Williams, 1924: 92). Whereas industry generally combined along 'vertical' lines, the coal industry in fact moved away from this form towards 'horizontal' associations (particularly after the decline of the symbiosis between iron and coal in South Wales). One famous example was the formation of the Cambrian Combine. In 1907 the Cambrian Trust was formed with a capital of £120,000. Within a year of its formation it had acquired a controlling interest in the Cambrian Colliery Company, the Glamorgan Coal Company, the Britannic Merthyr Coal Company, and the Naval Colliery Company. Each of these concerns retained its identity, and technical and economic relations generally remained unchanged. Financial control, however, passed to the newly-formed trust. In 1908, control was taken of the firm of L. Gueret, itself a 'mini-combine' and with it came four firms engaged in the distributive side of the coal industry. In 1913 the Trust transformed itself into 'Consolidated Cambrian Limited' thereby eliminating the veneer of autonomy held by associated firms; this organisation commenced operations with a capital of £2,000,000, 95 per cent of which was given in exchange for the shares of the amalgamated concerns (*ibid.*: 95–6).

The real significance of the Cambrian Combine was not its monopolistic character, nor even the extent of its consolidation, but that it represented in the coal industry the transformation that was taking place throughout the economy, that is, from the independent company to the capitalist corporation. After the failure of so many schemes it was generally thought that the coal industry was immune from monopolistic developments. The Cambrian Combine was a concrete refutation of that: it demonstrated that *ultimately* capital in the coal industry did not differ from capital in any other sphere of industry. In other words, it respects no organisational or personal boundaries in the inherent progression of accumulation. However, as has been discussed, this process was uneven and still had far to travel by the 1920s.

Textiles: Size, Location and Capital

The textile industry, particularly the woollen side, was dominated by the privately owned specialist firm involved in one stage of processing, and the individualist ideology of manufacturers (fuelled by the furious competition) was a serious material force in the history of the industrial structure. In the Parliamentary report on Artisans and Machinery in 1824 no long-standing combinations of masters are mentioned, and when the Manchester fine spinners combined in 1830 they chose as chairperson an employer from another trade. Chapman recounts how employers contributed to workers' funds in order to support strikes against competitors (1904: 207–8). Throughout the century combinations of masters emerged only in response to an outside threat: firstly, that of the trade unions in the 1820s, 1830s and 1850s; and second, that of the gathering competition from the USA and Germany.

The structure of the industrial process, a series of discrete operations, naturally encouraged a high *dispersal* of capital, together with considerable geographical concentration. So the history of Britain's first capitalist industry had a peculiar organisational form: an increasing number of units gradually coalescing around the North West. As Jewkes pointed out, this was partly due to the demands of expansion, particularly in the supply of labour. So whilst fundamental progress required a 'combination of processes', and thus a high proportion of fixed capital, immediate interests demanded a quicker return, and a lower entry ticket – facilitated by the 'natural' structure of the process (1933: 98).

By the 1850s the localisation of textiles was underway, a major factor being the availability of transportation and labour in certain areas (A.J. Taylor, 1948–9: 120–5). In contrast to the USA where 39.2 per cent and 56.7 per cent of the northern and southern states respectively combined spinning and weaving, the figure for Lancashire was only 16 per cent. Moreover, in the period 1884 to 1911 the number of combined firms fell again from 470 to 300: the particular suitability of the area allowed specialisation not to contradict with economies of scale. After all, the district also provided coal, machine-makers, lime-free water, and as long as the elementary labour used did not price these services beyond the economics of the specialist firm the industrial structure could prosper by proliferation. On a local scale, this in turn produced concentration in service industries such as the giant Platts engineering firm in Oldham (Chapman, 1904: 157).

Because the textile industry is thought of as the precursor of the modern industrial system, it is easy to overlook the continuing importance of pre-industrial methods at various stages of the production process. Even the mechanised tasks remained relatively labour-intensive and needed considerable experience for their operation in a standard manner. In this sense the under-developed, or uneven, character of production also contributed to the multiplication of enterprises. At the other end of the scale, the rising number of units did not impede the emergence of a few giant enterprises or the combination of factories under one company. In 1795 the Peels had 23 mills, whilst in the early years of the nineteenth century McConnel and Kennedy employed 1,020, David Dale at New Lanark 1,600 to 1,700, and A.G. Murry 1,215 under one roof (Clapham, 1915: 477). Nonetheless in Manchester, the centre of the industry, the average factory employed around 300 in that period, in Mansfield, 211, Preston, 115, whilst the estimated national average in 1816 was 175 persons per mill (*ibid.*: 476).

The available statistics over the next 40 years of expansion are patchy but do not suggest a rapid exclusion of the small firm, despite the geographical concentration. According to Marx, from 1838 to 1850 the number of cotton factories increased by an average of 32 a year, and from 1850 to 1856 by 86 (1976: 541). A chronicler of Oldham noted that from 1821 to 1825 the number of cotton manufacturers rose from 60 to 139 (Butterworth, 1856: 140, 183).

Table 2 ii compiles some of the figures for size and number of cotton factories. These figures reveal two points: firstly that the rise in demand was answered by more factories, rather than larger ones; and second, that (as an obvious consequence) the average size fell. This obscures the important differences between specialist enterprises and combined spinning and weaving concerns which were significantly larger in size than the above figures suggest; in 1841 for example the 313 such firms employed on average 349 persons. By the 1850s, as Jewkes suggests, their numbers were falling and the difference between them and spinning and weaving only was increasing, the former now over three times larger than the latter (Jewkes, 1933: 98).

National figures are not reliable until 1870, but regional estimates abound in contemporary accounts, Factory Inspectors reports and so

TABLE 2 ii

Year	Number of Firms	Average employed in England	Average employed in Chester Parish
1838	856	136	236
1850	1149	166	246
1856	1451	166	247

SOURCES: 1842 XXIII: 12; 1857 XIV: 202; Fong, 1930: 32.

on. The typical mill in Ashton in 1840 employed 75 to 200, in Oldham a majority had less than 100, whilst in Blackburn the figures were 100 to 200 in 1847 (1840 X Third Report: 62; Butterworth, 1856: 118–9; Farnie, 1953: 193).

Not unnaturally it is the larger stable enterprises that figure in local history and in the Blue Books. From these it appears that Manchester and Glasgow were centres of really large mills. In the early 1830s the average Manchester mill employed about 300 to 400 workers, some 30 employed over 500, and seven over 1,000. The six largest firms in Glasgow employed on average 833, although interestingly the introduction of steam power seems to have led to a reduction in numbers – 20 years earlier several of these firms had employed over 1,000 (Clapham, 1926: 184; 1834 X: 19). Statistics of this kind are subject to the traditions and customs of their time: for example McConnel and Kennedy, the fine cotton spinners, in 1833 had 932 employees 'on their books'; however 1,553 actually worked there, the other 621 being formally employed by the other workers, not the firm (Lee, 1972: 128).

At least an approximation of the national situation is available from the 1851 Census: in cotton, wool and worsted there were 411, 82, and 31 firms respectively employing over 100, and constituting 36, eight and 24 per cent of their trade. Of the 2,931 concerns in the whole of these trades, therefore, only 18 per cent employed over a hundred (Census Ages and Occupations I: Table cclxxvii).

In textiles we do not find steam power sweeping through the industry from the introduction of the factory system: the country water-powered mill maintained an important role up to the middle of the century (A.J. Taylor, 1948–9: 115). In 1850 water provided about one half and one quarter of the power in Derbyshire and Yorkshire mills respectively, and 11 per cent of that for mills in Lancashire (*ibid.*). Of course, it would be misleading to minimise the impact of steam, but it would be just as inaccurate to equate its use with a rapid move towards large-scale operations. Of the 2,887 mills mentioned in the Factory Inspectorate Report of 1862, 35 per cent used less than 20 hp and were

built during the period of prosperity after 1858, for the most part by specu-
lators, of whom one supplied the yarn, another machinery, a third the
buildings, and they were run by men who had been overseers, or by other
persons of small means.

(Marx, 1976: 584–5)

In the various other branches of textiles, steam power was even less
important. In 1857 a third of the power in English and Welsh woollen
mills derived from water, and in Scotland, two-thirds (1857 LVII: 338;
22). By 1871 the average cotton factory was using 118 steam hp but in
the manufacture of silk, hosiery and flax the average was well below 20
hp, and in woollens only 29 hp (1871 LXII: 302).

For the years 1870 to 1890 there are reasonably precise figures on
textile factories subject to the Factory and Workshop Acts, published
in the *Statistical Abstracts*, Volumes 31–33 and 47–8. Table 2 iii shows
the total number of establishments covered by the Acts, and the average
work force for England and Wales. Not until the late 1880s does the
number of enterprises begin to fall and the unit size rise. Of course this
series, by including cotton factories alongside jute, hemp, and silk, is
biased. Nonetheless the figures for the cotton sector alone show a
similar pattern, as illustrated in Table 2 iv. In the woollen and worsted
trades these same trends were repeated, although the fluctuations were
greater.

In Lancashire in combined firms these averages would have been
greatly exceeded, perhaps by three times, but they do reveal another

TABLE 2 iii

Year	Number of factories	Unit Size
1870	5968	120
1878	6189	125
1885	6359	127
1890	6180	139

TABLE 2 iv

Year	Number of Cotton Factories	Unit Size
1870	2483	181
1878	2674	180
1885	2635	191
1890	2538	208

side to the archetypal pioneer sector of industrialisation: increased output was until late into the last quarter of the century dependent on the multiplication of units, and as a consequence the work experience of many of the workers would have been of small 'personalised' factories. Averages always distort any series, and it would be incorrect to give the impression that even a large minority of, for example, cotton factories in 1885 employed about 190 workers. From what is known of the industry structure this represents a number in between a mass of small firms and several much larger ones. Thus, in cotton, not one, but two, typical magnitudes is the case corresponding to the type of product, its market and the technology required. Indeed the evidence suggests that the response to market swings and competition was towards speciali-sation rather than capital-intensive efficiency (Farnie, 1953: 147). Here the comparison with America is interesting. The American industry was more highly capitalised, often combining spinning and weaving, and aimed at a relatively stable home market protected by tariffs – geographical concentration did not lead to the separation of processes (and capital) characteristic of England (Chapman and Ashton, 1913–14: 508–9).

So the figures quoted show the fulcrum upon which the polarised structure of the industry swung and are a reminder of the diminutive size of the majority of concerns whose history, unlike the famous giants, died with them.

In terms of the capital requirements and structure of activity in the cotton sector two main points will be dealt with: the variability in the amount of capital required in spinning and weaving, and the degree of dispersal resulting from the character of the production process as it developed in the last half of the century.

Firstly, it seems of prime importance to note that where spinning and weaving were separate concerns (as was increasingly the case in Lancashire), entry into the latter was far easier in terms of both competition and capital. This, however, is an impression gained from primary material, business histories and so on, rather than from data which invariably lump the two together because of the way chroniclers and government officials constructed their statistics. From these sources it appears that the years 1834 to 1860 were the period of fastest fixed capital investment, and thus of falling labour costs per unit (Blaug, 1960–61: 360). This, of course, can be ascribed largely to the intro-duction of the self-acting mule. But Blaug's calculations highlight, by comparison, the relatively low cost of capital needed to establish a business in the first place, that is, buildings, materials, labour, and so on. After Crompton's original invention the factory could for nearly 50 years be supported by an army of outworkers owning their own means of production, employed or unemployed at will, and who, through force of circumstance, had little bargaining power to resist the burden of trade slumps or price wars falling on them. In 1834, of the 300,000 looms, two-thirds were still worked by hand; in Bolton a muslin manufacturer explained to the Select Committee of 1834:

One would suppose that the reward of labour would find its own level; but from the very commencement of it [muslin manufacture] it has been the power of any one manufacturer to set an example of reducing wages, and I know it as a fact, that when they could not obtain a price for the goods . . . they immediately fell to reducing the weavers' wages. (1834 X: 381)

Once the self-actor was introduced, or weaving mechanised, trade slumps were automatically passed on to the labour force – the extent of fixed capital was never sufficient to require some other strategy by the capitalists. In Bolton four years later, 30 out of 80 mills were either not working or were working only partially; during the cotton famine of 1860 to 1864 the Clitheroe weavers worked two or three months of the year, or on two instead of three to four looms (Ashworth, 1842: 75; Sharpe-France, 1953: 154).

Even if steam was available, the early factory pioneers did of course often use water power because of its lower running costs. Chapman's recent analysis of insurance policies of mills based on Arkwright's jenny and Crompton's mule show, for example, that in 1795 in Stockport there were 50 of the latter type with insurance machinery ranging from £50 to £2,000 (1972: 29). Steam often complemented, rather than replaced, water power in the larger country mills: the Quarry Bank mill at Styal in Cheshire installed a 10 hp Boulton and Watt engine in 1810 for precisely this purpose (Rose, 1978: 9). Turbines were used to update this equipment at Styal at a later date; or ingenious and complex waterflow systems constructed to regularise output, as at the Strutts' mill at Belper and Milford in 1816 (Fitton and Wadsworth, 1958: 221–2).

Further savings on initial outlay could be made by the use of parish apprentices from the local workhouses or families, on a seven-year unpaid bond; at Styal such workers made up about one-third of the workers until the 1840s, a practice still also extant in the Halifax woollen mills at that date (Collier, 1933: 120; 1844 XXXV: 20). The truck system, by mortgaging wages from one pay to another, also served to lower working costs, as did the opportune shortage of small coin which justified fortnightly, or even monthly payments. Payment in kind, whether direct or indirect, played an important role in en-suring the liquidity of the Strutts, Oldknow, Greg and Evans family mills, particularly in crises when, for example, as at Owen at New Lanark, wage 'tokens' were issued (Fitton and Wadsworth, 1958: 240–52).

As the cockpit of the partnership system, characteristic of British industrial organisation as a whole, cotton provides a good example of how such an apparently limited system could operate successfully in favourable circumstances. Where profits were high, investment required no further extension of company structure, but merely their retention and recirculation in a new form. Pollard's survey of business records (1964) shows how the small man was able to obtain, from both suppliers and wholesalers, credit or cash in advance, thereby reducing to a minimum actual cash in hand.

The slow progress of the joint stock principle outside Oldham has been the subject of much comment (Jeffries, 1938: 85–90; Chapman, 1904: 170–7; Clapham, 1932: 141–6). Here it is sufficient to note that it is another indicator of what Farnie has termed 'the dominance of small capitals in the industry' (1953: 199). Regional and family ties, particularly in the Manchester area, seem to have adequately financed the textile sector up to the 1890s, although the limitation of this system was felt earlier in spinning. Weaving, on the other hand, retained a substantial number of 'first generation' companies. An official of the Burnley Power Loom Workers' Association told the 1892 Royal Commission that local employers were known as 'mushroom men' because

they work with other people's capital. They begin with the maxim that we have all to gain and nothing to lose, because they had nothing to begin with . . .
(1892 XXXV: 762)

In contrast, 22 years earlier the Factory Inspectorate Report commented of the spinning industry that:

The manufacturers of textiles begin life with fortunes which those of the hardware districts are content to retire with.
(1870 XV: 152)

A survey of 1912 reported that, of 134 weaving firms in the Bolton and Rochdale area, 65 had less than 500 looms, and whilst to the disappointment of the authors this did not indicate significant inter-class mobility, they claimed it did show it was 'still possible to make a small beginning in industrial management' (Chapman and Marquis, 1911–12: 300). This disparity is also reflected in the progress of joint stock organisation: by 1895 it embraced 68 per cent of spindles, but only 38 per cent of the looms (Farnie, 1953: 318). Furthermore, this type of organisation was concentrated heavily in the Oldham area, and vertical integration (typical of this business structure elsewhere) was of little importance (Lee, 1968). The amalgamation movement which had begun in the 1890s in all branches of the industry tended to be one of 'horizontal' associations of family businesses, partnerships and a few limited companies (Clapham, 1938: 227).

Apart from Oldham, spinning firms remained locally financed, partly because of the abundant profits of the earlier years and partly because of the lack of any tremendous technological breakthrough (*ibid.*: 339–40). Also significant here was the active role, post 1860, of the mule spinners themselves in adapting to, and indeed encouraging, capital saving economies (Blaug, 1960–61: 360). Their action in 'absorbing' and retarding the introduction of ring-spinning is a good example (Copeland, 1917: 70–4).

To summarise: the spinning industry retained much of its early characteristics of informal marketing, capital and organising techniques, largely as a result of the heritage of the 40 years of untrammelled supremacy in the world market. In the course of that period it created its 'own' domestic mass consumer market in the factory class of Lancashire: Schulze-Gaevernitz in 1895 estimated that the German textile worker spent only £15 per annum on clothing, whilst his English counterpart purchased over £50 worth (1895: 200); he was also quick to note the coincidence of consumerism with conservatism in Lancashire, a relationship which will be investigated in detail later.

Investigations of the industrial structure of these three industries reveal the continuing importance of the smaller firm in supplying a specific need. There appears no 'rationalising' force or convergent development until at least the 1900s, and in coal much later. The experience of work in the factory trades of engineering and textiles would therefore have been on a limited scale, often cyclical in its recruitment of labour, or seasonal in intensity. Sheer numerical size is important, since both engineers and spinners would have been only a proportion of these total employment figures, and similarly in coal, the underground face-worker was in an analogous position.

It has been seen how, for different reasons, the consequences of pioneer industrialisation were the root cause of the atomistic and heterogeneus productive system, based as it was on the accumulation of *private* capital rather than on the advancement of capacity for society as a whole. The point has also been made (if only implicitly) that the ideology and class origins of the capitalists in a particular sector are a material force in industrial history and of equal interest therefore to the labour historian. Perhaps the mill owner of Preston in the 1850s would have felt considerably closer (in terms of 'social distance') to his spinners than to the aristocractic mandarins of the North Eastern coalfield, abstractly his class allies. But these interesting byways must not detract from the clear picture created by the substantive analysis: capitalist expansion was contradictory and uneven, leaving the diminutive enterprise the dominant force in all three sectors until at least the turn of the century. As such the organisational context of the work experience of engineers, miners and spinners is not open to simple linear generalisations; neither is the specific form of occupational action we would expect to find. In this sense exclusive action and ideology had a material basis in the 'irrational' and divergent form of industrialisation, the empirical outlines of which have been described. With this in mind the substantive analyses of work experience can be approached through the following questions:

1   Can a relationship be traced between pioneer industrialisation and the organisation of work?
2   If, as is suggested, the structure of these industries facilitated skilled occupational solidarity, what effect does this exclusive action have upon the nature of conflict?
3   Is the transition from the 'formal' to the 'real' subsumption of labour to capital empirically demonstrable?
4   Is it possible, from these examples, to construct a preliminary explanation of the corporate nature of working-class response to capitalism as a whole?

APPENDIX: **Ownership and Size 1900 and 1924 in the Coal Industry (1925 XIV)**

TABLE I: The average number of mines per owner 1900 and 1924

	1900	*1924*
UK	1.8	1.8
Durham	2.3	2.0
South Wales and Monmouth	1.6	1.8
Derbyshire, Notts. Leics.	2.5	1.7

NOTE: After Table 6: 176.

TABLE II: Percentage of tonnage raised of mines employing 2,500+ in 1924

	Percentage of tonnage	*Percentage of Mines at work*
UK	16.2	2.2
Durham	22.3	4.3
South Wales and Monmouth	8.4	1.1
Notts. and Derbyshire	24.1	5.8

NOTE: After Table 7: 177–8.

3 Engineers: The Craft Experience

Introduction

Trade union history uses as a benchmark the Webbs' famous *History of Trade Unionism*, although in the last two decades the priorities and methods of this work have been questioned. In particular the Webbs' concern to demonstrate the essential continuity of form between the trade guilds of the eighteenth century and the modern form of trade union – culminating in the formation of the Amalgamated Society of Engineers – is said to ignore the contribution to the formation of collective bargaining of the unruly, episodic and disorganised responses to industrialisation. Luddism and other forms of violence were not the antinomy of trade unionism, but in many trades its precursor. Moreover, these tactics, it is argued, were not a primitive stage through which a 'mature' state was reached, but on the contrary remained an integral part of the relations between labour and capital until well into the nineteenth century (Allen, 1962; Hobsbawm, 1976; Thompson, 1968).

This debate aside, it remains a fact that the ASE has been seen as the archetypal example of those qualities of 'responsibility' and 'accommodation' said to characterise the privileged sector of the emergent working class – an emphasis shared by labour historians as ideologically distant as E.J. Hobsbawm and A.E. Musson. Those taking a Marxist standpoint often begin from Engels's article 'England in 1845 and in 1885', where, for the first time, Marxism as a theory is applied to the reality of the apparent stability of capitalism. His analysis of the condition of the labour movement begins with a famous passage in which he says 'a permanent improvement' can be recognised in two sections of the working class. Firstly, the 'factory hands' whose 'local concentration' and legally enforced hours endowed them with 'a moral superiority' (1971: 391). Here he undoubtedly meant the textile workers, but since the legislation only covered certain products, and since the organisation of work remained hierarchical, it is fair to assume that this category was in fact the spinners – they certainly were the only organised section constituting around 25,000 workers (Turner, 1962: 125). The other 'protected' group identified by Engels was that *least* affected by the competition of women, children or machinery – 'adult men':

The Engineers, the carpenters and joiners, the bricklayers are each of them a power to that extent, that, as in the case of bricklayers and bricklayers' labourers, they can even successfully resist the introduction of machinery. That their condition has remarkably improved since 1848 there can be no doubt . . . They form an aristocracy among the working class; *they have succeeded in enforcing for themselves a relatively comfortable position* [M.H-J. emphasis] and they accept it as final.

(1971: 391–2)

This last sentence is crucial, and is the key to the whole section; it also differentiates the essence of Engels's approach from the previously annotated approaches. For here it is made clear that the position of this *latter* group is in part *actively maintained* by their own group activity and not simply or primarily a result of price falls, changes in work organisation or whatever. Thus the labour aristocracy is composed of two groups, the 'protected' factory workers, and those trades 'resisting machinery'. But the crucial point is that those in the latter category were in a transitional stage of their occupational history. They were neither elevated by factorisation and mechanisation, as were the spinners, nor as yet degraded to the level of the semi-skilled or unskilled. Their position was in part a function of the structure of industrial order, but this fact is subordinate to that of their role in the active maintenance of craft controls, occupational identity and trade cohesion.

What Engels only implicitly argues, but which has been stressed by later historians and sociologists, is that, of course, this activity had a dualistic effect upon the relations between labour and capital: on the one hand, craft control obstructed the employer in the rational exploitation of his resources, yet, on the other hand, in so doing, the workers responsible actively excluded the rest of the work force and, in part, were involved (sometimes directly) in *its* exploitation (Hobsbawm, 1976; Parkin, 1974). There is no need in particular instances to construct a *political* version of the labour aristocracy theory (Foster, 1977; Gray, 1975). These craft workers either partly or wholly paid their assistants, controlled an apprenticeship or occupational hierarchy system which did not guarantee (in the case of the spinners) ever achieving the superordinate position, hired and fired, speeded up or slowed down production as their interests demanded, and ultimately influenced local and parliamentary politics for their own ends. The argument is to what extent this dualistic role was a factor in the frustration of a wider class-consciousness. Did the craft workers provide a model of reformism for the unskilled masses to follow? (Bauman, 1972; Pelling, 1968.) Were they 'bought off' by the profits of imperialism? (Lenin, 1970, 667–763.) These and other questions posed at the level of society as a whole often hinge upon the experience of the engineers and their union, and for this reason the following analysis of their work experience must assume wider implications in labour historiography.

Era of the Millwright

Modern industry never views or treats the existing form of a production process as the definitive one . . . it is continually transforming not only the technical basis of production but also the functions of the worker and the social combinations of the labour process.

(Marx, 1976 I: 617)

'Engineering' as an occupation was the product of the sub-division and atomisation of the role of the all-round craftsman and small producer of the industrial revolution. Steel and high grade tools, available from 1750 onwards, gradually transformed his craft from a timber to a metallurgical one, though as late as 1818 the *Book of English Trades* lists the 'turner' as primarily a woodworker (Thompson, 1968: 270–1). This initial convulsion was expressed through the formation of a variety of Friendly Societies in the first two decades of the nineteenth century; the Iron-moulders, Vicemen and Turners, Mechanics, and, in 1824, the Steam Engine Makers Society which was the largest with around 5,250 members by 1836 (Jeffries, 1945: 19).

These small organisations were omnipotent within their own corner of a trade. The young William Fairbairn arriving in London in 1810, after a five-year apprenticeship, applied to join the Shipwrights Society whose rules specified a seven-year minimum. On discovering this Fairbairn attempted to falsify his indentures, a ruse discovered by the Society, and his application was duly turned down. His only alternative, with the metropolis thus closed to him, was to tramp out to rural Hertfordshire where the Society did not influence the trade, and there he got work (Smiles, 1908: 310–12). An established millwright by 1814, he was to write of his own craft years later:

In those days a good millwright was a man of large resources; he was generally well-educated, and could draw out his own designs and work at the lathe; he had a knowledge of mill machinery, pumps and cranes, and could turn his hand to the bench or the forge with equal adroitness and facility. If hard pressed, as was frequently the case in country places far from towns he could devise for himself expedients which enabled him to meet special requirements, and to complete his work without assistance. This was the class of men with whom I was associated in early life – proud of their calling, fertile in resources, and aware of their value in a country where industrial arts were rapidly developing.

(*ibid*.: 303)

Fairbairn apparently saw no contradiction between this eulogy of the skilled worker and the comment in his autobiography at the time of his rejection by the Shipwrights that 'the junta of workmen had no right to impose restrictions upon my free labour' (*ibid.*: 313). But of course the generic skills of the craft worker were dependent on precisely these restrictive practices; skills which it took 900 pages to describe in *The Operative Mechanic and British Machinist* (1828).

It was the growth of the cotton industry that really created the conditions for the emergence of the 'engineer' as a metal-working wage labourer; the basic division was between those concerned with powering and those with building the Jenny and the water-frame (Clapham, 1926: 152). The evidence suggests that by the 1820s the craft had retained the body of trade defences despite the repealing of statutory apprenticeship regulations. Interestingly, the employers argued that this measure had ended *combinations* and not the apprentice system itself, yet of course one predicates the other. Nonetheless, Alexander Galloway, a London employer, took this attitude in his evidence to the Select Committee of 1824 (V:27). Yet at the works of T.C. Herves in Manchester (employing 150 and probably one of the largest firms in the country) expansion of output was limited by the enforcement of the 'five year rule' – only 'legal men' could be taken on otherwise a 'turn out would result' (*ibid.*: 357). Galloway reported his men imposing fines upon themselves for swearing or bad behaviour, a certain indication of some form of association, although he himself deducted contributions to a factory sick fund (*ibid.*: 25–6). The engineers still remained well paid by contemporary standards, although by no means at the top of the artisan wage-tree (Hobsbawm, 1976: 277).

Labour costs were still the main ingredient in the production process. Galloway estimated an average of three-fifths, 'but in finer work we consider the wages to be seven-tenths of the price of every article' (1824 V: 13). Another estimate in the production of cotton machines, a major sector of the industry, put labour as nine-tenths of the cost (*ibid.*: 30). Of course these figures may have been political exaggerations or products of random book-keeping which did not recognise capital as a unit cost, but nonetheless they are indicative of the extent to which skill remained a premium (Pollard, 1968: 271–84) – that is, the degree to which the worker was able to dictate the *time* spent on each process and the rhythm of production. The importance of this is demonstrated when the case of engineering in Scotland is considered, where wages were significantly less than in Manchester or London. Despite this, profits were in fact generally *lower* than south of the border, and the reason for this illustrates the reality of Marx's statement (p. 41). Because Scotland as yet lacked a sizeable cotton industry, machine tools were relatively less developed, leading to proportionately less sub-division of labour and therefore to a higher percentage of labour cost in each article. Such regional differences show the route by which the exploitation of labour must follow and its relationship to the organisation of work, and then finally, as will be seen, to the payment of wages, and the rate of accumulation of capital.

The uneven rate of technological change displaced, but did not dispose of, the skilled worker. His ability was compartmentalised and moulded by external forces, but not as yet dispensed with. For example, machines in the cotton idustry required constant attention: the first bobbin-net machine required as much as two to three months of 'tuning' after delivery before it could function satisfactorily (1824 V: 19–21). Accuracy and precision, in the absence of the slide rest pre-1840s, required even more bespoke work at different stages than pre-factory machinery. The mainstay of the machine-maker, the Jenny, was subject to this limitation in its production.

The parts of the machine are made to fit the rollers and spindles and not the rollers and spindles to fit the parts; for it is chiefly in the roller and spindles that nicety and accuracy are required.

(*ibid.*: 397)

As long as this was the case, improvement in the design and concept stage remained fettered; plans and wooden models became common-place but it still needed a 'very scientific man' to produce them, and a 'very skilful man' to put the idea into practice (*ibid.*: 396).

However, whilst the 1820s and 1830s did not see the destruction of the generic craftsmen, the transistion from the wood- to the metal-worker was not achieved, it would seem, through the same personnel. T.C. Herves recruited his 'leading men' from clock- and cabinet-makers, opticians and other fine-working, though not 'factorised', trades. Herves compensated such men by wages: the expansion of his business relied upon them passing on their skills to the younger men below them – and hence his rage at their successful limitation of the numbers (1825 V: 15–20). Other employers noted how, despite tempting wages, craftsmen in handicraft outdoor trades could not be entreated from their independence (*ibid.*: 21). The relatively larger size of the Manchester firms is partly explained by the availability of labour: they had, of course, the longest tradition of 'factorisation' and thus a longer period of the break-up of the skilled outdoor trades from which the cadres of the first engineering factories came.

Another indication of the transitional stage of the occupation was the rapid turnover of labour. Skill of a new sort was at a premium. Collective bargaining took the form of a constant flow of individual negotiations; Galloway claimed that during the previous 12 years labour turnover had averaged 100 per cent per annum. Lump payments were commonplace – inducements to leading men to leave their present jobs

– and, it was said, up to £50 for foreign assignments (1824 V: 337). Of course, whilst this was going on, standardisation and accuracy suffered, and consequently so did the employers control over the labour process.

Watt endeavoured to remedy the defect by keeping certain sets of workmen to special classes of work, allowing them to do nothing else. Fathers were induced to bring their sons at the same bench with themselves, and initiate them in the dexterity which they had acquired by experience; and at Soho it was not unusual for the same precise line of work to be followed by members of the same family for three generations.

(Smiles, 1908: 180–1)

Perhaps this in part explains the famous paternalism amongst the early engineering firms, particularly those, such as shipbuilding, which were regionally concentrated (Allen, MSS).

It was the change in personnel and the high demand for these types of workers that ultimately laid the foundation for the introduction of piecework. The aetiology of piecework is found here rather than in advancing technology, because engineering was an occupation emerging rapidly, but unevenly, from a wage structure based on custom and statute. This can be demonstrated retrospectively by examining the labour market for, say, ironfounders and engineers up to 1840. These workers undoubtedly had an excellent bargaining position but 'traded off' some of this against non-economic benefits of day-rates, less supervision, mobility and higher status above the rest of the factory work force (Chadwick, 1859: 410).

Contemporary employers did not rationalise their introduction of piece-rates primarily in terms of standardisation, but rather as a method of stifling the emergence of unions. In the 1820s William Brunton, a Lancashire civil engineer, when faced with an all-round demand for a two shilling advance responded by *choosing* certain individuals (his fastest and most reliable workers) for the rise and denying it to the rest. According to him, uniform wages caused unions.

I have noted that whenever men are paid indiscriminately the same wages without reference to their qualifications as workmen, there combination more or less exists.

(1824 V: 323)

Similarly, at T.C. Herves's firm piecework only applied to the lesser crafts 'below the millwrights' who refused categorically to accept the system. Amongst their subordinates wages varied from 30 to 40 shillings, whilst the millwrights in a 'closed society' received a uniform day wage (*ibid.*: 361).

As will be realised most of these early schemes were not piecework in the sense of relating output to wages, or automatically regressive, that is, the payment for each increment in production being at a lower rate relative to the preceding increment. Their significance lies in the extent to which they indicate a need to *supervise autonomously* the pace of work, and thus that section of the labour force which at any stage, was abandoning custom in favour of conforming to, in Hobsbawm's phrase, the 'rules of the game'. In other words, these early schemes were instrumental in the progress of the Weberian work ethic in which effort was proportionate to reward and not to need (Hobsbawm, 1976: 361; Weber, 1929). Over the next 20 years various forms of piece-rate systems were introduced into engineering shops, but a consideration of their forms is here less important than a consideration of whom they involved, and the purposes for which they were introduced.

By the 1840s the evidence begins to suggest a less favourable bargaining position for the skilled worker, as a generation of young workers trained in the 1820s and 1830s began, in turn, to apprentice the next layer of engineers. This, coupled with the advancing use of the planing machine (invented in 1812 but little used up to the 1840s), and a general improvement in tools, increased the available labour. Once again cotton was the initiator. T. Ashton of Hyde mill, probably the largest in the country, reported to the 1841 Select Committee on the export of machinery, that

a very great increase took place in consequence of the demand [for machinery] and now there is an abundance of artisans and preparation for making machines to any reasonable extent.

(1841 VII: 22)

In Manchester, the centre of technological improvement, Chadwick noted a distinct worsening of the conditions of 'machine' artisans from the mid-1840s. No longer protected 'by the market', they were, it was said, turning towards the use of combinations aimed at reducing the supply of labour into the trade (1859: 412–15). W. Jenkinson, a Lancashire employer, stated to the 1841 Committee that tools, which 20 years earlier were no more than

'hammers, files, chisels . . . are now in fact machines . . . I consider that the tools have brought a great revolution in machine making in many points . . . machinery is made by almost labourers.

(1841 VII: 96)

Yet from other witnesses it becomes apparent that progress was not quite so sweeping. Numerous preparatory and concluding tasks remained handicraft, and the production of spindles, a mainstay of many machine-makers, was a 'wholly manual operation' (*ibid.*: 99).

The progress of piecework was uneven. In some areas it still remained the prerogative of the 'lesser trades' below the millwrights. However, in some of the larger establishments we find an interesting reversal of the situation at T.C. Herves's in the 1820s. Now piece-rates were accepted by the highest grades and the lesser workers reverted to day wages. At Fairbairn's of Leeds, employing 550 men, 'piece-hands are generally first class men and some of them will earn as much as £3 to £4 a week' (1841 VII: 104). This amounted to a differential of up to 150 per cent over the other skilled tradesmen and 200 per cent over the labourers. In other words, whereas once the craftsmen accepted a small differential in favour of higher status (primarily in terms of a uniform day-wage), now the leading men, in this firm at least, took piece-rates as a symbolic and material confirmation of their high status (*ibid.*: 104; 120–5). This separation between the piece-men and the rest was to become the foundation of the hated piece-master system which evolved in the 1850s, and which represented the first example in this industry of the 'pacesetter-supervisor' role so disliked by the ASE (1856 XIII: 139–40).

However, the large enterprises, whose employers came to the notice of the various Parliamentary Committees, were by no means typical. In most shops such practices would still be unheard of, and the advances in tools and machinery negligible. Thomas Wood, newly recruited in 1845 to the huge Platt's firm, described himself as a man

who had never worked in a shop with eight or ten men, and with country-made tools, the very best of which, Platts would have thrown away as utterly useless.

(Burnett, 1977: 310)

Another account of a shop in the mid-1840s described it thus (Stone-well-Brown, 1887: 49–50)

There was no steam hammer; all the forging was done by hand, and it was a fine sight to see seven or eight strikers, at the forging of a crank-axle plant use their hammers in rapid succession upon the spot indicated by the smith . . . All the light turning was done by hand without a slide rest.

Not that this meant inaccuracy:

I have seen two pieces filed so perfectly when placed one upon the other the lower piece would hang to the upper by the force of molecular attraction, as if glued to it.

Old customs still prevailed: on reaching 21 Wood was called upon to provide a supper for the whole shop although his poverty precluded the use of the usual venue, a public house. Young apprentices would traditionally be asked to stand a gallon of ale on their first day, and on occasion had to present the leading hand with a gift of some sort, often an expensive tool or book (Burnett, 1977: 308; Stonewell-Brown, 1887: 48–9). Other accounts describe similar practices in the 1860s and 1870s, particularly those relating to apprenticeship (Taylor, 1903; Wright, 1867).

Tramping was still usual; an important part of the initiation into the various societies was the obligation of hospitality towards these men. Wood, after just over a year at Platt's was 'stopped' because of lack of orders and set out on a fruitless search for work. He eventually found a position in a small shop 'with no proper order or economical order of working' (Burnett, 1977: 311). In such situations there was much less pressure and supervision. Hugh Stonewell-Brown described his shop in the early 1840s:

I cannot say we worked very hard . . . In the fitting shop we took our turn to watch for the foreman as he came up to the sheds . . . Another man who made cross-heads rarely did an hour's work a day.

(1887: 51)

Whilst apprenticed Brown managed to teach himself Greek during his working hours (*ibid.*: 57).

Thus, by the middle of the century there co-existed firms which reflected the future and the past in engineering. As suggested earlier, the survival of these firms was not an incidental freak of industrial progress but a necessary consequence of the structure of engineering, its capital market and the limited nature of consumer demand.

Technological Change 1850–1900

The development of textile machinery, particularly the power loom, and of railway locomotives, underlay the transformation of the engineering industry between 1830 and 1850. The major change occurred in the utilisation of machine tools which brought some element of automation and standardisation into the work process. However, the heritage of written history tends to obscure the difference between potential use and actual use. This bias comes from two principal sources: the accounts of employers and inventors, and technical histories. An example of the former is Nasmyth's account of the progress of machinery in his factory (although it is interesting to note that most changes were motivated by worker recalcitrance or strikes):

The machine never got drunk, their hand never shook from excess, they were never absent from work, they did not strike for wages, they were unfailing in their accuracy and regularity.

(Smiles, 1883: 193)

The existence of a tool, or a new method or system of working tells us nothing of the extent to which it was in use. The standard text on the history of machine tools dates the introduction of the turret lathe to between 1860 and 1890, regarding its use as a crucial indicator of the degree of mass production (Steeds, 1969: 55–70). Yet contemporary accounts of the 1890s and later mention it only occasionally as a new invention. At a bicycle works W.F. Watson recalled:

In those days in 1897 all components were made by hand on centre lathes, each unit being separately handled, and the tools constantly changed for each operation.

(1935: 12)

When finally introduced, the turret lathe did revolutionise the work, but its use was restricted by the refusal of the ASE journeymen to do the skilled task of setting it up for a run of work (*ibid.*: 13). A survey in 1928 dated the 'widespread use' of this machine to post-1900 and, even then, 'It is impossible to give any exact idea of the extent to which semi-automatic and automatic lathes have replaced the ordinary types' (Rowe, 1928: 265). The principles of Whitworth's standardisation scheme were finalised by the early 1830s, yet 20 years later, in a series of lectures to commemorate the 1851 Exhibition, his system was being advocated rather than praised as a

process which would have the effect of making the construction, application and repair of all work into which screws enter vastly more easy and expeditious than it now is.

(Clapham, 1926 I: 44)

As late as 1886 the President of the Institute of Mechanical Engineers was still impressing upon his colleagues Whitworth's other contribution, the recognition of the importance of 'working to gauges throughout' (*ibid.*, 1932 II: 75).

With the reservations made above, the main developments in working methods can be summarised:

1   The hardening of steel was greatly improved by F. Taylor's tungsten alloy which allowed the cutting speed of tools to be increased by 300 per cent to 90 feet per minute. These were commercially introduced in Britain from the 1900s, but were not established until after the First World War (Rolt, 1965: 200–220).

2   Traditional driving methods were based upon the steam engine, power being transmitted to each machine through overhead belting, examples of which were still common in the 1930s. From the 1890s electric and gas engines working a geared headstock allowed greater flexibility – although their use led both to the facilitation of mass production *and* to an extension of the small shop, since they required less capital outlay (Steeds, 1969: 118–119; Allen, 1929: 209).

3   By 1850 the lathe had become 'an industrial machine tool of precision and high capacity' with all the essential developments of its modern form (Woodbury, 1961: 117). The self-acting slide rest, established by the 1840s, 'really marked a far greater step forward than has any subsequent improvement' (Rowe, 1928: 264). The extension of the slide-rest principle in the form of the turret or

capstan lathe has already been discussed, but also worth noting is the emergence of 'speed and feed' rates, fixed by the office, for the most advanced lathes. These systems appeared in the 1880s and depended on a high degree of specialisation amongst the work force – otherwise these rates were bargained individually between the worker and the foreman under the rubric of the existing piece-rates. The two systems – 'fixed' and 'analytical' piecework – co-existed up to 1914, but it was the adoption of the latter in the 1890s that was a causal factor in the strike of 1897 (Burton, 1899: 174–5).

4 Up to the 1890s boring was done on a modified lathe, and then, with the invention of the radial drill, it became a specialised operation. The radial drill allowed the work to remain stationary whilst the drill moved to obtain the correct position. Up until 1861 the drill itself was simply a pointed piece of metal, with no cutting edge; the twist drill greatly increased the capacity of boring machines (Rowe, 1928: 266; Floud, 1976: 28).

5 Slotting and planing machines remained basically unchanged from their invention in the 1830s until 1914. The planer could travel faster across the work by using the improved cutting steels, but the principle remained the same, as did the semi-skilled status of the operator (Rowe, 1928: 267).

6 The milling machine, on the other hand, was largely developed during the period from 1850 to 1914. It differed from the planer insofar as the tool revolved and the work remained stationary. The Plain and Vertical machines were introduced into Britain from the 1890s, and the Universal model some 10 years later, the latter allowing the work to be tilted to any angle desired (Floud, 1976: 29).

The reasons for the slow permeation of new ideas and methods throughout the engineering industry seem to be threefold. Firstly, there is the opposition by a strong craft union to new techniques which weaken its position (this is dealt with in detail later). Second, there is the fact that many workshops made their own tools, particularly in the key 'motor' sections such as textiles and railways. This insulated developments from one another and lessened the likelihood of complete re-tooling (Saul, 1970: 162). Third, there is the state of the market. Long runs are essential to cover the cost of special machine tools, the elaborate jigs and templates, and the time taken to set them up – and this applies as much to the makers as to the users of machine tools.

Having noted these possible factors, what is significant here is the lack of fundamental change in methods and machines from 1850 to 1890 – major inventions occurred before or after these dates. This supports Jeffries's assertion, at first rather startling, that:

The spread of the processes and inventions in the first half of the century rather than the developments of new methods, was the main characteristic of the years between 1850 and 1890. The fitter and turner in an up-to-date shop of the 1850s would have been quite at home in a shop of the 1890s.

(1945: 55)

Thus the context of the work experience of the engineers is not a revolution in methods, but a long process of attrition, an interregnum within which engineering expanded by eroding, but not by eliminating, craft control.

The 1852 Lock-out

The progress of unionism in the 1840s reflected the uneven state of the industry. The 'second generation' of factory engineers were now emerging as the majority of the adult skilled labour force, whose apprenticeship had been based on the two prime tasks of fitting and turning. It was 1842 when the Friendly Society of Mechanics changed its name to the Journeymen, Steam Engine and Machine Makers and Millwrights Society (JSEM), the nomenclature being indicative of its new industrial composition. This union became the first to assume national proportions, dominating the Northern centres and having branches in Greenock and London (McLaine, 1939: 137, 156). Unlike its various predecessors the JSEM did not require the customary seven-year apprenticeship but allowed any man to join who had worked five years at the trade (Burgess, 1975: 16).

This body, however, remained distanced from the London mill-wrights whose industrial heritage and attitudes were founded on the tradition of high quality specialist manufacture in the production of scientific instruments and clocks (Burgess 1970: chap. I). However, the two were brought together by the prosecutions of engineers involved in a strike led by the JSEM in Newton-le-Willows in 1846. Nine convictions for 'intimidation' and 'conspiracy' provoked a national outcry and committees were established within the trade to finance an appeal, the London body being led by one William Newton. The successful outcome of this agitation (all nine were acquitted on appeal) did much to promote the idea of amalgamation as well as to create the first opportunities for personal meetings between the various societies. This was the context in which the Amalgamated Society of Engineers was to emerge, but, given its disparate composition, its formation was not to be easy.

The negotiations began in 1850 against a backdrop of a series of important local disputes concerning the principles of the engineers' trade policy. These events, described in detail by Burgess, demonstrate how strong factory level organisation was in certain areas, and the survival of craft instincts. For example, one such incident involved the fining of a man working on a self-acting lathe for 'skulking' at his work. As in other disputes, this initiated a successful strike against the whole system of fines – designed as they were to complement capital-intensive methods of working (Burgess, 1972: 646–9). In contrast, another important inaugural dispute concerned a Bingley firm employing only 41 men and boys, and was related to the number of apprentices and the raising of adult wages to journeymen status (*ibid.*: 646).

These two conflicts reflected precisely the combination of the 'old' and 'new' problems facing the engineers. It was also the uneven state of the industry which nearly frustrated the appearance of the ASE itself. After months of negotiations riven by sectional interests, the grand 'new model union' was launched with a meagre 5,000 members, some 2,000 less than its parent body, the JSEM (Jeffries, 1945: 29). However, within eight months of its inception the Webbs' assessment was that, perhaps partly through these successful local strikes,

by October [1851] Newton and Allan were at the head of a united society of 11,000 members paying 1s. per week each, the largest and most powerful Union that had ever existed in the engineering trades . . .

(1920: 213)

Burgess (1969) has made a strong case for the argument that the 1852 lock-out was essentially the product of the methods and practices of the 1830 to 1848 boom period being applied in the subsequent three years of trade decline, and with this, very importantly, a slowing in the rate of technical change. This interregnum was initially caused by the sharp drop in railway building requirements from the late 1840s – during its peak railway building was worth five to 10 million pounds per annum (Mitchell, 1964: 328). However, the expansion of machine tools during the boom had begun, and in some cases, completed the transition from a labour- to capital-intensive industry. This compelled the employer to persist with a high labour utilisation, for example, piecework and systematic overtime even during 1848–51, when trade was slack. The Parliamentary Committee on masters and operatives of 1856 (XIII) reported an ASE official to the effect that both shift and Sunday working was common in London in 1851 (*ibid.*: 144). Burgess concludes that:

the issues in dispute during the 1852 lock-out arose from the hostility of skilled workers to capital-intensive labour utilisation in a period of depressed trade.

(1969: 231)

The introduction of unskilled labour, piecework and overtime had been cushioned by the runaway demand of the 1830s and 1840s; now the depressed state of trade meant the skilled engineer found himself with little bargaining power. In another article Burgess shows how the final confrontation came as the ASE rank and file began to take independent action to restore their former position towards the close of 1851 in the context of a slowly improving trade cycle (1972: 646–654). A survey of the membership in August revealed overwhelming opposition to piecework and systematic overtime, both of which were considered to cause unemployment and bad work. And it is clear that the leadership, at least, considered that many employers would view the concession of these points as an easy method of curtailing competition (Hughes, 1860: 173). As for the rest, an ASE circular (*ibid.*) declared:

The amalgamated trades are strong enough to meet any storm of opposition which may arise, and to support those who are faithful to their order . . .

The events of the lock-out have received considerable attention in recent years, and in general terms are well established. Whilst exact interpretation in terms of the impact on the ASE and industrial relations in general is not unanimous, most observers seem to agree that, in Burgess's words:

Technological change had undermined in a fundamental way the privileged position of engineering workers who found themselves isolated and divided.

(1972: 660)

As a consequence, 'independent craft autonomy in the engineering industry more or less came to an end' (Foster, 1977: 227). But this question cannot be judged on the facts of the 1851–2 lock-out alone, but must also be considered in the context of the years preceding the 1897 strike. In purely formal terms the contest was an outright victory for the employers. The ASE members returned on humiliating terms, and were forced to rescind Rule XXIII of their constitution which forbade piecework; membership fell by some 2,000 and the funds from £21,705 to £1,721 (Hughes, 1860: 186). Yet almost immediately when work resumed after the four-month lock-out the Society began to recover; eight new branches were established in that same year, and by 1858 the fund had risen to £30,000 and membership was over 17,000 (*ibid.*: 187). It would seem worthwhile, therefore, to examine the next 50 years of the Society to determine to what extent the craft tradition persisted despite the employers' hostility.

Custom and Tradition

The work experience of the engineers in the years 1850 to 1914 did not simply consist of paradigmatic changes in technology, methods of payment or trade union structure. What was involved was the transition of the 'inner life of the workshops', that subterranean complex of beliefs and attitudes which together with skill and collective action make a craft union. As a revolutionary form of social organisation capitalism overthrows, at all levels, traditional modes of activity and behaviour – and, especially in the sphere of work, this revolution can be dramatic. It is not therefore surprising to find opposition to capitalist methods of work resting upon custom and tradition: resistance through rituals.

At various points this ritualism surfaces in the orthodox histories of unions or industrial disputes, but its role is subordinate to convention: if a custom is formalised, either in a legal or civil agreement, it becomes 'history'. But history is much more subtle. In the example of the issue of piecework and the 1852 lock-out can be seen a custom formalised into a convention embodied in Rule XXIII of the ASE which was rescinded at the end of the dispute. As will be shown, this was by no means the end of the matter. Resistance, successful resistance, continued in the day to day life of the workshop, occasionally emerging into open conflict as written 'history'.

The maintenance of the idea that conventions depend upon custom is crucial for labour historians. Without it the history of work experience, for example, would be a one-dimensional descriptive discourse. For the same reason that it is important, it is also largely hidden from the usual historical sources, and any account of it is somewhat episodic.

The significance of custom and tradition is that they represent an implied collective attempt to 'keep alive' the other side of the worker not required by capitalism – the capacity to discuss; enjoyment and improvement; pride in the work. For example, the practice of shop discussion around the symbolic grindstone in the dinner hour – subjects including philosophy, literary and cultural topics, as well as trade concerns – was seen in the Blackwood and Gordon works in the 1850s (P. Taylor, 1903: 60). Then there was the 'ringing in' ceremony – the banging of tools against the machines reaching a thunderous climax – to celebrate marriages or the end of apprenticeships. The whole work force would congregate in the main shed, usually on pay day, whilst the celebrity made his ceremonial exit or entry (Wright, 1867: 100). These events were also the occasion for an all-round collection for beer to 'wet' the newly-married or newly-apprenticed. This practice, often called 'footings', originated as an obligation paid each week, but by the 1860s seems to have been restricted to special occasions (*ibid.*: 96).

Apprenticeships, for the greater part of the century, were maintained via custom; in particular the ratio of learners to skilled men was a point of contention and only settled through local activity. Whilst the ratio worsened from the workers' point of view, traditions associated with it seem to have survived, indicating that at least the men themselves did not simply view the introduction of a new young lad as an addition to the work force, but saw this as part of an initiation into a trade. Significantly, it was his qualifications as a look-out for the foreman or as a smuggler of drink, rather than his mechanical aptitude, that impressed his superordinates in 1867:

> . . . if he does well in keeping 'nix' for the foreman whilst the workers read, smoke or do 'corporation work' he will be regarded as a treasure, a youth of promise. If he fails at these initial tasks he will be regarded as one concerning whose capacity to learn his trade there are grave doubts.
>
> (*ibid.*: 85)

Hugh Stonewell-Brown apprenticed at 14 in 1854 found his 'engineering' consisted solely of making tea and standing at shed doors as look-out for the first three months. On his first day he was expected to spend 10 shillings on drink for the journeymen and forced to suffer a ritual of pranks and jokes, including being sent on the still popular errand to fetch the 'left-handed spanner' (1887: 48). The ritual of jokes and pranks symbolised the superior position of the journeyman by emphasising the mystery of the craft. An apprentice of the 1900s, even with a quick wit, could be fooled:

> One hesitated only to be damned for indolence. How to decide in a milieu where a rubber hammer was a foolish joke and a leather hammer a legitimate tool?
>
> (Roberts, 1976: 166)

This superiority was also confirmed in another way by the meniality of the initial tasks detailed to new arrivals: 'In three minutes the charge-hand had taught me all I needed to know "Now gerron with it" he ordered . . .' (*ibid.*: 159).

Peter Taylor, apprenticed in 1855, found himself operating a hand-bellows for the furnace as well as acting as teaboy (1903: 46–7). The emphasis on character in the 'inner life of the workshop' is indicative of the attitude of the craft workers to apprentices: they wanted particular types of *people*, not just mechanically able youths. Of course the system benefited craftsmen, particularly up to the 1880s (before apprentices began to be used on semi-automatic machines), and their limitation was seen as a vital part of trade policy, and thus linked up with the ASE's recruitment criteria which stressed moral and social virtues as well as the obligatory training.

The observance of 'Saint Monday' is often solely associated with the outdoor trades and non-factory occupations, such as coal-mining. There is, however, evidence to suggest it was common amongst the engineers, at least up to the 1890s, as part of a wider non-industrial attitude towards time (Wright, 1867: 107). E.P. Thompson has distinguished between time as 'currency' and time demarcated by *tasks*. In the former, 'the employer must *use* the time of his labour, and see it is not wasted: not the task but the value of time when reduced to money is dominant' (1967: 61). Where time is governed by tasks – 'task orientation' – activity is determined by necessity, and 'work' and 'life' are intermingled. Obviously, as Thompson points out, conditions of industrialisation generally, and factory life in particular, demand new attitudes and behaviour. The pre-industrial legacy, despite the assiduous socialisation propaganda campaigns of employers and moral reformers, persisted. Employers in engineering often found it difficult to 'cash in' on trade booms, for the higher wages they paid to their workers resulted in greater absenteeism. James Nasmyth, overloaded with orders for the Liverpool to Manchester railway, bemoaned the fact that:

The workmen attended less regularly, and sometimes when they ought to have been at work on Monday mornings they did not appear until Wednesday. Their higher wages had been no good to them, but the reverse. Their time had been spent in two days extra drinking.

(Smiles, 1883: 192)

W.F. Watson relates his experience in an ASE shop in Manchester at the turn of the century. When a Monday morning had been worked, in the pub at their dinner hour the men would toss a coin to see if they should return for the afternoon: 'If the coin stayed up they went to work, if it fell to the ground they stayed out' (1935: 34).

There was also a conflict over time in general between the employer and the engineer, the most obvious manifestation being the piecework issue. The rational regulation of work requires the organisation of time and effort – the more so the greater the capital intensity. But craft workers brought to their work situation a residue of the 'task orientation' attitude to time. In 1856, according to *The Engineer*, the shipwrights of the north were striking *against* a reduction in hours with the same pay, a move instituted by the employer 'in order to prevent the frequent interruption during work hours, by allowances of time for refreshment.' The workers however, preferred longer hours with frequent breaks (apparently every two hours or so), which allowed them to organise their time and effort (June 13th 1856). In a well-known dispute in 1907 the Engineers' Executive signed an agreement ending the breakfast break by starting work at 7 a.m. rather than 6 a.m., but this was turned down 2:1 in a national ballot. Clearly this issue, coinciding as it did with a series of disputes over 'clocking in' and piece-rates, remained linked in the engineer's mind with the general issue of autonomy (Croucher, 1971: 40). W.F. Watson experienced the transition to 'American' conditions of labour in 1904 in one of his many jobs. Formerly tea had been brewed on a gas burner as and when it seemed propitious. Of course the new work schemes could not allow this and the management (just to make sure) threw away the tea brewer, 'but age old customs are not so easily abolished. We soon made new bunsens . . . made tea surreptitiously and hid it under the bench' (1935: 28). In a later job at Thorneycroft's where trips to the toilet were limited to two seven-minute sojourns, 'passive resistance and sabotage' were widespread (*ibid.*: 92). In time, of course, such attitudes towards time and effort were tamed as the incentive principle became accepted. Alfred Williams described the scramble in 1912 to be offered extra work in a rail shed:

The putting on of a few new hands and the addition of a night shift would obviate much overtime and give the unemployed a chance, but the daymen are offended should that proposition be made. I have actually heard men volunteer to work double-handed at the fires and promise to turn out considerably increased quantities of work on their turn rather than for the foreman to run a night shift and so prevent them from working overtime.

(1915: 294)

Also indicative of the engineers' attitude to time was the widespread practice of 'corporation work', that is, their own work, often making tools or home gadgets. An important role of the apprentice was to warn of the approach of authority when such work was underway, and occasionally aid in secreting it out of the factory (Murphy, 1914: 25; Wright, 1867: 85). In some shops this activity was 'overlooked' by employers, in others efforts were made to stop it. Amongst the London engineers in the 1900s these 'jobs for the King', as they were called, required considerable unofficial organisation. At the time the rather apocryphal story was circulating that a man at the Woolwich Arsenal had made himself a complete lathe in this way (Watson, 1935: 23).

It would be wrong to interpret these shop customs as incipient demands for *control* in a political sense; they are much more akin to symbolic acts of a labour community. As such they strengthen the sense of separate identity and autonomy, and thus indirectly solidarity, and must therefore have a material impact on the relations of labour and capital. Whilst in essence they are conservative and corporate responses to the restrictions and petty tyranny of factory life, once threatened alongside other 'orthodox' matters, such as wages, they undoubtedly contributed to the character of the ensuing disputes. This dialectical process is best summed up by Carter Goodrich:

There is a certain distinction between the resentment *against being controlled in a certain way* and the resentment *against being controlled at all*. But even more significant than the distinction is the fact that the one passes so readily over into the other.

(1920: 30)

This was nowhere better shown than in the regional pay disputes of the period from 1897 to 1914. In particular the 1908 strike in the North East represented a good example of these struggles to maintain the *district rate* for the craftsman, irrespective of the vicissitudes of trade. Newcastle District Committee established 36 shillings as the minimum wage at which a journeyman should labour, and neither appeals by the ASE leadership, nor the five-month strike that ensued could change their view. The final ballot showed 40 per cent still against a return on the basis of a one shilling reduction (Jeffries, 1945: 153; Croucher, 1971: 40–64). This sentiment originated from the strongly held belief that a craftsman was defined by the fact that his wage – set by the District Committee – was not subject to seasonal or market fluctuations. It was not, as Jeffries suggests, merely 'the first fight for a fixed minimum wage', but a reflection of the *principle* of a craft wage. The speeches and propaganda of the engineers relied heavily on this idea. At a meeting held in Bishop Auckland market place in May 1908 *The Socialist* (June, 1908) reported an ASE branch official to the effect that: 'Without doubt the employers wish us to be reduced to the level of labourers . . . the 36/- is our defence of our trade.' A local ASE member made the same point in a different way in a letter to the *Northern Mail* (February 21st 1908):

We have been put on long enough . . . We have been compelled to work alongside non-unionists – that is one of the terms of employment – and many a man who has been known to belong to the ASE has hardly been able to call his soul his own.

Further support for the view that this was a struggle over principle comes from the fact that the bedrock of the strike were the highly skilled day-wage marine engineers of the Tyne basin. Croucher also shows how there was almost exact correlation between the prevalence of piecework or premium bonus and the first weakening of resolve in the dispute (1971: 78–80).

The view the engineers had of themselves was probably strengthened by the wave of social investigation and reforms characteristic of the era. An important assumption of the time was that the unskilled and semi-skilled were a product of the disorganised state of the labour market. Casual and seasonal employment were said to be the domain of the labouring poor whose condition of life turned upon the irregularity (rather than the overall paucity) of their income. A Charity Organisation Society report stated (1908: 9):

First, casual labour causing thriftless forms of life, and causing by this irregularity considerable deterioration within its ranks, with the consequent of inefficients and unemployables; second, casual employment regarded as itself produced by the existence of those whose work value is so low that their only chance of employment is to fill up the gaps caused by the fluctuations of industry and to do the odd jobs for which neither brains, physical strength, nor character are required.

This 'theoretical' stance undoubtedly permeated through to the emergent trade union leaders and into union policy, via the Fabians and

Lib-Lab politicians, underpinned by an implicit form of Social Darwinism (Semmel, 1960: 128–141). Up to the 1900s the Society had been able to contain average unemployment at around five per cent, and pay, according to a union official speaking to the Labour Commission, 'has remained stable for the last twenty years' (1893 XXXII: 153).

The encroachment of piecework, of course, opened up the craft to pressures of trade and subsequent fluctuations of wages, without, however, bringing them to destitution. In a London shop in 1902 'slack time' made up three to four months each year, leading to a 25 per cent reduction for the pieceworkers.

In a busy week 72% of these men earn 40s. and 86% not less than 30s. The proportions are nearly reversed in slack time – 85% earning less than 30s. and only 13% reaching 40s.

(Booth, 1903 IV: 363)

To the skilled day-wage men of the North the rising tide of self-help propaganda, combined with the worsening status of their craft, must have identified the employers not just as the perpetrators of low wages, but also as agents of those forces reducing them to the level of the 'residuum'. A participant, Robert Allen of Prennoldsons Shipbuilders, wrote in his notes on the District Committee of May 1908:

There is an overwhelming sense of shame of even discussing acceptance. Bro. Walker has left the room twice this evening on the advice of the Chairman to cool his temper – are we engineers or navvies? is his response to all efforts at conciliation . . .

(Allen, MSS):

The heritage of 50 years of the ASE – its stubborn refusal to accept change, its very conservatism in industrial life – gave custom and tradition a great importance in the work experience of the engineers. The sense of continuity, of a collective memory of the craftsman's role and status in society and work, contributed considerably to the fierce resistance to employer offensives from an otherwise very politically and industrially corporate union.

Apprenticeship: the Hidden Struggle

From the earliest forms of trade union the policy of the craft worker was based upon the regulation of entrants into the trade. The Webbs argued at length that it was the repeal of the Apprentice Statutes in 1814 that galvanised the moribund journeymen combinations of the towns into action – forcing them unwillingly into the first examples of modern trade union action. The 'Old Mechanics' had no formal policy or ratio, although 1:4 combined with a five-year minimum training seems to have been their custom (Jeffries, 1945: 21). At Manchester's largest machine makers in 1824 this policy was in effect – much to the chagrin of the employer who wished to expand his business (and therefore the labour force) but admitted a strike would result if the *status quo* were disturbed (1824, V: 357).

Wages were not the main interest of the pioneer societies amongst engineers. Following the guild tradition they concentrated upon regulating the labour market:

The rate of wages paid was seen as the equation of the amount of labour available to the amount of work to be done; if labour was scarce, wages would rise; if plentiful, wages would fall.

(Jeffries, 1945: 23)

There is no need to label this attitude as 'inculcation of capitalist economics'. No doubt some of the first leaders were aware of 'supply and demand' theory, but far more telling were the practical effects of labour abundance in certain trades in the period 1815 to 1850 – the degradation of the weavers was probably far more influential than the writing of Adam Smith.

The apprentice issue was an important part of the 1852 lock-out. One of the successful local actions in 1851 had been the restoration of the 1:4 ratio at a Manchester firm, resulting in the sacking of 25 boys (Burgess, 1972: 647). Another aspect of the question – the employment of 'illegal' (unapprenticed) men – was the reason for several disputes, particularly in the large northern firms. Whereas the rank and file called for their dismissal, the ASE Executive equivocated on the matter. Being based in the smaller London firms, the latter saw them as less of a threat and furthermore did not wish the strike to be seen as interfering with the employer's right to manage his factory (*ibid.*: 654–6).

Another result of the defeat of 1852 was the expunging of the rule limiting apprentices. True to form the leadership, with a view to alternative strategies of controlling the labour supply, turned to co-operative workshops and emigration schemes. They were neither popular with the membership, nor effective. As with piecework the initiative was very much with the District Committees, the evidence suggesting a considerable degree of success. As Secretary, W. Allan stated to the 1867 Commission that apprenticeship was now governed by 'custom' not rule; for example in London it was 1:3, *more* restrictive than the formal pre-1852 Society rule which specified 1:4. The purpose of this, he candidly informed, was 'to keep wages up; no question about it' (1867 XXXII: 46).

The significance of apprenticeship goes beyond the labour market; its observance by entrants to the trade served as an ideological preparation for the Society as a whole, ensuring its stability. Whilst hand work remained at a premium the apprentice was very much the servant of the men, not of the employer: the latter could not teach him his trade. Thomas Wright observed in 1867 that though it nominally is the master to whom he is bound, who has to teach him his trade, it is on the goodwill of the skilled workmen of the establishment that he really had to depend for being initiated into those little 'wrinkles' and specialities the knowledge of which makes the difference between the good, and the bad or only ordinary workman.

(1867: 86)

The implications of this were spelt out in the 1864 *Rules* and went far beyond a statement of trade policy.

If constrained to make restrictions against admission into our trade of those who have not earned a right by probationary servitude (apprenticeship), we do so knowing that such encroachments are productive of evil and when preserved unchecked, result in reducing the condition of the artisan to that of the unskilled labourer, and confer no permanent advantage to those admitted. It is our duty, then, to exercise that same care and watchfulness over that in which we have a vested interest, as the physician does who holds a diploma, or the author who is protected by a copyright.

(Webb, 1920: 469–70)

The skilled engineer did not simply have a pecuniary advantage over the labourer; there was a moral superiority – an ideological distance. For each improvement they secured was to an extent at the expense of those below them, as much as the employer.

The artisan and labourer were both employees; but there the similarity ended. The mid-Victorian engineer saw himself as the custodian of a trade, on a par with the organiser of that trade, the employer. The ASE supplied the skilled labour, the employer capital: each were masters of their territory. Other unions concerned solely with wages were viewed as crude parodies of a craft society; this was the essential division in the union movement. W. Allan boasted in 1867 that during the previous twelve years there had been only three or four strikes over wages, most disputes 'in defence of the trade' concerning apprentices and piecework (1867 XXXII: 42–3). Clearly the regulation of labour supply was fundamental, and as Hobsbawm has said, 'the whole point of a classical craft union', so that the Society took recruitment very seriously. Character, as well as ability, were assessed,

men who were forced to wear glasses were not allowed to join, and the Bridgewater Branch felt it necessary to consult the Executive Council before admitting a 'worker who is a little round-shouldered'.

(Jeffries 1945: 59)

How successful then was the ASE? An easy guide to this is the extent of unemployment that existed in the union. Between 1852 and 1889 it averaged 4.2 per cent, an extremely low figure (Howell, 1890: 498). This is supported by an official report which examined the 'Vacant Book' of several Society locals (all unemployed members had to sign daily). During 1888 to 1890 (years of bad trade) 78 per cent of the

Society's membership were in full employment; 3 per cent lost three months or more; 1.5 per cent, six months, and the rest under three months (1895–6 IX: 57). These figures could, of course, be due simply to external demand for labour, so it is necessary to discover the actual ratios of apprentices to artisans.

Of the 24 replies to the questionnaire sent out by the 1886 Royal Commission to 'working class organisations' in engineering, it appears that apprenticeships were maintained at five to seven years, but a number of answers were qualified with comments such as, 'Not taught so well, payment gone up by 50 per cent'; 'deterioration in standards, piecework allowed'; 'apprentices put at one class of work only'. It is interesting that those districts which complained most of piecework and systematic overtime were also generally those where apprentice regulations had been allowed to lapse; for example, 'because of the importation of young men at the age of 18 who have served 3 years, the proportion is about 7 apprentices to one journeyman' (1886 XXI, App.II: 7–16). This generally favourable state of affairs was not maintained without difficulties. Three years earlier the Sunderland branch launched an offensive against the 'overcrowding' of the trade: in seven main shops there were nearly 500 apprentices to 700 men. Wage demands put forward at the same time were conceded but the men struck, declaring they were, 'ready to sacrifice part of the advance of wages rather than give up their position on the point of apprentices.' After nearly two years, in the midst of a shipping trade decline, and £100,000 of ASE money later, the strike was abandoned and the issue lost, and with it most of the Sunderland branches (Jeffries, 1945: 103; 1893 XXXII: 353).

At the 30 firms who completed the schedule of the 1892 Labour Commission, 2,788 persons were categorised as 'apprentices or young learners' giving an average ratio of 4.6:1, close to the Society standard. However, as the Chatham and Rochester Society branch stated, real apprenticeships were 'constantly evaded' through 'patronage and verbal agreements' (1892 VII: 178–188; 60–61). From the unions the schedule information is patchy; only seven gave the actual ratio in their area. It averaged at 3.3:1, but in one area, Stanningley, it was actually reversed with one journeyman to two 'apprentices' (*ibid.*: 16–18). In shipbuilding particularly, the fluctuating demand increased the attraction of a high proportion of apprentices for they could be retained more cheaply, whilst the journeymen were laid off. This was another inducement to the Society to limit the number of apprentices (1893 XXXII: 399).

The 1880s also saw the decline of the 'premium apprentice', that is, one for whom a considerable sum was paid to the employer to ensure he was fully trained in all departments, including technical instruction. Of them it was said: 'They come from a different class altogether from our general apprentices' (*ibid.*: 323). *The Engineer* reported in 1908 that William Armstrong's was one of 'the steadily diminishing number of firms which lay themselves out to premium apprentices . . . who do all the departments for a premium paid yearly in advance.' Then there was a second and third grade of young learners, the former attending classes but confining themselves to one department and subject to the same rules as workmen; the latter class was for 'artisans' who were accepted on the basis of a literacy test (February 28th 1908). In 1892 at John Fowler and Co. there were no indentures, but

two classes of apprentices; those who are the sons of farmers, or people of that class, with which we largely deal. We bring them in and teach them the trade as best we can. Then there are the ordinary workmen's sons, what we call boys.

Only the former, 'as a favour to them because their fathers are customers', pass through several shops, the other were trained in one task only (1893 XXXII: 358–9). The practice of 'buying' a trade was not, however, entirely dead. In 1896 W.F. Watson, unable to afford the £40 necessary for his indentures, was initially employed as a 'shop boy' (Watson, 1935: 9).

The general trend was to de-skill the apprentice procedure and, perhaps more dangerous for the Society, to lead to faster turnover of labour in the industry. In Scotland, during depressions,

you would find three to one journeyman. The result is they come to the trade, and afterwards begin to perceive that it is futile as far as they are concerned . . . And the result is that we turn off every year hundreds and hundreds of men . . . in a time of prosperity there is a great number of people come into it, and they do odd jobs at it and there, instead of getting up the wages you will find the result is that the employer has them all at command, and so does not require to raise the wages.

(1893 XXXII: 183)

A writer to the Society's *Journal* (June 1904) reported his own experiences in trying to recruit these young workers:

The main objection given by apprentices when asked to join . . . [is] . . . the possibility of being out of employment as soon as they finish their time, and being non-free members, in receipt of no benefit.

Those who made it to apprentice status could rapidly find themselves victims of mass production. W.F. Watson was put on to piecework making clock-parts and earning 14 shillings a week at only 16 years of age. J.T. Murphy recorded his fight for a proper apprenticeship at Vickers' Sheffield in the early 1900s:

After a spell on a drilling machine and then a shaping machine I moved to a miller. In all cases the process was simple and there was considerable repetition to it. I began agitating to be transferred to a universal miller where the work was more varied and skilled. So began the fight for variety of work and training.

(1941: 23)

In response partly to these changes the Society, in 1892, allowed apprentices to be recruited at 18 years, although, as has been seen, this was not wholly successful. In 1901 a further concession was made allowing 'machinists' who had served in the trade for two years to join at three-quarters of the craftsman's rate. It was left up to branches, however, to decide to recruit such persons. Despite the obviously huge potential reservoir of members, only 4,000 were enrolled in this section by 1904, and in 1917 it was abolished entirely (Jeffries, 1945: 166; Webb, 1950: 486).

An apprenticeship was still the majority's avenue into the ASE. The average age at recruitment between 1900 and 1914 was just under 25 years, a sure indication that some training period had taken place. Characteristically the Webbs' *Industrial Democracy* regarded the whole system as having collapsed because the formal agreements declined, even though shop by shop initiative had not (1920: 470). The non-apprenticed W.F. Watson was faced with outright obstruction: 'I tried to learn something by overlooking the turner next to me, but he checkmated me by standing between myself and the job' (1935: 20). Amongst the London engineers in the early 1900s the seven years was a minimum, plus another two or three years as an 'improver' before full rates would be expected. Significantly, most apprentices remained the sons or relatives of journeymen (Booth, 1903 V: 312–13). Further evidence of rank and file vigilance is the constant stream of letters on the subject to the Union's *Journal* (for example, August 1911; June 1912; October 1913). A Society official (1893 XXXII: 181) explained that the 'Apprentice Union' was begun by the Society in order that

when they became strong enough, and their funds became large enough, [they] will bring pressure to bear upon their fellow apprentices . . .
To prevent them coming into the trade? – Yes.

He suggested the excess should emigrate:

I am not concerned with training outlets for the lads. What I am concerned about is to prevent them having inlets into our trade. The other trades protect themselves.

This in many respects summarises exactly the insular self-sufficiency of the Society's response in many areas. This official's answer to the apprentices was the traditional solution of controlling the labour market; when pressed further he could only propose a limitation of the population as a whole if the problem persisted. As has been seen, these views were based on 50 years of trade experience in an industry whose rate of change was sluggish and whose work force clung tenaciously to a non-instrumental, but highly exclusive, attitude to work and work organisation. The symbolic importance of apprenticeship accordingly lasted well beyond the period when its 'material', 'technological' or 'contractual' basis ceased to exist. As such it continued to influence the shop and society policy of the engineers and thus to shape their struggle for occupational interests.

The Piecemaster System: Authority Deferred

It has been suggested that one of the consequences of the 1852 lock-out for the ASE was the growth of the piecemaster system. In this system a leading hand contracted for a particular job at a rate dependent upon the amount produced, and his receipt of a bonus depended upon his speed in completing the work. The men below him were paid a day wage – sometimes by the piecemaster, sometimes by the office. It was up to him if, or how, he shared the surplus. This form of piecework was particularly insidious: management could choose a few selected men to whom to offer the piece-rate, thereby indirectly affecting the total work force without actually introducing payment by results, and thus incurring the opposition of the men as a whole (1888 XXI: 525–30). The piecemasters became, as it were, 'NCOs' of piecework and the incentive principle which statistical surveys could not reveal, since individually the workers would still be on a day wage, and only as collectives could they earn a proportion of a bonus. Their actual numbers and influence are obviously very important, therefore, in establishing the degree of acceptance, *de jure* or *de facto*, of piecework.

Foster has argued that the piecemaster system was

the central institution of the new type of labour force . . . It meant that the skilled engineer was now actively involved – as pacemaker and technical supervisor – in the work of management.

(1976: 227)

Clearly, if a large minority were involved in the disciplining, supervision, pacing and in some cases, payment, of the majority on behalf of the employer, one would expect this to form an important mediator of authority. But Foster has here generalised too easily from the situation in Lancashire. In 1861 a Society survey showed that of the 533 piecemasters, 75 per cent were in Lancashire and another 10 per cent in Yorkshire (Jeffries, 1947: 40–1). Certainly the system was correlated to size; in 1852 the average number of men employed in Lancashire firms involved in the lock-out was 290. But equally, considerable numbers of larger enterprises in London (the average firm there employed 263) could not therefore have used the piecemaster system at all (Burgess, 1969: 233). Jeffries reports that:

Fourteen of the eighteen questions on piecework concerned piecemasters and the piecemaster system. Only 22 districts replied to these questions as in the remaining 151 districts, in the words of the Belfast branch secretary, there were 'None, God be thanked'.

(1947: 40)

Furthermore, although the piecemaster was formally part of the skilled work force, the evidence suggests that hostility (rather than craft solidarity) was the general attitude of the ordinary ASE member. Two Oldham members of the Journeymen Steam Engine Makers were expelled in 1842 for acting as piecemasters (McLaine, 1939: 192). The 1861 survey revealed strong opposition to the system on three main counts: piecemasters were inclined to employ youths instead of journeymen; they tended to 'drive on the men'; and when the job was finished the 'settling' (bonus) from the employers was rarely equitably distributed. In response to this the Executive Council passed a resolution making it compulsory for the 'settling' to be evenly shared.

It was this latter issue which caused most trouble, and which had initially prompted the Manchester District Committee to send a motion to the Executive from which the whole survey sprung (Jeffries, 1947: 41–2, 28). It is perhaps significant that the brunt of the main objection in Manchester stemmed from a failure to share out the bonus, and was not, as was suggested in other areas, to the system as a whole. The Executive's response seemed to reflect this equivocal attitude. John Burnett described the Union counter-measures:

Any member taking work by piece and not sharing equally in proportion to his wages any surplus over and above his weekly wages paid to members and other persons . . . shall be summoned before his branch or committee . . . if he does not comply with this regulation he shall be fined, in the first instance 10s, in the second 20s and in the third be excluded, subject to the approval of the local council . . . Any member working for or under any piecemaster, and not receiving an equal share of any surplus in proportion to his wages . . . shall be summoned before his branch . . . on refusing to leave such employment he shall be fined for the first offence 20s and for the second offence excluded.

(1888 XXI: 530)

There are several points of interest here. Firstly, the ASE's strategy was to obviate the iniquities of the system through the internal discipline and vigilance of the rank and file, rather than through a general conflict with the employers by demanding its abolition. There were two reasons for this. A small minority of engineers, mainly in the machine and locomotive works of northern England, were actively benefiting through both piecework and the piecemaster system. In addition, as the piecemasters were after all engineers themselves, the Society regarded it as 'their' problem. As Burnett expressed it, a well organised trade can make both sub-contract and piecework 'unobjectionable' (*ibid*). Also of interest is the clause in the rule which specifies 'equitable' as meaning the bonus being distributed in proportion to the existing differential. This is another reflection of the Union's ambivalence: it was as resolutely hostile to piecemaster 'profiteering' as it was to interfering in the local hierarchy of wages and did not want these measures seen as a first step towards equalising wages. The rules passed in 1864 seem to have given official backing to rank and file activity; where the ASE was strong the piecemaster would be held in line, though still receiving five to 10 per cent extra. The main success of the ASE lay in forcing payment through the office, rather than abolishing the system altogether; in the words of William Allan it then became not a form of sub-contract, but a 'clumsy method of discipline' (1867 XXXII: 40).

The view that the roots of the piecemaster system lay in control rather than in productivity is supported by a survey of the sectors in which the system proliferated. It seems to have been confined to erecting, fitting or assembling jobs in the production of steam engines or locomotives; in other words, tasks in which both the character and the pace of work was undetermined: it could not as yet be standardised (Jeffries, 1947: 41). In such conditions individual piecework was impossible, and working in team conditions made the worker less vulnerable to 'outside' pressures. The use of an 'internal' supervisor in sole possession of the knowledge of the amount of bonus, and responsible for the decision on how it would be distributed, was virtually the only method of exporting the incentive principle, given its absence in the labour process itself, and of retaining some element of quality control. Schloss gives an example from an engineering works of an improvement of 21 per cent in productivity (1907: 149). However, by the 1880s the system seems to have become less popular; an enquiry by Iron Trades Employers in 1876 of 157 firms in the Manchester area showed that 26 employed piecemasters, only 15 permanently (1876: 12–14). *The Engineer*, December 3rd 1880, argued that, in the context of a well organised work force, the use of piecemasters could result in a *loss* of control and lack of supervision – an analysis reflected in the views of William Glennie, a Tyneside Society member to the 1892 Labour Commission:

. . . a man works best where he is personally interested. At the present time the division of labour has reached such a stage, that a man automatically does his work without any personal interest in it whatever. . . . The employers attempt to remedy that by the introduction of a taskmaster whose duty is to flog the men up to highest pitch. But the men simply adopt other methods to evade his whip. The result is simply irritation and bad feeling between the employers and the men, and there is no more work turned out than before because the workman as a rule knows his trade sufficiently well to be able to evade the taskmaster.

(1893 XXXII: 178)

At Armstrong's on the Tyne the piecemaster system was, up to the 1890s, 'universal' in the works where, according to the managing director, they used, for

> the erection of certain work, to let it to a man and this man employed a number of men . . . and a certain number of labourers. I am not sure as to if the labourers were paid piece by piece. We did not interfere in the distribution of it, and we paid the headman.

This delegation of responsibility relied exclusively on the foreman and the piecemasters to enforce co-operation:

> . . . a good deal of opposition was taken to it by the men, and the foreman found it difficult to carry out. It was a very satisfactory way of doing the work, and no doubt some of the men made very large profits by it.

> (*ibid.*: 329)

The terminology used here by management is indicative of the authority relations inherent in the system: 'men' employed by the piecemaster are the skilled workers while *their* subordinates are 'labourers'; the headman received 'large profits'; the vagueness of the management's understanding of the methods of payment. All these point to the maintenance of a layered system of autonomous but subordinate groups, held together by the uncertainty of the rate offered and the actual wage earned. At the Thames Shipbuilding Company at Blackwall a collective bonus scheme was tried with the aim of allowing the workers to become 'capitalists for themselves', by tying in the extra increment to the efficiency of the entire firm for each contract. In the words of the employer this was 'piecework on a gigantic scale'. It was adopted because individual piecework 'worked so badly', for 'in times of brisk trade it is difficult to get the men to do the work' (*ibid.*: 316). The piecemasters here simply collected production figures and submitted contract prices for the work available, while pay went through the office.

At a non-union shop in the early 1900s the piecemaster paid the men in the local tavern, and, according to W.F. Watson, cleared £10 to £12 a week – four to five times the average skilled wage (1935: 53–4). Complaints over the attitude of piecemasters persist in the ASE records into the present century – in 1902 workers at Vickers reported the piecemaster paying them directly instead of through the office – but overall the system seems to have declined in almost direct correlation to the rise in individual piecework (Weekes, 1970: App. IV).

It is difficult not to conclude that the rise and fall of the piecemaster reflected the acceptance of the incentive principle amongst significant sections of the Society membership; individual piecework was greater amongst those same sectors where once the piecemaster system was prevalent. However, it is not possible to argue at this stage that the role of the piecemaster reflected some new decisive change in the structure of industrial authority; what is really demonstrated was the *breakdown* of the internal discipline of work and the labour force through the sub-division of tasks. The uncertainty of the task and the hostility of the skilled men blocked individual piecework – the piecemaster became a transitional figure until the hostility of the latter was undermined by the uniformity of the former. As Schloss was to find in his survey of the extent of this form of wage contract in the 1890s, it was more usual in trades where union organisation was weak and the work semi- or unskilled, that is, where the workers had no craft pride in their work (Schloss, 1907: 166–179). The ASE remained a craft union; opposition to the system was often motivated in terms of the pressure to 'scamp' work. In the words of a Society official in 1911: 'If a man's not worth 36/- a week the union has rules to deal with incompetence' (*Monthly Record*, June 1911).

Piecework and the Craft Union

The purpose of this section is to marshall the scanty statistical evidence on pieceworking in engineering and combine this with the frequent references, by both managers and men, to its effects on the character of work. As indicated earlier it is contended that the extent of the defeat of 1851–2 can only be estimated by analysing the degree to which the formalities of the employers' terms were translated into the 'inner life of the workshops'. Furthermore, the progress of the incentive principle, although not synonymous with payment by results, is at least indicative of the workers learning the 'rules of the game' (Hobsbawm, 1976: 361). As the engineer belonged typically to a high status group within a larger subordinate work force, his attitude and responses were an important agent in diffusion of these principles. It should be stressed at this point that the ASE saw its role as a union very much as a custodian of custom: it did not recruit – the fully qualified worker *achieved* membership – and trade policy was occupationally defined, and, as with the industry itself, regionally directed through the District Committees. Overwhelmingly activity was directed to restoring the *status quo* of the craft. This heritage came from the founder unions whose formation dated back to the 1820s and before – the Journeymen Steam Engine and Machine Makers (the 'Old Mechanics'), the Steam Engine Makers Society and the General Smiths (Jeffries, 1945: 28). But within 10 years or so the union had expanded well beyond the boundaries of the old craft societies, incorporating, for want of a better term, the 'skilled machinist', that is, those whose apprenticeships were based upon the slide rest and the machine tool.

At its inception the ASE's first secretary William Newton stated that the first object of a trade society was 'to destroy redundancy in the labour market'. As a result the leaders set up a fund to establish co-operative workshops, the great strength of amalgamation being 'to supersede the necessity of the strikes and turnouts' (*ibid.*: 32–34). As has been referred to earlier, amongst the larger more capital-intensive shops, the rank and file saw the amalgamation (coinciding as it did with a period of good trade) as a chance to re-establish craft rules in the works – an end to systematic overtime and piecework, restoration of the ratio of one apprentice to four journeymen and the repudiating of 'illegal' (unapprenticed) men working in the shops. The schism between the leadership and the rank and file was not over policy but how to effect this policy. After the experience of 1852 both co-operative shops and emigration were pushed by Allan and Newton but with little enthusiasm amongst the membership whose prime concern remained their own position and status.

The progress of piecework in the 1850s and 1860s reflected the uneven development of the industry and the contrasting working methods employed in different sector. Thus both in London and on the North East Coast payment by results was almost unknown, but for different reasons. London workshops were small with a mixed general output, repair work often being a central function; on the Tyne the highly skilled marine engineers were largely involved in bespoke work on ships, boilers or other large 'one-off' orders. In neither case was piecework a practicable or useful incentive for the employer, and in both areas workers were better placed to resist its imposition (*The Engineer*, January 12th 1862). In the words of an itinerant engineer of the 1850s, 'Some of the shops want quality, others speed' (P. Taylor, 1903: 75), clearly implying, of course, that the two are incompatible.

Table 3. i summarises the statistical evidence.

TABLE 3 i   Percentage of Engineering Workforce paid by piecework

	1861[1]	*1886*[2]	*1891*[1]	*1906*[2]
All grades	10.5	7.5	16.8	27.5
Fitters and Turners	–	6.0	–	33.0
Machine men	–	11.0	–	47.0

NOTES: 1 Jeffries, 1947: 43.
       2 1911 LXXVIII Pt. VI.

As would be expected, these figures hide big regional differences. In 1861 in Wales, Ireland and Scotland, piecework was almost unknown, whilst in Yorkshire 11 per cent, and in Lancashire and Cheshire 16 per cent of the membership were employed in this way. There was a close connection between the type of production in different towns and the percentage. The large-scale textile machinery and stationary engine centres of Manchester and Oldham, Rochdale, Bolton and Leeds returned an average of 25 per cent of the skilled men. In railway towns this rose even higher, for example, 66 per cent in Rotherham and 57 per cent in Swindon. But, interestingly enough, other locomotive building centres, such as Crewe, Wolverton and Doncaster averaged only 11 per cent, again demonstrating the heterogeneity of technique. Agricultural machinery towns of the eastern counties averaged 40 per cent amongst journeymen. Finally, in the armaments industry piece-rates were just beginning – an area in which they were to progress the fastest in the next 20 years (Jeffries, 1947: 39).

Individual piecework was far more common than the piecemaster system. In 38 of the 60 districts reporting some form of piecework the former was the only system, and it existed sometimes predominantly in the other 22/27.5 per cent of the total Society *districts* therefore reported some variant of the system. The increment varied considerably and seems to have been governed by prevalence, that is where piece-rates were most widespread the percentage extra earned was lowest. Thus in Lancashire and Cheshire it ranged from 20–25 per cent, but in the northern counties it was up to 40 per cent (*ibid.*: 40).

As a result of the survey the Society took action against the piecemaster system, but it was not until 1874 that formal action was taken against individual piecework, banning its extension into new areas. There is some circumstantial evidence to suggest a slight diminution between 1850 and 1886. Apart from the percentage reduction shown in the table, William Allan reported to the 1867 Commission that 'we have a decided objection to piecework and endeavour to do away with it where we have the opportunity . . .' In Manchester, a stronghold of the system, he said 'there was not so much as formerly' (1867 XXXII: 36–8). From the other side, a shipyard employer claimed unions now *fixed* piece prices to their advantage: 'they are in fact the masters of the situation not ourselves . . . the bonus payments bring average pay up to 31s, where in 1832–5 it averaged 23s per week (*ibid.* XXXIX: 385). In the final report the Commissioners reported piecework as common in iron works, collieries, printing, tailoring, cotton and lace, but generally 'not the practice' in engineering, building and the ironfounders (*ibid.* XXXII: 272). But such evidence is susceptible to polemical excesses.

Piecework was also opposed by the ASE because it created opportunity for the craftsman wage to be affected by trade fluctuations. An official of the Society from Manchester reported to the Labour Commission a form of task-working, suitable where handwork was still predominant. The system was applied

upon work which the men themselves have absolutely to do by their own labour, and the same applies to many other shops in the machine trade. When there comes a depression in trade the employer reduces the piecework prices, but when an improvement takes place he rarely advances them, and the men can only obtain the same rate of wages by additional physical exertion. It has got to its limit now.

(1893 XXXII: 160)

By ignoring pieceworking and refusing to negotiate about it the Society set its craft standards against pecuniary gain. To the same witness it was said:

Then I was right in my conjecture that if the Union were to make piece-prices a matter of negotiation the probability is that you would get a rise? – Yes, we could deal with them. We would rather have it abolished.

(*ibid.*)

This form of stoic resistance seems to have been remarkably successful up to the 1890s, and of course it allowed the Society to avoid a national debate on such a potentially divisive issue.

According to a leading Tyneside shipbuilder in 1885, the previous 20 years had seen a steady rise in wages: 'No matter what we do to reduce the wages, there is a steady and persistent advance' (1886 XXXII: 144). From 1871 to 1886 his time wages advanced 17.4 per cent and piece-rates by 21.8 per cent. The records of the Palmer Shipbuilding and Iron Company show pieceworking restricted entirely to the Boilermakers and their subsidiary grades. The Engine Works Department wage figures are given as a weekly wage. Perhaps even more importantly the *proportion* of the grades remained stable over the years from 1865 to 1882, reflecting the lack of radical change in the structure of the labour force. The owner described the period:

. . . we have with the steady increase in the cost of labour, . . . a constant conflict going on, a perfectly peaceful one, between employers and skilled labour; and it is shown in endeavours to substitute skilled labour by machinery.

(*ibid.*)

Table 3 ii shows how the Society was able to hold the line.

TABLE 3 ii   Proportion of the major grades in Palmer's Yards, Engine Works Department, 1865–1882, as a percentage

Grade	1865	1873	1882
Fitters	18	21	18
Machinemen	13	10	13
Patternmakers	3	2	2
Labourers	14	14	16

SOURCE: 1886 XXXI App. A: 298.

Of course, the Tyne was an ASE stronghold within which the Nine-Hour Movement had originated, and where, in 1892, the District Committee claimed none of its 4,042 members were paid by piece (1893 XXXII App. XLVI: 467). A more representative picture comes from analysing the schedule of replies to the Royal Commission on the Depression of Trade sent to all 'working class organisations' which covered 23 ASE districts. The results show again how patchy was the progress of pieceworking. The system does not seem to be related to any specific sector, except perhaps to locomotive building. Fifteen districts claimed to be paid entirely by the hour or day, though most of these complained of systematic overtime. In the rest, comments such as 'piecework being introduced which goes against the interests of the employers, but they cannot see it', and 'piece-rates recently introduced for skilled grades', are typical. In the majority, however, successful resistance is the theme: 'piecework not recognised', 'all skilled work by the day', 'machine-making and millwright's work by time only'. In two examples, bicycles and textile machinery, piecework had been introduced for the unskilled grades – but in the main where it did not operate for the craftsmen it did not apply to the labourer (1886 XXI App.II, Pt.II: 7–16).

In strong union areas overtime was curbed by a *de facto* limit which fluctuated with the 'state of trade,' that is, employment of Society members. The general manager of Palmer Shipbuilding at Jarrow speaking of this 'trade regulation' (itself an indicative term) said:

We have never seen it as an advantage. It destroys that relation between us and our men which we strive to cherish . . . they give us an intimation when it is exceedingly inconvenient and damaging to us, that for the present and for so long in the future they will not work overtime, and that is generally as I have already said, when we need it very much.

(1886 XXIII: 154)

Whatever the paucity of evidence for the 1870s and 1880s, we are fortunate in having a wealth of detail, albeit unsystematically catalogued, in the reports and evidence of the 1892 Labour Commission. This can be supplemented with academic research and an increasing number of personal biographies of engineers from the 1890s onwards. The early years of this decade also represent something of a social and technological watershed for the industry; working methods began to be rationalised, employers became more organised, new mass-production sectors, such as bicycles and sewing machines, were getting underway. The evidence, therefore, of 1892 represents a summation of the interregnum and a useful counterpoint to the information of the 1850s and 1860s.

A Society survey, similar to that of 1861, undertaken during 1891 for presentation to the Commission is a good starting point. This showed the overall percentage of pieceworkers had risen to 16.8 per cent but again this conceals regional disparities. Over one half of these workers were in Lancashire and Yorkshire – but the intervening increases were not evenly spread among all the districts. In Lancashire the proportion increased from 16 to 26 per cent, in Yorkshire from 11 to 17 per cent; in the South West from 16 to 22 per cent; and in the East Midlands from 14 to 25 per cent. But in the West Midlands the proportion of piece-workers rose from 14 to 44 per cent and in the eastern counties from 19 to 57 per cent. In Coventry, for example, where pieceworking was unknown in 1861, 83 per cent of Society members were now employed in this way – largely as a result of the growth of the cycle industry (1893 XXXII App. XLVI: 466).

The Commission itself issued a questionnaire to districts from which the industry's representatives came (10 in all) concerning wages, con-ditions and hours. The replies from the ASE, other unions and em-ployers cannot be said to conform to the statistical requirements of a sample, but the areas and type of work covered were wide-ranging. From the replies, only four of the 10 areas admitted to Society members working by the piece, and in one instance only, Stanningley, they were in a majority (the branch secretary adding the remark that the system was nonetheless 'the ruination of both trade and men'). Other areas reported payment by the hour with some piecework, particularly in non-union shops where also, according to the Gloucester Branch, 'fines and other petty tyrannies are commonplace'. This evidence has to be seen in context – it was the public face of the Society – and in one case at least, Oldham, it is contradicted by the employers' replies. However, in the main this second group of answers, although not from exactly the same areas, confirms the general picture.

Thirty firms, employing on average 453 persons, sent in returns, nine of which mentioned piecework of one sort or another, and two others the occasional use of sub-contract. The overall summary was that: 'In the engineering shops there is sometimes piecework but not always and in some shops it is not allowed by the union' (1892 VII: XVII). In only one firm, an Ironworks in Lincolnshire, was piece-working predominant, '40 per cent day; 60 per cent by the piece'; and in a locomotive works it occurred 'very extensively'. But in the main the comments say 'by the hour' or, for example, 'very little piecework, chiefly drilling is by hand'. Perhaps most significant is the return from Thomas Platts of Oldham which employed at that time 1,100 men and was the best known of Britain's textile machine-makers. This shows the firm had minimum and maximum wages for each grade of work, but this was not primarily decided by piecework, for only 27 per cent of the work force were paid in this way (*ibid.*: 185).

Although only small percentages were involved in piecework, 71.7

per cent of Society members were subject to systematic overtime. This confirms the view that the essential extensions of labour power were achieved through increasing hours rather than the intensity of work – which is consistent with the earlier analysis of the lack of technological progress from 1850 to 1890. Upon this rested the ASE's maintenance of other craft shibboleths: piecework and apprenticeship had 'held the line' but at the expense of allowing overtime to become widely used. As the Webbs argued, overtime induces pieceworking because it destroys the concept of 'normal time' upon which collective bargaining (the regulation of effort to wages in a *specified* period) rested (1920: 346). Not surprisingly, where the two were already combined, *standard* wage rates were the lowest, but *earnings*, however, were high (1893 XXXII App. XLVI: 468). Further such differentials weakened the tradition of craft custom and attitude. Swindon and Oldham, centres of piecework, were equivocal in their attitude towards it. An ASE official reported to the Commission (*ibid*.: 149):

Swindon, representing 772 members or 1.3 per cent, the majority of whom accept piecework, do not consider it an evil, or that it leads to scamping of work, and they are of the opinion that if abolished it would be detrimental to the interests of the Society.

    Oldham representing 1,858 or 3.3 per cent, while not agreeing that it leads to a scamping of work, are of the opinion the working of piecework is detrimental; but are afraid in Oldham the work done in that district would revert to other districts where piecework is the practice . . .

Crucially Swindon also did not consider overtime detrimental 'since they do not work it systematically' (*ibid*.). In other words, where methods based on the incentive principle were well established, less overtime was necessary because the work force had 'learnt' to increase effort beyond the 'craftsman's rate' to that required by the firm: the rationality of capitalist social organisation absorbing the ethos of the craft. Conversely, the Society's influence was strongest (as reflected through the monitoring activities of the local District Committee) where the skilled day-wage worker in a non-repetitive task situation was sovereign. The minutes of the District Committees of London and Barrow-in-Furness – both centres of skilled marine engineering, and the former an important repair centre — for 1889 to 1897 show how they were able to enforce standards without strikes. (*ibid*. App. XLVI: 468; Weekes, 1970: 9–10).

    But does this relationship between low overtime and high piecework hold on a greater scale? Out of the 76 ASE districts reporting piecework only 41 gave an exact percentage. On average 33.5 per cent of members were at any one time paid in this way, but of the top six districts 18 per cent, and in the lowest six 26 per cent, were on systematic overtime

(Holbrook-Jones, 1979: 186). This suggests that, as yet, payment by results was not generally associated with rational work organisations and capital-intensive firms which should, ideally, have dispensed with systematic overtime. As one Leeds employer put it, working this way

is simply ruinous . . . It was caused by a sort of unbalanced condition of the shops, one set of tools being in advance of another, and so on. We have gradually brought in a little more capital, and balanced as well as we can, so as to do away with the necessity.

(1893 XXXII: 355)

The survey also offers the opportunity to test the converse hypothesis, namely: was the strength of ASE locally related to the prevalence of piecework? If the 1891 Census figures (for 'engine and machine maker', 'fitter and turner' and 'spinning and weaving machine maker') are divided into the Society branch membership an estimate is obtained of trade-union density – a ratio of non-union to union labour. This only works for 11 districts, that is, where the census area (an 'Urban Sanitary District') matched an ASE branch which made a full return. For example, the ratio in Leeds is 4.3:1, whilst in Newport it is most favourable to the ASE, being 1.1:1. Overall, however, the five pieceworking districts average at 2.3:1 and the non-pieceworking areas at 1.7:1. In other words the latter had a 26 per cent better 'density' of union membership. Given the aforesaid qualifications and limitations, this does seem to indicate a relationship between effective resistance to payment by results and local Society membership, demonstrating that in the early 1890s the issue was still a political rather than a technical one (Holbrook-Jones, 1979: 187).

The uneven development of engineering in this way benefited the craft worker in his defence of the trade. In no way had the industry fully rationalised its form of the wage contract along individual piecework/capital-intensive lines. The intermingling of explanatory factors – the market, craft restrictions, regional insularity and the 'insulating' qualities of the industrial structure – are subordinate, in this discussion to the role of the *active* workshop, demonstrated above, achieved by workshop vigilance of the engineer. The fact that union density is clearly associated with the form of the wage contract demonstrates beyond doubt that the crystallisation of the capitalist form of work organisation is not a 'rational' process implemented from above. On the contrary, the work experience of the engineers, the leading actors of the modern age, illustrates a *continuous* conflict, not resolved by contracts or agreements. As such it is the responsibility of the researcher to examine more closely the 'material' origins of this process, and thereby to highlight the covert struggle of ideals it represented.

The Form of the Piece-Wage

The real basis of piece-wages is the separation of time from remuneration, output alone deciding the wage earned. In certain outworking industries or highly mechanised sectors (boot and shoe making and spinning would be examples) this was indeed the case. The defence of the craft trade was to insist (usually informally) on the output attainable with reasonable exertion being based on the hourly day-rate. 'Time and a third' or 'time and a half' piece-wage level would result in the worker earning a third or half more than the time wage per hour, assuming a higher intensity of work. In the Royal Gun Factory the wage was formulated thus:

A piece-work price is placed on each article, or on each operation through which the article passes in the process of manufacture. These prices are so calculated (though there is no inflexible rate on the subject) that an average workman may be able to earn about one-third more than his daily rating.

(1887 XIV: IX)

This is confirmed by the ASE whose official stated it ranged from 10 to 50 per cent per hour extra, but in many cases prices were automatically reduced if a worker exceeded time and a quarter (1893 XXXII: 167). The Society was not concerned with the prices themselves; these were decided shop to shop.

We fix the minimum rate of wages . . . the man must have his wages guaranteed where he is employed, even if it is a piece-work shop; so that if he is earning 34s a week it is immaterial to us whether he makes that in piecework or not but he must have 34s a week.

(*ibid.*: 160)

The defence of the concept of time thus formed the foundation of the unofficial local policy on piece-rates: the Union set the basic wage, the districts and branches debated the prices, or did so at least when the prices fell below the Union minimum. This fitted in with the structure of the Society, which up to 1897 left the districts to regulate the craft standards via representatives of the district committee in the shops who reported infringements (Weekes, 1970: 11). Thus the Society's response to piecework was in a sense as unco-ordinated as the employers' use of the system.

An early example of an all-embracing scheme, of which piecework formed one part, was instituted at the Thames Shipbuilding Company in 1891, with the idea of 'getting everybody to pull in the same direction' (1893 XXIII: 302). The material basis of this was to divide up each department and give each a fixed sum for labour in every tender for work. This, it was claimed, solved the problem that

where 3,000 or 4,000 people are involved it is difficult to bring home to any individual workman the sense that his work is affecting the profits of the concern.

The men were then paid a daily wage at the Union rate for the district, but if they produced the work for less than the fixed cost the difference was shared proportionally to their wages. The system involved fundamental reorganisation of the accounting system and organisation of the work, and was not simply an addendum like individual piecework:

the men realise now if they choose to work and produce more, the money will not go into our pockets, but theirs. One very interesting result is this, that as they are working in fellowship they are not paid piecework, but they are all paid together . . . the result is that these fellowships will not have bad men working with them . . . 300 or 400 men have been discharged out of the various trades at the request of the fellowships themselves, and the supervision exercised by the men is more valuable than we could exercise, because they know the men better than we do.

(ibid: 302–3)

This refined the notion of uncertainty considerably: the individual worker never knew what the relation between effort and reward was; only that if he exceeded the norm all the extra earnings would accrue to his group. Thus, added to the indeterminacy of the increment, were the pressures on the team to keep up with the expected rhythm of work from within the work force itself – an integral discipline. In the words of its initiator,

fellowship is a sort of cross-breed between day-work and piecework; it has the motive of piece-work, but it also has the responsibilities of day-work.

(ibid.: 313)

The same principle of collective responsibility was used to control quality: products rejected by foremen were taken out of the fellowship scheme and done again, thereby making the group pay for mistakes twice, and equally increasing its investment in ensuring it did not happen again. The principle of group self-selection under the pressure of an undetermined reward, apart from its disciplinary character, was also a form of 'industrial social Darwinism' in which the trade *itself* rejected those 'unfit' for the system *(ibid.:* 303).

Shipbuilding was particularly suited to this type of wage contract: each tender was a separate one-off job for the vast majority of the workers and, provided careful planning went into the costing, the employer was usually sure of the actual premiums he would be paying in advance. Furthermore the 'fellowship' or group working was only a refinement of the gang system common in shipyards where the group leader bargained for a job and distributed any bonus himself.

However, in the engineering industry as a whole the majority of employers were pragmatic in their attitude towards payment by results; the relationship between this and the 'new economic order' was not perceived. Comprehensive piece-rate schemes were regarded favourably, but still as experiments. At Hull only the shipyard working was by the piece:

it is the only class of work of which we know the cost beforehand . . . We generally let the plating of a ship to a squad of men; that is to say, there are six to eight possibly, they form an association or company, and will take the plating of the whole of the ship at a price that has been arranged by their Association beforehand or in accordance with a schedule.

(ibid.: 340)

The engineers however worked on day wage, 'where the men are working under supervision, and where there are no disturbing elements . . .' *(ibid.*).

Hobsbawm has suggested that justifying payment by results under supervision rather than by efficiency was characteristic of the early stages of industrialisation (1976: 353). However, in the attitudes of employers in engineering in 1892 we find the latter has by no means overtaken the former. According to the managing director of William Armstrong's of Newcastle:

In some particular cases it is necessary; it also is very necessary in some particular classes of work. In others it is not so necessary; for example, if you have a large piece of work put into a large machine, the foreman knows the rate at which the machine should go, and if he exercises proper supervision he can ascertain without much trouble whether the proper amount of work is done or not; but in other cases it is very much more difficult, and piecework is the only available means of knowing that you are getting the proper amount of work out of the men employed . . . it emphasises the difference between good and indifferent workmen.

(1893 XXXII: 321)

Or, in the words of an 'engineering and toolmaker' employer of Manchester,

we find we get more work and we get good work. Less supervision is required in the works as to the details of the carrying on of the work. That is to some extent compensated by a considerable amount of supervision being required to see that the quality of the work is there . . .

(ibid.: 351)

Five years earlier the superintendent of the Royal Gun Factory put the issue explicitly to the Committee on the Manufacturing Departments of the Army:

if you have day work, you at once want a tremendous lot of supervision to keep the men at work. For instance, in a night shift day-work would be almost impossible – you would find all your men asleep – therefore, we put every man who is on night shift, with one or two trifling exceptions, on piece work.

(1887 XIV: 104)

These quotations sum up many of the contradictions of payment by results – the necessity of the *prior* knowledge of costs and standardisation; the transfer of authority (at one level) from the supervisor to the labour process/wage contract – but equally the emergence of the problem of *quality* whilst handwork is still important. Although gaining increased productivity the employer was nonetheless forced to employ extra staff concerned with the 'labour of superintendence'. The piece-meal approach to payment by results up to the 1890s suggests very strongly that it was control, rather than efficiency, that prompted its introduction. A Leeds employer argued:

> The business of a foreman who is over a piecework shop consists in seeing that he gets the quality of work done; he has no trouble in getting the quantity. In a day-work shop, as far as my experience goes, the difficulty is getting the quantity . . .
>
> (1893 XXXII: 358)

The regulation of effort is seen as the prime advantage where it is possible to calculate in advance the increment to the worker and impossible to entirely eliminate the skill element. Schloss already noted in the 1890s a few areas where the domination of the machine was so complete (thereby reducing the cost of labour), that 'the manufacturer has so great a margin of profit that he does not think it worth his while to put the people on piece-wage' (1907: 54).

Overwhelmingly piecework up to the 1890s in engineering was an *ad hoc* method of maximising effort in a period where handwork still remained important. Although an ever-present threat to the regulation of craft, for as long as it remained unrelated to revolutions in the *method* of work its meritocratic effects could be cushioned. The results of our investigations into the extent and the form of piecework suggest strongly its adoption and implementation had more to do with control and discipline than with efficiency and effort, at least up to the 1890s.

The Engineers 1807–1914

> . . . the most valuable workman is the man who identifies himself with the machine.
>
> (Engineering employer, Tariff Commission 1909 IV: para. 714)

The period of the 20 years up to the First World War has received much attention from historians; the effect of technology, the internal structure of the Union and the relationship of the industry to the economy have been investigated in detail. Primary source material is more easily available, business records, official statistics, Union records and personal memoirs are all far more informative from the 1890s onwards. This section sets out therefore to reinterpret these sources in the light of the examination of the period from 1850 to 1890.

In most branches of engineering change was obvious, if less dramatic, in comparison to the main overseas competitors. Orthodox accounts rely heavily on the restraining influence of the market structure in explaining the slow rate of progress: very little specialisation; production on 'short runs' leading to a reliance on skilled labour which perpetuates out-of-date methods, which leads to little specialisation, and so on. (Saul, 1970; Harley, 1973–4). There is considerable *prima facie* evidence for this. For example, the major steps were taken in the one sector of the industry which *did* have a stable mass market – bicycles. Both sub-division within the factory and between factories progressed much faster than in other sectors – with sewing machines running a close second. In 1909 in a factory producing bicycle chains,

there may be from twenty to thirty operations on every length, and each one of those operations is performed on a highly specialised machine by one operator . . . frequently no more than a child . . . [who sits] hour after hour, day after day, pushing with deft fingers a small atom of steel into the insatiable mouth of the machine.

(*The Engineer*, December 1909)

Many established firms jumped into the cycle boom in the 1890s, causing more diffusion of new methods amongst the industry as a whole. The rationalisation and fierce competition led to the 'modern' process of rapid concentration (in Birmingham and Coventry). *The Ironmonger* (November 26th 1904) foresaw the end of 'the small man who will be deprived of the fruits of his labour in assembling'. Again the mass market facilitated the elimination of the small manufacturer who, in other engineering sectors, survived so successfully (G.C., 1929: 159–64).

The motor car industry provides an example of a reverse trend. In 1900 there were no less than 53 firms, two-fifths of whom remained in business up to 1914. Output was generally very low and the production runs short. In 1907 only five firms made more than 500 vehicles a year. Whereas the cycle industry had utilised some existing regional skills (for example, tubular frames in bedstead making) the car industry began very much from scratch. F.W. Lanchester recalled in 1899 that: 'No ancillary trades had then developed and we have to do *everything* ourselves, chassis, magnets, wheels, bodywork, etc.' (Kingsford, 1960: 47).

The undivided structure of output and the skilled labour needed to produce it, reinforced the 'bespoke' character of the industry. A manufacturer told the Tariff Commission (1909 IV: 108): 'At least 90 per cent of the cost of a motor car is labour pure and simple'. In recruiting the engineers the employers found themselves inheriting a tradition that would have proved totally hostile to mass production and standardisation, had it been attempted. F.W. Lanchester recalled:

In those days when a body builder was asked to work to drawings, gauges or templates he gave a sullen look as one might expect from a Royal Academician if asked to colour an Engineering drawing.

(Kingsford, 1960: 49)

These two examples illustrate the two ends of the engineering spectrum in the two decades up to 1914. The essential character of change lay in the consolidation of advanced machine tools – the capstan and turret lathe, the vertical, horizontal and universal milling machine, grinders and radial drills – combined with a marked rationalisation of factory and workshop organisation.

To what extent were engineers affected by this? The first point that should be made is that the consequences were not felt uniformly by the different grades of workers. Patternmakers, for example, remained relatively unscathed; their rate of output was quickened but the element of handskill remained. A report on the relation between wages and skill in engineering in 1928 stated that

these machines [planing, grinding and drilling] have relieved the patternmaker of much heavy manual work, it is difficult to believe that their use has lowered his high standard of skill and craftsmanship.

(Rowe, 1928: 93)

In 1892 around 6,000 such men existed, two-thirds of whom were organised (half in the ASE, half in the United Pattern Makers Association), piecework was 'almost unknown' and wages fluctuated only in marine engineering, but averaged about 36 shillings per week (1892 VII: 29). Their role was to make 'a pattern for the purposes of moulding a casting in iron, steel or brass. A joiner on the other hand produces the finished article' (1893 XXXII: 42). They described their work employing:

Planing machines, circular and band saws and lathes, are the only machines used. Most work done by hand. Improbable that any further introduction of labour saving machinery will be made.

(1892 VII: 70)

In London at the turn of the century the patternmaker was said to usually own a large set of tools 'of considerable value . . . His duty is to cut in wood . . . the patterns, drawings of which have been supplied to him from the draughtsman's office . . .' (Booth 1903 V: 306).

The fitter was more directly affected, particularly by the spread of semi-automatic lathes in the turning shop. Interchangeability rather than dead accuracy was the demand of standardised production. 'Erecting' became more important than 'fitting' parts, and whilst large employers manufactured sufficient spares to allow for a certain percentage to be scrapped, in many shops, as has been stressed, the necessary machinery was not used. In time there emerged two types of fitter: the bench worker doing the more traditional task of aligning work from the turner, and the 'erector' who assembled a specific machine or type of machine. In some respects the former's responsibilities were increased in light engineering where the complexity of the product outran the ability of the lathes to work at fine tolerances (Levine, 1954: 490–3).

The turning shop and its personnel suffered a similar form of polarisation. The new lathes once 'set up' could be run by a semi-skilled youth after a few hours' instruction. It was this type of issue which dominated ASE activity particularly after the 1897 lock-out. In 1897 a Manchester firm introduced a number of automatic milling machines, which, according to *The Engineer*, November 26th 1897),

once the correct cutter was put in position, and the tool set for the work to be done it only required the article to be dropped on to a spindle and a nut screwed up, the rest being automatic until the work was finished. A labourer was put in charge of four of these machines. The Amalgamated Society of Engineers demanded this work on the grounds it was displacing their labour.

This attempt to stop the substitution of Society men was very much a second line of defence of craft prerogatives – shop by shop vigilance and the steady retention of status and privileges remained paramount. But the turner's job was divided by the new tools: 'setting up' of work remained a highly skilled and influential role in the production process; the actual job of 'turning' (manual dexterity applicable to all general engineering tasks) was less so. In particular, the task of 'marking off' work was done by a specialist and not each turner. As early as 1880 at the North East Marine Engineering Company it was said that 'a man's whole shop life is spent in marking off and setting out work and in doing nothing else . . .' (*The Engineer*, August 1880). Yet still 20 years later in the London turning shops, lathes were worked single-handed: 'Here are finished off the parts which require to be accurately rounded off or which have to be screwed' (Booth, 1903 V: 307). Or again, it was said that tables replaced the *ad hoc* calculation of the individual turner as to how the work should be organised: 'speed and feed' specifications would be issued with each job from the office. But according to W.F. Watson writing of the situation in about 1905:

A journeyman must be familiar with the formula for working out a set of wheels to cut any thread coarse or fine, odd or even, on any type of lathe.

(1935: 39)

Each sector leaves a different impression: for example textile machinery makers using standardised equipment, but conservative methods; locomotive builders, more advanced in an engineering and work organisation sense, but having to conform to customer preferences. Alfred Herbert recalls the shop at Jessop's, a textile machine maker, in about 1910:

They turned out really good work by the standards of their time, but by comparison with a modern shop their equipment and their methods were primitive. There were no milling machines, no capstan or turret lathes, no grinding machinery, no gear cutting machines for all gearing was cast, no twist drills, no jigs or fixtures, and not even a blueprint.

(Saul, 1970: 166–7)

At T.S. Prennoldson's, shipbuilders and engineers of the Tyne, Robert Allen recorded that in the 1900s all the really large jobs remained based on handwork,

> even cutting key ways, in crank shafts, tail end shafts and propellers . . . we made our own templates and even made all the iron water pipes . . . The overhead crane was handgear . . . Even the jib crane on the Quay . . . was operated by hand . . .
>
> (Allen: MSS)

Another indication of the success of the skilled man in resisting the meritocratic effect of technology is the stability of differentials from 1886 to 1906. Despite huge increases in the number of 'machine minders', piecework, and self-acting machinery, the ratio between the main grades, according to Rowe, 'remained virtually unaltered'. Whereas,

> If wages had moved in accordance to skill, there should have been little appreciable change in the differentials between patternmakers, moulders, smiths, machine men labourers, and the boiler shop grades . . . on the other hand the turners should have lost ground considerably, and the once more or less homogeneous grade of fitters should have disintegrated into a series of groups, at rates varying from a little above the labourers rate up to, and beyond, the smith's rate.
>
> (Rowe, 1928: 109)

The policy of resisting substitution rather than the machine had paid dividends at one level – exclusion. In the words of one of Booth's investigators, 'the mechanical engineer has adapted himself to, and to a large extent appropriated, the new industries' (1903 V: 296).

The New Forms of Piece-Wage and Workshop Organisation

> The modern factory system demands a different method to the old-fashioned watchfulness of the old man, and requires an incentive which appeals to men's natural cupidity, and converts each workman into his own taskmaster.
> (F.G. Burton, *The Commercial Management of Engineering Works*, 1899)

It has been seen that a pre-condition for the introduction of simple incentive schemes, largely unrelated to the method of work, was prior knowledge by the management of the precise increment to the worker. Without this, piece-wage based on 'time and a third' could, with careful organisation by the work force, rebound on the employer. The fulcrum of such a system was the price negotiated for each job, the details of which the workers were more likely to grasp than the management – hence the need for increased supervision. On the other hand, because of its variable nature the craftsman was open to wage fluctuations via the cutting of rates if trade were bad or production low. Furthermore, overtime was generally not paid at an increased rate and in most cases there was no formal minimum (Jeffries, 1945: 154).

The Society's ability to contain the degree of pieceworking suffered a set-back with the terms of the settlement of the 1898 dispute, but again as in 1852 the employers did not capitalise on their formal victory. In particular the fear that a form of 'scientific management' would become the normal practice did not materialise (ASE *Journal*, November 1898). Also, whilst engineering was temporarily on the upswing, disruption and guerilla warfare in the shops was the last thing management wanted. The Society officials still wished to arrive at some compromise over payment by results, especially in view of the constant tendency for the traditional system to lead to price-cutting, and (from their point of view) a wasteful 'eyeball to eyeball' struggle with each employer (Weekes, 1970: 174–6). Amongst the officials of the newly created Board of Trade Labour Department and employers generally, interest in American wage systems associated with the ideas of Frederick Taylor had been growing. However, even though 'Taylorism' itself was insignificant, the rationalisation of the wage contract took most of its inspiration from American theorists and industrial experiments.

This combination of circumstances led to the signing of the Carlisle Agreement between the Union and the Employers Federation in 1902 – the first nationally negotiated recognition by the Society of the principle that wages should be related to output. The nub of the bargain was this: in return for an end to all restrictions, the employers agreed to introduce a 'standard' scheme of payment by results (mainly the Rowan premium bonus), and a guarentee that, once fixed, prices would only change if a method or means of manufacture changed (*ibid.*: 180).

The Rowan system was hailed by Sidney Webb as a breakthrough in industrial democracy since it included a clause to the effect that prices would be 'mutually agreed'. In fact its choice was far more to do with the fact that it compensated for the old problem of the lack of expert rate-fixers and the tendency to err in establishing prices and times for complicated jobs: it fixed a rate that was attractive enough to act as an inducement without actually increasing earnings beyond the extra time 'saved'. The Rowan system had the added advantage of offering initially high rewards for increased effort, which did not afterwards, however, increase proportionately as individual output increased. The system worked by giving a standard time for each piece of work, and if the work was completed in less time the worker received a percentage bonus equal to the percentage of the time saved. It should be noted that the wage was calculated in terms of the time-rate, the bonus being calculated as so many hours to be paid for, in addition to the hours actually spent on the job. David Schloss, in a report to the Labour Department, stated that this is the foundation stone on which rests all the merits of the system, since by it, if an hour is saved on a given product the cost of the work is less and the earnings of the worker are greater than if the hour were not saved, the worker being paid in effect for saving time.

(1895 LXXX: 30)

To take an example, if the standard time is 10 hours and the work completed in eight, the worker receives his hourly rate for the eight hours plus a 20 per cent bonus which amounts to payment for an additional 1.6 hours. If he completed in seven hours, the bonus would be 2.1 hours, and in six hours, 2.4. In other words, no matter what error is made in fixing the time or the effort expended by the worker *there is no way he could earn double his time-work wage*. This is achieved automatically – not by a rate-cutter or a 'chiselling' foreman – and the first increments are quite high, but of course the rate of premium still remained to be established in the first instance. It is on this point that the Rowan system is similar to all other forms of the piece-wage: the starting figure or percentage is arbitrary and uncertain for every given case. But unlike its primitive forebears there is no way an error could lead to a really decisive change in the relationship of wages to effort in favour of the employee. As Schloss put it, each premium is unique: 'Nothing but good sense and judgment can decide in any case' (*ibid.*: 31). Contrary to orthodox piecework the system offers a minimum, that is the day wage of 'standard time', and, formally, a provision that overtime should be paid at a higher rate.

There is nothing compulsory about it and nothing tangible to oppose. It is simply an offer to gratify one of the greatest passions of human nature . . .

(*ibid.*: 32)

Although nationally agreed, because of the vagaries of engineering work, actual premiums could only be decided locally. The lack of uniformity returned the initiative back to the shop stewards, who over this period were transformed from district agents to shop representatives. Parity could only be maintained by constant monitoring of past prices and comparison with neighbouring works through the local committee, which naturally became the focus for opposition to the Executive. Of the many letters on the subject to the Society's *Journal* this best summarises their general tone:

As a body of men we are suddenly plunged into the above system [premium bonus] of sweating without having the least warning . . . by our Executive Council. From a theoretical point of view they quoted Sidney Webb and from a practical point of view 'nobody'. Now, having worked on this particular system for over 18 months, I think I may say that I have learnt a few of the practical points of it. The greatest germ of this disease is the feeling of jealousy it creates amongst our members, which is undoubtedly desired by the employers. A time is fixed called an agreed time, but it is not agreed to between the workmen and the master . . . but between the rate-fixers and the foremen who try to outshine each other in giving as low a time as possible . . . There is no published list whereby a workman can check over his card . . .

(June 1904)

An official booklet on the system, issued by the Employers' Federation, made this clear: 'The time allowed for any job will be fixed by the managers and heads of departments' (Barr and Stroud, 1902: 4). The bonus was supposed to be set to allow 'the average man' to earn 'time and a third', but in fact 'debts' on one job were carried on to the next and in one case a man ended up 'owing' his firm £20 (Watson, 1935: 97–8).

By 1917 even Sidney Webb had recognised this loop-hole in industrial democracy and advocated monitors, similar to those in the checkweighman system in the pits (1917: 66). It is interesting that this proposal is echoed in Murphy's famous pamphlet, *The Workers' Committee*, published in the same year, though here it is a call for their *extension* throughout industry, implying that unofficially this was already underway (Murphy, 1917: 19). In at least one engineering works in Bristol the firm employed a rate-fixer elected by the employees. Much more usual was the concession of a Joint Committee to which disputes were taken, for example, at the Bradford Dynamo Company and throughout the Barrow-in-Furness area (Goodrich, 1920: 169–171).

Despite ASE agreement to such a potentially disadvantageous scheme, inertia, once again, seems to have played a part in hindering its implementation. A few of the larger firms introduced it, as did the Royal Dockyards in 1904, but by 1906 the Wage Census showed that only 4.6 per cent of engineering workers were paid in this way. An ASE inquiry in 1909 revealed 9.2 per cent of its members working the system, which, given the larger population of the latter over the former, suggests very little progress indeed. Opposition amongst the membership reached a climax in 1909 when the Executive tried to stop district committees campaigning against the Carlisle Agreement. Since the issue had never been voted upon in a Final Appeal Court, judgment ruled the ban as illegal, and anti-premium bonus circulars regularly appeared from the committees in Barrow and Newcastle. The delegate meeting of 1912 instructed the Executive to hold a ballot on the issue which resulted in a 5:1 majority in favour of its abolition (Weekes, 1970: 202; Jeffries, 1945: 155).

Less spectacular, but perhaps just as important, was the gradual 'tightening up' of piecework systems and their attendant restrictions such as time-clocks, 'feed and speed systems', and increased supervision. Hardest to quantify and reconstruct historically was the impact of all this on the 'inner life of the workshop'. Fragmentary evidence is convincing however: gone was the almost casual but consistent integral control of the work group. In 1915 an old engineer reminisced:

A decade and a half ago one could come into a shed with perfect complacence; work was a pleasure compared with what it is now . . . The supervisory staffs have been doubled or trebled . . . before the workman can recover from one shock he is visited with another.

(Williams, 1915: 205)

Robert Roberts, a newcomer to a Manchester firm of engineers which employed about 150 just before the First World War, writes of the turners' shop where men driven to escape the intractable boredom assumed schizophrenic characters for the benefit of the apprentices.

It was our duty to visit it frequently to borrow micrometers and other small instruments. Men down the aisle, 'repetition workers', had done pretty much the same task day in, day out, since coming 'out of their time'. In an effort to escape boredom, and with their chargehand's connivance, several denizens had taken to acting out fantasy roles for the wonderment and perplexity of every new boy.

(1976: 166)

In this context it is interesting to note the tone of contemporary agitation against the effects of mechanisation. A pamphlet entitled *The Machine Monster: A warning to all skilled workers* commented that 'the machine has mechanised humanity and induced habits of thought and body which destroy alike the opportunity and the taste for good reading' (Rose, 1909: 7).

The awareness that the conditions of factory life were destroying independent capacity for thought is also reflected in Alfred Williams' graphic account of a railway factory:

A regrettable dullness is discovered by very many of the men which may be bred of the labour itself and the extremely monotonous conditions of the factory . . . he is never free from the effects of the hurry and speed of the machinery.

(1915: 306–7)

Significantly, however, this recurring theme of the book is qualified in relation to the fitters and turners who, he says, 'take the greatest pains to protect themselves and their interests', and from the ranks of which were appointed nearly all the foremen (*ibid.*: 102–3).

The Society expressed similar concern, typically from an exclusive point of view. In 1895 an official wrote that 'the artisan is reduced to a mere machine minder, engaged in constant repetition of a process often little more than mechanical . . .' (Galton, 1895: 101). The meritocratic impact of payment by results led to the 'scamping' of work, at odds with the non-instrumentalism of craft.

It is in piecework shops that 'those hateful words – *that will have to do*' (as a working engineer once called them) are heard on frequent occasions.

(Schloss, 1907: 70)

Increased supervision and the imposition of rules incensed Society men more than the resultant pressure upon wages, and industrial action over such issues was as resolute as if their whole trade were at stake. A classic example was the strike in South Shields in 1906 over the introduction of a Bundy Time Recorder: the issue was whether the men should have to clock in and out in their own time. The fervour with which the dispute was fought (and won) can only be understood in the context of the drive to 'Americanise' working conditions cumulatively producing militant responses from an otherwise industrially compliant work group (Croucher, 1971: 18).

Much of the informal strength of local shop organisation had originated from the fact that in many cases foremen were life-long ASE members. Such men were responsible for hiring labour, and one of the first 'tips of the trade' a journeyman learnt was the knack of catching the chargehand on his way to or from work (Watson, 1935: 29–30). There are fleeting glimpses of how such men could temporarily thwart the progress of new methods:

> When the managers recently attempted to bring about sweeping reductions in the prices throughout the smithy he [the chargehand] opposed them at every point, swore that he was master in his own shed and that no one but he should be allowed to fix prices.
>
> (Williams, 1915: 98)

This situation, a practical example of the dictum that piecework was an alternative to management, resulted from the tendency for local knowledge to become disproportionately important in an otherwise centralised factory system. 'Empire building' at the periphery, which crude piecework systems encouraged, had therefore to be broken. At the Swindon railworks new foremen were appointed, not from the most skilled or long-serving employees, but from the 'young and comparatively unknown' because

> they will have a smaller circle of personal mates in the shed, and consequently less amount of human sympathy for them. That is to say they will be able to cut and slash the piecework prices with less compunction . . .
>
> (*ibid.*: 75)

Not all foremen were traditionalists; they could be 'sweaters' and still remain union men. At a Manchester firm in 1904 the foreman was a 'quick production enthusiast, he was forever telling us to increase our speed' (Watson, 1935: 32). Nonetheless, the employers considered that the problem was sufficient to warrant the Federation proposing a scheme to 'buy out' the foremen's contribution to the Society and financially aid in the formation of their own Clubs (Jeffries, 1945: 128).

These then were the main pressures upon the craft basis of the engineering trade in the 20 years up to the First World War: an uneven, sporadic application of rational piece-wage systems; a general speeding up of workshop conditions; the first signs of the breaking of the hierarchy of skill and promotion; and the emergence of mass production industries in which the semi-skilled machine minder was to be the dominant figure rather than the fitter and turner. A young newcomer to the trade at this time, overwhelmed by the profane materialism of the workshop, was nonetheless awestruck by the weight of tradition and history as he waited to be called to join the Society:

In a chapel-like calm about fifty men sat in rows, fronting office-holders on a dias. Many of our own journeymen were present, giving us nods of recognition and welcome; no ribaldry now! . . . One felt proud to be a member. And men, we heard there, called each other 'Brother' and meant it . . . Sitting after induction, on a back row, I saw my father rise and speak on a minor issue of the time. He gave his views cogently and with a force and wit that delighted the audience. Once some injustice was 'damned' – a word he withdrew immediately, with apologies to the chair.

(Roberts, 1976: 187)

Within the workshop many shibboleths of the trade were violated by the development of the capitalist form of factory organisation. But in the private 'trade life' of the workshop the sense of ceremony and continuity persisted – a final symbol of the solidarity *and* the separate identity within the working class – roots which were to launch the paradox of the militant war-time movement, as documented by Hinton (1972).

4 Custom, Community and Status in Mining

It is paradoxical that orthodox economic historians have so often defined emergent capitalism in terms of the spread of 'free' wage-labour; with the individual money contract between employee and employer implying only effort-reward obligations. For in the foundation industry of coal itself pre-capitalist methods of social and industrial organisation persisted until the late nineteenth century: the yearly bond, truck, coerced labour (from the workhouse) and a 'feudal' type of fusion between employers, the legal system and the state. It is impossible therefore to account for the emergence of traditional forms of wage-bargaining in the 1870s without briefly considering the origins of the pre-industrial mining communities.

There is considerable agreement amongst observers as diverse as Marx, Sombart, Weber, Kerr, Inkeles and Barrington Moore, that there exists a powerful rationalising and centralising influence in the progress of capitalism. As a result, it is argued, economic restrictions, monopoly and state interference are overthrown, as are the social aspects of custom, reciprocity and tradition. Some historians have pointed to the manner in which this process was biased against the 'restrictive' practices of skilled workers and 'monopolies' of labour in unionism. Other accounts, even the most factually worthwhile, contain this contradiction:

Notwithstanding this evidence of the existence of privileged positions it seems probable that the changes in the structure of distribution extended competition . . . A striking feature of economic life in the eighteenth century is the prevalence of combinations.

(Ashton, 1977: 66, 122)

There are other potential theoretical antinomies in the orthodox view of capitalism (which appear, it is only fair to say, in parts of Marx's work, particularly *The Communist Manifesto, Introduction to a Critique of Political Economy* and Volume I of *Capital*). These can be expressed as follows: free trade and slavery, technology and handpower, textiles and outwork, development and under-development between nation states and regions. It is not possible here to investigate them all. Suffice it to say that we begin with the assumption that this lack of linear development is *normal*, and not the product of a specific combination of factors in each case. This approach (latterly called the 'centre-periphery' model) finds its heritage in the field of economics with Lenin's *Imperialism*, in the field of political economy with Trotsky's *Permanent Revolution*, and in the field of working-class consciousness with Gramsci's critique of Bukharin in the *Prison Notebooks*.

In this context the survival of 'feudal relics' in mining communities, particularly in rural areas, presents no theoretical problem: they require only description and analysis as integral antecedents of the 'modern' form of socio-economic organisation characteristic of the last 40 years of the nineteenth century. In particular the close relationship between work and community, surviving the Industrial Revolution, had an important influence on the structure of unionism. The real and legendary independence of the lodge, and the symbiosis of leaders in this field and the village (and later local politics), cannot be explained at the point of production. The 'independence' of lodges was also, of course, a form of insularity; and whilst the Durham Miners' Association (DMA) was noted for its 'vertical' solidarity, within the national miners' movement its role has been ambivalent: at once an example but not an exemplar. At another level this insularity contributed to the weakness of *rank and file* opposition to the leadership, even at its most unpopular (Welbourne, 1923: 300; Douglass, 1977: 247–82).

Equally the heritage of the DMA which was formed to replace the yearly 'bond' with 'normal' wage-labour cannot be overlooked. The rapid transformation, within six years, from a non-unionised work force, subject to the bond, to a modern system of industrial relations obscures the extent to which the change was one of content rather than of form. To be sure, the pressures of a trade boom and the strife caused by the bond were influential, but they don't explain the recognition accorded the DMA, and the Joint Committee, or at a more symbolic level, the building of a hall for the local lodge meetings by a Newcastle coal master (Welbourne, 1923: 134). The absorption of the union officialdom at a county level, whether conscious or not, exacerbated the tendencies of the DMA to operate, particularly in its first years, as a direct limitation on the volume of industrial unrest. The defeats of past unions in lost strikes was also a powerful inducement. Furthermore the Union emerged in a struggle against the bond, as an *alternative* to it. As a result the Union cadres were trained in an annual formal contest over the signing of the bond, rather than in the cut-and-thrust of local disputes. In this context the Joint Committee could be interpreted as an extension of the paternal despotism of the bond; of course a double-edged sword but at least its officials, it can be argued, if not the men, remained 'bound' to the masters via the cabinet system prevailing on the Committee.

Mining as an occupation cannot be viewed historically through the prism of technological change. Unlike the cotton and engineering workers the work experience of the miner did not, at least up to 1914, depend upon the paradigms of scientific improvement. Although his occupation was neither created nor destroyed by industrialisation, the social world in which he lived was, of course, affected by it. The industrial villages of the mining industry are the usual location given to the 'pre-industrial' practices of truck, coerced labour, penal discipline, and so on. It is argued that the combination of a declining agricultural sector with the expansion of coalfields in sparsely populated areas produced these practices, which were eventually erased by the arrival of modern capitalism in the 1850s. This 'domain' assumption of social history is not untrue, but incomplete: a more comprehensive picture can be gained from the reports by the Mines Inspectorate of some of the mining communities of 1840s.

The major fact which emerges from these reports is that the so-called 'pre-industrial' practices were actually the reverse: they were open and *conscious* attempts to enforce and sustain a total industrial discipline. Truck, for example, in most instances, was not to do with profits, but with obtaining, and holding on to, labour. A 'Tommy shop' manager in Airdrie claimed that:

Without a store we could not get many of our men to attend the work, before we had one they got advances in cash daily from the office, got drunk and kept their families starving.

(1844 XVI: 25)

Elsewhere it was justified in terms of controlling drinking habits either by restricting the availability of alcohol, or at least by cutting down the time lost by providing it 'on the spot', and in set amounts per week (*ibid*.: 24, 26). Thus, not only was the Scottish miner bound legally for a year to his employer, but through the truck shops up to 20 per cent of his monthly wages were mortgaged in advance (*ibid*.: 20). Not surprisingly paydays were celebrated with symbolic acts of freedom: an exodus of the villages for the nearest town, attacks on police houses, a two-day drinking bout and the singing of 'bawdy and irreligious' songs (*ibid*.: 31).

The 1842 Act ending underground female labour (women were incidentally largely paid by the colliers) opened up new opportunities of socialisation through family and home life. At one mine the owner paid a woman to teach his ex-female miners how to cook, sew, wash properly, and so on; the Inspectorate also noted the spread of competitions for the tidiest cottage or best domestic baking where the prizes were donated by the mine owners (*ibid.*: 5, 11).

Truck meshed in with the system of fines at source which was widespread in the iron and coal trade. Employers claimed this was the only method to enforce discipline and achieve quality. Another less well-known form of control in Scotland was the employer's right to 'arrest wages', that is, if a local trader had a debt with an employee he could ask the employer to deduct a weekly sum to be paid directly to him. At the Govan Ironworks between June 1843 and February 1844 there were 212 such cases (*ibid.*: 28).

It is interesting that the Inspectorate also couched their opposition to truck in terms of social order, but demonstrated a much wider perspective than did the concerns of the mine owners. According to them truckshops were an

obstruction to the growth of the middle class precisely in those localities where their influence and instrumentality are most wanting as the connecting link of society between those who gain their living by the work of their hand and those who accumulate vast fortunes by the skilful direction of that labour.

(1852 XXI: 436)

They also noted how they inhibited market forces in labour: in good times men didn't move to the most efficient pits, and, additionally, in bad times inefficient pits survived because labour was tied to them (*ibid.*: 439). Fourteen years later it was reported that truck had established 'a network over the entire works of Scotland', involving the widespread printing of token money and the drink trade almost entirely in the hands of employers (1866 XIV: 215–18). Further inquiries in 1871 and 1887 showed it to be by no means dead; prosecutions against it remained a civil affair and thus dependent on the initiative and expense of the individual workperson.

The fact that the employers were often landlords, magistrates and patrons of local churches, schools and libraries cannot be overlooked. Mass evictions were the most spectacular consequence of this position of power, but its effect was more insidious and far reaching. For example, the type of housing provided reflected the status at work, reinforcing these divisions within the community. In 1880 Heworth Colliery recorded in its books

30 large cottages
97 small cottages
 1 house for underviewer
 1 house for Engineman
 1 house for Overman

(DRO NCB IX/65)

The provision of housing also helped to maintain labour. Most companies provided accommodation to married men only, and in some areas this was restricted to face workers. In the northern counties housing was rent free, as 'an invariable custom'; elsewhere the ownership was nominally separate from the colliery and a rent charged (1907 XIV Pt.II: 6, 76). Marriage – 'settling down' – not only secured a house but in many districts of the North East also a rise in pay. This was, alongside the free housing, a considerable inducement, and was also a recognition of the lack of female employment in the area, in contrast to the South Staffordshire area, where it was said, '. . . the women work in the factories, and a lot of them work at home, nail making and chain making' (*ibid.*).

In the areas where organisation was weakest, housing provision, the evidence suggests, was used as a deliberate antidote to union progress. The combination of traditional selective victimisation at work and the over-arching potential threat of eviction seems to have been particularly important in Scotland. Certainly, the miners' witnesses to the 1892 Labour Commission reflected this view. The contrast with the North East with its higher productivity, lower accident rate and politically corporate work force was not lost on the Commissioners. Their final report drew attention to the relationship between the political radicalism of the delegates from 'unruly' areas, and the unsubtle tactics of the mine owners (1894 Fifth Report XXXV: 24). In Lanarkshire, for example, about one-third of the work force lived in colliery houses for which rent was deducted at source. According to the leader of the small Larkhall union:

> The workmen's houses are used as a lever in bringing down wages and carrying out other injustices. The employers do not scruple as to the means to get the workmen into the houses, and if any dispute arises they at once threaten to turn them out.
>
> (1892 XXXVI: 44)

Of the 34,000 underground workers, no more than 2,000 were unionised, but as progress was made, the witness claimed, so the proportion of miners in tied accommodation increased. 'Knowing the power which it gives them, employers are rapidly increasing the number of colliery houses' (*ibid.*: 50). Favouritism in the provision of tubs and working places also put pressure on the miner:

> . . . the men who were in the employers' houses were to get as many tubs as they wished while the other men, who were not in an employers' house were going to the pit day after day, and earning almost nothing.
>
> (*ibid.*)

At a more direct level Keir Hardie claimed that it was an unwritten law of contract in many collieries that the newly engaged worker and his family would reside in an employers' house. Since many homes had more than one member working in the pit, the proportion of the work force in a tied house was higher than those actually in tenure, and in certain villages this was as high as three-quarters (*ibid.*: 196).

The mine owners were enthusiastic advocates of religion, particularly Methodism, even when normally it was not their own. At Lambton Pit in the 1850s, George Parkinson recalled that

the colliery viewer, Tom Smith, had the good sense to see the converted men were punctually at the pit on Monday morning instead of lounging in a public house. He offered to alter Jacob Speed's cottage, at the end of the row, so that it could be used as a chapel.

(1912: 16)

In a similar vein a standard work on colliery management of 1896 (but still in print as recently as 1951) offered advice to managers.

An unfortunate task of the viewer is to carry through unpopular decisions. It is well, therefore, that he should cultivate relationships with them [the miners]. This he may do by taking a personal interest in their reading rooms and institutes, their athletic clubs, their musical bands, or in some of the various institutions which usually exist in colliery villages . . .

(Bulman and Redmayne, 1951: 65)

Perhaps more than any other industry mining was subject to legal authority. Under the Master and Servant Act the mine owner was empowered to prosecute individual colliers for transgressing the innumerable provisions of the Mines' Acts, as well as his contract of employment. In a South Wales colliery, to avoid the 'inconvenience and publicity' of the magistrates' courts, the worker was given the option of paying his fine to the local Library. Community pressure was overtly used by one colliery, where the offence was

posted up in some conspicuous place in the colliery so that his fellow workmen can see what the man has done . . . [this] has a far more deterrent effect upon him than any punishment he may receive at the hands of the magistrates, while it prevents a great deal of friction between the management and men.

(1892 XXXVI: 156)

Less subtle tactics were probably more common, and certainly are the predominant historical image: the owners were quite willing to use the Law on a massive scale if necessary. In 1896, in one week 395 Boldon miners were taken to court – and a further 560 at Marsden summonsed – for 'breach of contract' (*Newcastle Daily Chronicle*, February 15th 1896). As the local press and union officials observed, the use of the Law invariably escalated a dispute: after six men at Felling Pit were prosecuted for refusing to operate the 'token system' of time keeping, 1,800 of their colleagues struck successfully for their release – despite the opposition of the Durham Miners' Association.

Authority was also maintained by the universal use of the character note (either formally or informally), though this broke down when demand for labour was high. In South Wales the 'discharge note' was only given if the worker had 'satisfactorily completed his contract', and without it employment was difficult (Morris and Williams, 1958: 286). In Derbyshire the leaving certificate would be clipped at one corner to signify to a potential employer the miner's undesirability (J.E. Williams, 1962: 166).

The progress of the industrial villages reflects the contradictory impact of industrialisation upon the social structure. Coal was the first industry to undergo the transformation of scale (if not method) typical of the capitalist form: the appropriation of all physical means of production, the unleashing of market forces, the separation of workers and employers, and the creation of trading and financial structures. Yet its impact on the lives of the coal-workers was far less dramatic or linear in effect. In nearly all respects coal created a social organisation of its work force far from the ideal textbook 'proletariat'. The miners were not urbanised, nor in especially large numbers; their wages were subject to all sorts of deductions, and housing and situation contributed to the element of coercion in the nominally 'freely made contract'. Their labour was not eased or mechanised, and discipline remained largely punitive, rather than based upon incentives. All these pressures contributed to the famous parochialism of mining communities (Chaplin: 1978). But, of course, parochialism in the context of the organisation of pitwork led as will be seen, to a fierce determination among miners to control 'their' working and 'our pit'. These traditions, pre-capitalist in origin, sprang, not from a desire to *overcome* the authority of the capitalist, but merely to limit it to certain areas.

In Durham there was the paradox that rank and file movements were rarely effective, yet local autonomy was probably greatest precisely because of the tradition of the lodges. The stronger the latter, the smaller the need for rank and file bodies, given the insular structure of the industry and thus the ability to raise and solve local issues. So it is that both the august Welbourne and the radical Douglass discuss rank and file opposition entirely in terms of militant lodges (Welbourne, 1923: 206–24; Douglass, 1977: 272–82). United action between lodges was common, particularly on questions outside the frame of reference of the Joint Committee. However, it was in the main episodic and pragmatic: its history, for example, is not to be found in the DMA archives (except by reading between the lines of Executive circulars). It would take a separate study to evaluate its extent and exact character, but the overwhelming impression from both published and private sources is of a readiness to combine over specific points, without this ever coalescing into a 'movement'. This assessment was to be modified in the decade up to the First World War as the Independent Labour Party and the Socialist Labour Party began to recruit, but even their strength was based on traditionally militant large pits, such as Boldon, Usworth and Washington (Marshall, 1976: 303–3).

Wage-Labour and Custom

In mining, perhaps more than in any other industry, custom and tradition remained significant in the formation of the wage contract. The essential continuity of the method of work, the rural setting of many collieries, and the absence (until the last decades of the century) of formal bargaining procedures, all contributed towards this fact. In the Midlands particularly there survived the heritage of petty production methods and multi-dimensional sub-contract. Where unionism was established the defence of normative agreements was often the foundation of union policy, and defensive reaction to innovation was much firmer than offensive action to improve conditions. A DMA leader argued, in the *Newcastle Weekly Chronicle* of April 10th 1892:

Our best policy is to do what we can do to conserve our trade . . . to work so far as to secure an advantage . . . rather than to make demands for which no substantial reason can be assigned . . .

Such conservatism had its roots in the character of the work: 'Custom is one of those things that in the South Wales coalfields unfortunately seems to govern everything,' claimed a witness to the Miners' Eight Hour Day Committee. New methods and increased division of labour were resisted automatically as an 'invasion of privacy'; established practice was a 'tremendous nut to crack' (1907 XIV: 255).

On the other hand the employers were not noted for their innovatory attitude towards industrial organisation or methods. The sluggishness of technical progress indicates a reluctance or inability in making investment decisions. The atomistic structure of mining enterprises operating under conditions of extreme competition, led to stagnation and the universally held belief that costs could only be reduced by reducing wages, rather than by improving other factors of production. The success of coal-cutting machines in the USA, for example, did not change the view of the British owners as late as 1925 that,

Generally speaking, the saving of labour charges at the face is absorbed by the capital charges on, and the running cost of, the machine.

(Taylor, 1968: 59)

One heritage from the past was that, like many other skilled workers in this era, the miner provided his own picks, at least two (one for use while the other was being sharpened), but on average four to six (Durham *Proceedings*, 1912: 176). The responsibility for sharpening and repair was the men's. 'Pickpence' were deducted from wages by the management to pay a smith, only the stonemen receiving the service free (DMA, 1893: 12). Shovels and small hammers were also widely owned, whilst heavier hand tools such as sledge-hammers and shot-punchers were provided by the management. The ownership of face tools could act as an important feature of job control: in a colliery in Derbyshire in 1871 the owners compelled the use of forks (instead of the miners' own shovels) so that the amount of slack loaded into tubs was reduced (1873 X: 39). Or again, management could ban the use of implements *altogether* to achieve the desired effect. In South Wales,

The workman and 'butty' or boy, as the case may be, having cut the coal put it into an iron box with their hands. No shovel or other means is used in filling the box.

(Gascoyne-Dalziel, 1895: 109)

The provision and use of gunpowder was in the main organised by the workers, and even after the Mines Act of 1872 considerable autonomy remained although supervision was made compulsory. For example, at Boldon a committee of the lodge was in charge of enforcing the safety rules and arranging to buy in bulk at the cheapest price. The men then purchased it at a discount (DRO Minutes MS, DH/Ph/71/12).

Until the introduction of the Davy lamp the miner also bought his own candles, and even afterwards he preferred these since they gave off more light and more swiftly warned of a rise in the gas content of the air. In many districts a payment called 'lamp money' was negotiated as a compensation for the loss of lighting power. To the management's frustration this became a 'custom of the colliery' which remained for decades, and its removal was fiercely contested (DRO NCE I/CO/141).

Perhaps custom and tradition were most important to the worker in bargaining for contract prices as the state of the seam enlarged. The essential uncertainty of the task at the face worked both ways: the workers were unable to establish formal, exact rules even when their bargaining position was strong, but, even when it was weak the management could not entirely remove front-line control and initiative. In consequence the central pivot of the struggle between miners and employers has been the regulation of effort to wages: the former have attempted to maximise uncertainty at the face and minimise it at the pit bank, the latter, *vice versa*. Carter Goodrich recounts how an overman was unable to testify under oath whether a certain worker did his job properly, even though, as the magistrate pointed out, his duty was to visit each working place twice a day.

They always stop work when they see an overman coming, and sit down till he's gone – even take out their pipes if it's a mine free of gas. They won't let anyone watch them.

(1920: 137)

This problem for the employer was compounded by fierce inter-regional competition characteristic of the industry until well into the twentieth century. The great difference in the costs of production between regions and even between neighbouring collieries prevented any tendency to limit output and control prices. The Inspector for Derbyshire commented, 'Yes they have meetings, and they fix the price; but they go home and do directly opposite' (1873 X: 37). The mine owner aimed at the maximum output per shift so that in good times he could make more profit, and in bad times the cost of production per ton would be kept down to a minimum. But the miners' attitude was quite different. When trade was good and prices and wages rising, his effort declined to a level sufficient to maintain his usual standard of living, and he may also have had in mind a concern not to 'spoil the market'. In bad times, following the 'ratchet effect' (whether a scale was in force or not), wages would not fall as rapidly as prices, and the miners may anyway have found it preferable to work three shifts a week at a higher wage, than six days at an imminently lower one. The owner would therefore have been faced with increased costs of production as well as falling prices. For these reasons productivity was inversely related to wages, independent of trade conditions as such (A.J. Taylor, 1961–2: 51–3).

Thus both sides had a vested interest in the maximisation of uncertainty albeit as *different levels* of the organisation. Paradoxically, this was more apparent in the unionised regions, such as Durham. Here the local strength at work and in the community enabled the miner to constantly improve county standards, and at the same time defend established practices. The schism of the miners into 'two camps' from 1893 to 1907 over the issues of minimum wages, sliding scales and the legal eight-hour day, in reality revolved around the extent to which contracts should replace agreements. The DMA, born in part in the struggle to oust the law from industrial relations, saw in the Miners' Federation policy a weakening of *their* conditions and advantages, particularly at the face.

In the genealogy of industrial relations custom is often assumed to be the antinomy of contract: the natural progression is towards a rational contract in which the conditions of the parts are subordinate to the whole, which is then conducted on a larger and larger scale until complete national bargaining establishes industry-wide agreements and standards. But in Durham mining, which should be a 'classic' example of this, the emergence of 'mature' county bargaining between Union and owners is evidently characterised by the *expansion* of customary and local agreements. From the 1870s the Joint Committee produced, at regular intervals, a handbook of 'Wage and Trade Customs' running to over 300 pages: each class of labour both over and underground, and by pit and seam was specified, and for each a wage-rate given. For example, the 1876 edition specifies at Wheatley Hill Pit, Five Quarter Seam,

10 putters paid 1.10d for 80 yds. + 1d extra for each 20 yds by HAND
38 putters paid 1.3½d for 80 yds. + 1d extra for each 20 yds by PONY
(DRO NCB I/CO/92)

This scale of detail is evident throughout the book, representing a series of on-the-spot negotiations: in Durham custom was symbiotic with the formation of the Joint Committee, not an alternative to it.

Of course, these variations were partly a result of the unstable character of production, but they also reflected the struggle over uncertainty. The miner needed a reference point from which to argue the case for each alteration in work which affected his earning capacity (alterations which could occur daily), but he did not want a formula. Equally, the management wished the smooth changeover to new working conditions, but at rates not disadvantageous to itself (a need reinforced by fierce competitive warfare). The 'county average wage system' ensured that these adjustments did not get out of hand, but also gave the miner the kind of minimum wage, as will be investigated in detail later.

This equilibrium relied on a certain balance of forces. Where either side could resolve the issue to its own advantage it did so. In South Wales the owners found great advantage in leaving allowances unspecified and unregulated, since in practice this meant they were set by the pit management. One mine owner recounted how, during the price rise in the 1890s, the extra wages were made up by the multiplication of these allowances and not by an increase in the basic rate. Not unnaturally a strike ensued over the formalisation of these temporary gains and their publication (1892 XXXVI: 153–4). Similarly the manipulation of custom relied on a close equality of wages throughout the field, that is, wages not primarily dependent on the viability of each pit. This was essentially the case in Derbyshire in the 1890s which reduced the 'stakes' in each dispute to a contest between miners and management in each pit (1892 XXXIV: 702). In Durham, the sliding scale, the Joint Committee and the whole panoply of arbitration weighed down upon local contestants, restraining their options and curtailing the issues. In this context it is interesting to note that several mine owners attributed the failure of sliding scales to the *weakness* of unionism in their area; a Derbyshire employer reported that a scale would be tried again at a later date when the union had 'sorted itself out' (*ibid.*: 701). In differing contexts organisation can be seen as a prerequisite of the conflict over exactitude.

From this 'equation of uncertainty' comes the employer's hostility towards the appointment of a checkweighman and the various strategies of the former to vitiate the effectiveness of the latter. The face worker's wage depended on the weight of the tubs, and from 1860 miners had the legal right to ask for one of their number to check that the tubs were being correctly weighed. However, as Alexander Macdonald pointed out to the 1867 Royal Commission, 'the employer has the power of turning him off . . . and they keep turning the man off' (1867 XXXIX: 313). Keir Hardie considered that by 1892 one third of Ayrshire pits had not exercised their statutory right because of the 'system of terrorism exercised by the employers over the whole trade union organisation' (1892 XXXVI: 198, 195). Even in the union areas the change introduced by the 1887 Mines Act (which made the *election* rather than *appointment* of the checkweighman obligatory) caused a fresh series of disputes. According to the *Shields Daily Gazette* of March 3rd 1887 the action of the Hebburn owners in evicting their checkweighmen was justified since the Act 'had changed the position of these employees in regard to the owners . . .' The significance of the eviction was, of course, that the management no longer considered them as employees (and therefore no longer eligible for a colliery house). A spate of similar disputes followed throughout the year, careful investigation of which would provide a useful clue to the degree of paternalism.

Elsewhere miners found themselves able to elect whomever they wished to represent them, but they had no legal rights if the employer did not agree with their choice, and simply dismissed his entire work force only re-engaging them on condition it was changed. The voting procedure itself allowed more selective victimisation; 27 participants of the Lanemark Colliery in Ayrshire were dismissed on these grounds (1892 XXXIV: 49, 196–7). It has been suggested that the checkweighmen were the foundation of conciliatory attitudes insofar as they were the first examples of a group of full-time workers' officials (Challinor, 1967–8: 28–30; Webb, 1950: 300–1). This may be so; but their greater significance lay in their role as a transitional non-manual layer, an organisational 'buffer' between the union leadership and the rank and file, irrespective of the ideological consequences. Very few miners were elected straight from the pit to full-time officialdom – however, in different contexts this had different political effects. For example, checkweighmen seem to have played an important role in the South Wales Unofficial Reform Committee in the period from 1910 to 1920, but in both Derbyshire and Durham they were identified by militants as 'employer's men' (Woodhouse, 1970: 30–65; J.E. Williams, 1962: 409; Douglass, 1977: 282–3).

The owners countered the miners' fight to impose certainty at their level of the organisation by a number of strategies. During the price boom of 1872–5 the riddling device, known as 'Billy Fairplay', spread from South Wales to other areas. This was designed to allow the management to decide what constituted 'slack' or small coal in each tub, and therefore what was underweight, by the use of an 'impartial' machine – rather than to be seen to be deliberately tightening regulations as coal prices rose (1873 X: 208). In addition, during a depression at a Derbyshire pit in 1895 the men were told to use forks instead of shovels to load coal, and a man was employed to travel the pit to listen for the sound of the offending tool (J.E. Williams, 1962: 371). Checkweighmen were often not allowed to get close enough to the weighing machine to check its readings, which were anyway only shown to the nearest quarter hundredweight. These and other petty harassments gave a disproportionate advantage to the management (1892 XXXVI: 60). The weaker the union the more blatant these attempts to undercut the miners. The Blantyre Miners' Association of Lanarkshire (numbering 800 members out of a work force of 34,945) stated that

Nothing is more frequent than partial reductions when men are plentiful, or in anticipation of an advance, made on the excuse that a place may be softer, the coal easier got . . .

(*ibid.*: 67)

Finally, restriction of output, a trade custom that originated in pre-industrial times, but which became the cornerstone of Martin Jude's Northern Miners' Union in the 1840s, had, by the 1870s, been abandoned by respectable established unions in favour of the sliding scale, but in both Derbyshire and South Wales lived on in various guises. It is interesting that in the weakest union area, Scotland, it became almost an alternative, that is, a way of regulating the *prices* market if failing with the *labour* market:

. . . whilst it [Lanark] is the worst organised county in Great Britain, I will claim for it that it is the most progressive in means of united action and spontaneous action in obtaining advances of wages . . . by limiting their output and limiting their days. If they anticipate a reduction, I have frequently known them to reduce their output by two tons a day; and they thereby take command of the market . . .

(*ibid.*: 66)

This old tactic was absorbed into syndicalist theory, and presented as a new alternative to the 'outmoded' stoppage of work: the aptly named, 'Irritation Strike'. Whatever the nomenclature its popularity stemmed from its simplicity: only the external pressures of the price of coal could compel the miner to higher productivity and, whilst this was so, the full rationalisation of the wage contract remained impossible.

This examination of custom and community leads to several conclusions concerning the experience of mining in the nineteenth century. Firstly, there was an intense regional separatism, not entirely due to geological differences, but in fact a product of the industrial structure and markets. Second, the system of cultural and social attitudes towards work was part of a wider non-capitalist consciousness which was strengthened by the 'industrial village' setting of much of the industry. Third, regional peculiarities expressed themselves in an important way through differences in the wage 'floor' set by alternative, or female employment (agriculture in South Wales, textiles in Yorkshire, are examples). Accordingly, it is assumed that, in one sense, there is no such thing as *the* miners. Their occupational identity, social cohesion, internal hierarchy and work organisation are all empirical factors determined by the local conditions of the general system. As such, *similarities* in patterns of behaviour between (say) Durham and South Wales miners are of as much interest as are their differences.

One important consequence of this approach is that it becomes impossible to historically reconstruct the experience of work, and its implications, through the institutional histories of the miners' unions. Taken to its logical conclusion this approach would assume the miners had no history at all before the 1870s (even later in many cases). This *is* the impression gained through otherwise excellent miners' histories by Page Arnot (1949, 1955, 1967), E. Edwards (1961) and Griffen (1955); the notable exception is J.E. Williams's study (1962). The above assumptions are reflected in the following pages, where little emphasis is given to the organisational history of unionism. Instead an attempt is made to analyse fundamental sources of the development towards combination, of the continuous interaction of work with community and capitalism.

The Miners: Work and the Wage Contract

The previous section showed some of the unique problems involved in investigating the work experience of miners. Work, community and custom are inter-related, and at the level of each industrial field this is more so rather than less. With these premises it is impossible to deal with the miners as a homogeneous group; but it is also impractical to give an individual description of each of the twelve coalfields at the necessary level of detail. Three examples will, therefore, have to suffice, only two of which are given in detail.

The Durham and South Wales miners are used as theoretical 'benchmarks', and form the basis of the substantive analytical material. Here are found certain comparative features: a sliding scale system, charismatic leaders, long histories of coal extraction, social isolation of the mining areas, the dependence on one market for the output, and the early associations of both master and men (although under very different circumstances). However in reality these two areas and the miners within them, *in practice* had very little in common, and the purpose of this discussion is to compare: not to seek a 'model' or 'common basis' between them, but rather to illustrate the reverse – that no such approach is possible.

The inclusion of the Midlands fields in this examination of miners' experience is purely for comparative, rather than for factual reasons. Unlike Durham and South Wales, it is not possible in this instance to identify one group of geographically or trade defined miners and link to it the growth of a particular union, owners' associations, method of wage regulation, and socio-economic constraints. The Midland field is thus included to demonstrate the full spectrum of forms of working, particularly the types of charter or butty systems, and to show the continued vitality of these forms in the midst of the Industrial Revolution. It reveals that the indirect or intermediate form of wage contract was not a relic of pre-capitalist times: the history of the Midlands fields shows how this is, on the contrary, subordinate to the social relations of production, or rather to the antinomies of these relations.

The Durham Coalfield and the Wage Contract

Historically this field has been bound up with export. Firstly, via the Tyne to the London consumer, and then, increasingly in the nineteenth century, to feed the boilers of the world's steamships and engines. Whilst in South Northumberland a certain amount of 'soft' or domestic coal is found, the main output was from the 'hard' seams which provided a clean ash burning required by the steam engine (Rowe, 1923: 16; Clapham, 1926: 435). By the 1850s this area produced nearly one-quarter of the nation's coal; subsequently the differential with other fields closed, although it was not until 1914 that South Wales and Yorkshire exceeded the tonnage of Durham alone (Rowe, 1923: 17). In County Durham geologically the typical seam is thin, irregular and in the northern areas likely to be wet. As a result the traditional bord and pillar system of working lasted well into the 1920s; longwall working, which required at least a three-foot seam, was impossible in the seam structure dominant here (Fairbridge MS, DRO D/MRP21/2).

Prior to the adoption of the sliding scale in 1877 the Durham miners had, after ending the bond system in 1871, been involved in a fortnightly Joint Committee with the owners. Through this both the advances of 1871–2 and the reductions of 1875 were negotiated, with the DMA Executive vainly attempting to 'police' its own agreements. According to Welbourne the system ended because it 'excited too keen an interest amongst the men, and provoked serious discontent' (1923: 177). Its successor, the sliding scale, had two important consequences: firstly, it removed direct responsibility for wages from the union, and, second, it established the principle that prices, rather than any custom or an agreed minimum, govern wages. Given the high proportion of wages per unit cost in the industry, the decision to revolve remuneration around the fulcrum of price assumes a particular importance. Unlike other scale systems, it is independent of the effort involved by the individual worker, and in contrast to other wage schemes emerging during this period, it was not primarily concerned with incentives. In other words, it is in no way connected with the *basis* on which work is paid for (by piece, day or whatever), but with changes in the rate concomitant on the market price. It thus operates as a 'stick' rather than a 'carrot'. When market prices are rising the miner's wage increases with the same output; but when they fall he is forced to work harder to maintain his income. Also, the percentage price rise did not equal that of the wage increment, so that, for example, in the scale fixed in 1879 by the DMA a 38 per cent price rise meant a 15 per cent addition to the tonnage rates for the miner (Wilson, 1907: 163).

In contrast to South Wales where the adoption of a scale greatly weakened unionism, in Durham, it must be stressed, in formal terms the reverse was the case. The recognition of the DMA was embodied in the operations of the Joint Committee which dealt solely with union officials. Yet the union was also strong enough at local level not to become swamped by the complexities of the scale. Perhaps the crucial difference between the two is that in Durham the body overseeing the wages' question also dealt with all other issues of dispute raised by lodges or managers. In South Wales, however, the men elected their representatives, whether unionised or not, to the 'sliding scale committee' which dealt with that question only; the union was thus totally embroiled in a system over which it had no control, and which it could not counter at a local level (Evans, 1961: 122–9). Furthermore, in South Wales the scale worked to the disadvantage of the miners, particularly in the first 10 years after 1875, whereas in Durham the system initially operated more favourably. Durham's regional unity, longer traditions and the single market also aided trade union cohesiveness, as did the agreement to alter wage rates by only 2½ per cent at any one time; in South Wales the statutory change was 7½ per cent for every shilling per ton rise or fall in coal prices (Welbourne, 1923: 181; Evans, 1961: 119).

The adoption of the scale in Durham at the instigation of the DMA occurred at the apex of a wage explosion which had begun in 1871, and during a period of sustained growth of unionism. The owners, reaping the benefits of a trade boom, conceded advance after advance through the Joint Committee, where, of course, the DMA was the recognised miners representative. In the years from 1872 to 1876, wages had risen 58 per cent, according to Lord Londonderry's superintendent of mines. On May 5th 1879 the latter wrote to his employer urging him not to withdraw from the Coal Owners' Association.

It is my opinion that had there been no Association the advances would have been far greater for no coal owner would close his pit during the continuance of good trade.
(DRO: D/LO/C60454–87)

He did however agree with his Lordship's view that

The sliding scale agreed in 1877 has been a great mistake, it has in fact [been] most advantageous to the Workmen, and the reverse to the Coal Owner.

(*ibid.*)

The minutes of the Durham Coal Owners' Association (formed in 1872) for this period reveal the considerable authority this body exercised. Individual collieries were sacrificed for the cause of employer unity. At the height of the trade boom in the 1870s the owner of Shipcote Colliery was 'instructed' to accept a 12½ per cent rise in hewing prices despite his claim that it would be 'ruinous' (DRO NCB I/SC/625(i)).

Also important for wages was the 'county average wage' system in Durham. This was a notional figure arrived at by dividing the numbers of hewers into the total county wages bill each quarter. If the wages of a group of hewers consistently stayed five per cent above or below this amount the men or the owners could ask the Joint Committee to alter the rates. (In 1912 this figure was 6s.1¼d per shift.) In practice, however, where working places were bad it was the custom to bargain 'consideration money' with the deputy of the district to bring earnings up to the county average. A DMA survey in 1912 reported that 147 out of 190 lodges used this system (Durham *Proceedings*, 1912: 14, 58–9).

This procedure (along with the cavilling system) did much, as will be seen, to ameliorate the inequities and uncertainty of piecework, and was a further boost to local rank and file organisation, placing it beyond the influence of 'the Durham lot', as Boldon Lodge minutes once called the DMA leadership (September 19th 1879: DRO DH/Ph/1/12). With less fluctuation built into the system, and local extras won, the scale, at least in reasonable trade periods, neither removed the need for collective bargaining nor led to rapid and demoralising wage cuts.

Both Union and employers expressed similar sentiments toward the Scale (in public at least). W.H. Patterson, Secretary of the DMA, told the Labour Commission:

I have always believed long before it was introduced, that it was the safest and most beneficial system to all parties concerned.

(1892 XXXIV: 323)

J.B. Simpson, speaking on behalf of coal owners before the Commission on the Depression of Trade, was involved in the following exchange:

– It [the sliding scale] entirely abrogates the wholesome natural effect of the scarcity of labour, or of the super-abundance of labour upon the price of labour.
– Certainly that is the effect, but the Sliding Scale has been adopted as a sort of easy method of adjusting differences and preventing strikes.

(1886 XXIII: 211–2)

During the first 10 years of the scale's implementation, earnings and coal prices remained congruent and stable. It was when prices took off in 1889–90 that discontent finally surfaced, that is, not when the scale was actually at its most oppressive 'objectively' (in terms of actual income), but when it appeared to the miners 'subjectively' as most inequitable (which of course coincided with the apex of their bargaining position in the labour market) (Holbrook-Jones, 1979: 286). After a clumsy attempt to arrest the rising antipathy towards the system (by rigging the questionnaire to lodges when the scale came up for renewal in spring 1889), the Executive issued a ballot paper which included an option for outright abolition. This was adopted by a huge majority. There then followed a series of bitter local disputes: the managers wished to introduce a greater sub-division of labour, in particular the creation of a 'putter-hewer' class, whilst the miners countered by demanding more uniformity of hours, and the accurate definition of working customs (Welbourne, 1923: 257). In October of 1890, in the wake of the abolition of the scale, the Joint Committee also ceased to meet. Immediately following the fall in prices in January 1892 the employers switched from nibbling away at local 'restrictive' customs to a demand for an overall wage cut. There followed a 10 week strike during which the Durham leadership was hopelessly outmanœuvred by the owners. Not that it had much confidence in the first place; three days after the humiliatingly large majority for the strike it had issued the following exemplar of economic orthodoxy:

No trade however strong, however powerful, can resist a reduction in a falling market when a fall is clearly proved.

(DMA *Circular*, March 21st 1892)

A compromise was reached after a doggedly solid but tactically inept struggle: a 10 per cent cut and agreement to a wages board. Out of this experience came the new leader, John Wilson MP, who wrote some years later that 'the gain would be greater by the avoidance of the struggle' (Wilson, 1907: 182). This somewhat cryptic logic was to become the basis of the next 15 years of his leadership. The main vehicle for this philosophy was the new Joint Committee, reconstructed 'under new rules which departed little from those of the past', the significance and importance of which was greater than that of the more historically dramatic sliding scale, (Webbs, 1950; Welbourne, 1923: 289). According to the 1892 *Rules* the 'powers of the Committee' were as follows:

The Joint Committee shall have full power to refer to arbitration or otherwise settle all questions (except such as may be termed county questions, or may affect the general trade) relating to wages, compensation for alteration in practices of working, and all questions or disputes of any other description which may arise from time to time at any particular colliery between the owner of such a colliery and his workmen, and which shall be referred for the consideration of the Committee by either party concerned, and the decision of the Committee shall be final and binding upon all parties.

(DRO NCB I/CO/4)

This referred specifically to the Miners' Joint Committee (there were separate bodies of a similar nature for the Mechanics, Enginemen and Cokemen) and is the nearest to a 'framework of reference'. The proceedings were published annually, often running to over 100 pages, with up to 12 agreements per page; in 1890 the Committee had 25 meetings and dealt with 1,016 cases (1892 XXXIV: 411).

It has been argued that the Joint Committee

counted for very little at the level of the colliery itself . . . In effect what happened was that wherever the lodge did not ignore the Joint Committee right from the outset, they would ignore it if the results were not to their liking.

(Douglass, 1977: 264)

In one respect this is correct: the customs of each colliery often varied from one to the next and were defended tenaciously. But as has been stressed, the last quarter of the century was the period where traditional methods were, in some areas, under attack. For those issues for which there were no agreed methods, Committee decisions were important at a local level, for example, on the compensation set for the introduction of Davy lamps at Leasingthorne Colliery in December 1881 and Brancepeth in August 1877 (at six shillings per score of tubs); or again, concerning the rates for a 'new method' of long-wall working in July 1876 at Nettlesworth, and in the use of a 'wedging machine' at Tursdale in October 1886. In other instances, the Committee resolved disputes with the phrase, 'subject to the custom of colliery', particularly those over working arrangements and prices (*DMA*, 1893). Of course, these may have been ratifications of already locally agreed decisions, but even as such, especially in the 'new areas', would have had a 'knock on' effect into other pits.

These decisions, alongside the detailed lists of 'Wage and Trade Customs', were the backbone of industrial conciliation. The breadth of subject matter created a constant formal fortnightly forum (usually between the same six representatives for years) concerned with a bedrock of specific and thus soluble problems. An 'oasis of calm in a stormy sea', as John Wilson called it in 1893 (DMA *Circular*, June 1893). With a county court judge as chairman with a casting vote its role was described as simply taking up local questions not general ones. When a general question as to the alteration of hours or wages affecting the whole county arises, it is taken up . . . by the Federation Board composed of Miners, Cokemen, Mechanics, Enginemen and the Owners' Association.

(1892 XXXIV: 313)

The fact that the Joint Committee dealt with these minutiae gave it its strength. Issues which would have otherwise been spread 'horizontally' between lodges went 'vertically' to the Committee. For example, whilst in Northumberland the *total* average wage of a colliery had to be under the county rate before an application to the Committee could be made, in Durham if *any* 'flat' (part of a district within a pit), with perhaps as few as six men involved, was below the county average they could apply separately (1892 XXXIV: 416). Apart from the tendency to prolong issues this was also said to weaken the authority of management. If summoned to the Committee, miners were paid the usual rate for a shift, not surprisingly, as one owner observed, 'they like it' (*ibid*. 432).

The establishment of the DMA as the sole representative, through the Joint Committee, of employees in the mines was conducive to the formation of sectional unions. In December 1872 the Mechanics and the deputies applied to the owners for wage increases, but were told to go through the Joint Committee, that is, in practice, the DMA. As a result, the latter along with the Colliery Mechanics formed their own organisations in 1876 and 1874 respectively, thereby ensuring themselves a place on the Committee (DRO NCB I/SC/625(i); Hall, 1929: 11). These were important developments in the structure of trade unionism in the county, and reveal much about the nature of the DMA itself. They also provide the backdrop to the argument of the next section, that is, that the Durham Miners' Association was a union essentially representing the interests of the hewers.

The Durham Miners' Association: the hewers' union As a result of the character of the Joint Committee the DMA became more exclusively a union representing the interests of hewers. At a Miners' Federation of Great Britain (MFGB) conference in 1913 the DMA delegate prefaced his comments on the Minimum Wage Act:

Unlike my colleagues from other areas I can only speak for the practical miner of Durham, other classes of labour have their own organisations and their own policy . . .

(MFGB, 1913: 566)

In fact the 'density' of overall union affiliation was probably highest in Durham. Of the 80,595 recorded as miners in the 1891 Census of the county, 48,000 were in the DMA, and no less than 30,000 of these were hewers (1893–4 CVI: 330; 1892 XXXIV: 334). In other words, *six out of 10 miners were in the DMA, and six out of these 10 were hewers*.

The status of the hewer was in part a product of the traditional method of working coal in the North East, that is, the bord and pillar system. There are many technical descriptions of this, but the clearest comes from the memories of a miner at Leasingthorne Colliary. John Kell, born in 1877, began work at the turn of the century in the Brockwell Seam which was four-foot thick. The coal was won thus: first a 'winnin' was cut three or four yards wide and up to two miles long; then cuts, five yards wide, were made into the coal on each side; and from these the miner cut left and right to leave a pillar 30 foot square. 'When you are working bord the coal is facing you, when you are working pillar, the coal is end on.' The best comparison, said Kell, was the difference between sawing *across* wood and *down* its length (DRO Kell MS, D/MRP23/2).

By the time Kell became a hewer three-shift working was introduced, so that the usual group of 'marras' became six, two to each shift. His group was typical in that it was linked by family ties (Kell had a brother and two cousins and two others in his group). The total pay for the six would be collected by one man, usually the eldest, and he would distribute it amongst the rest. In stable groups the division would be equal; differentials for skill or inexperience were low, the essential divide being a member or non-member of the group itself (Burt, 1924: 110–12).

From the 1880s the newer pits, particularly on the east coast, began to work on the longwall system. It has been suggested that the adoption of this method reflected a new 'technical' or 'scientific' approach to coal extraction, in contrast to the traditional bord and pillar methods (Trist *et al.*, 1963). In fact it originated naturally in Shropshire in the seventeenth century because of the wider more accessible structure of the coal veins, and, until the 1820s when it spread to other areas, was known as the 'Shropshire method' (Galloway, 1898: 203). Working this way the face is cut 'face on' in walls of 10 to 60 yards long, the waste being used to pack up the roof as it advances or, when not available, by pit-props. It is more efficient than the bord and pillar system insofar as none of the coal is left behind as support, but in the northern fields where the seams were deeper, thinner and uneven, required more mining technique. Coal cut longwall was, all other things being equal, open to more rational exploitation. Mechanical cutters could be used, supervision and ventilation was facilitated, and the autonomy of the hewing group was lessened and its job control and thus overall status declined.

By the 1900s many Durham pits were working both longwall and bord and pillar, the introduction of the former causing hewing prices to fall since extraction was easier from the face (DRO NCB/4/6–1912). However the majority of faces in Durham remained only three or four feet high and the bord and pillar method used was determined by geology and custom. Despite this, and the shorter than national average hours spent at the face by the hewer, his productivity was generally, until the 1900s, very good (Holbrook-Jones, 1979: 285). The explanation for this is that the hewer in Durham was a specialist: tertiary jobs at the face, such as stoneworking and timbering, were generally done by other specialist groups, in the latter case by the 'deputy back-bye' (*Colliery Guardian*, January 22nd 1909; Durham *Proceedings*, 1912: 19). For about six months four to six hewers would work solely upon one small face, each shift preparing the work for the next. As Wilson put it, by retaining their inter-dependence, 'each works to the other's hands', and thus the work was done overall in the best way – rather than the individual maximising his output to the detriment of the next shift. If preparatory work was necessary, or timbering required before the face could be continued, this loss of time was borne by the 'marra' group as a whole, for it would in the long run increase their output (*ibid.*: 152). Autonomy was exchanged for efficiency: on the hewer's side, high status, job control and safety; on the employer's side, good productivity and self-regulation of the work.

The employers were well aware of this. After the 1912 Minimum Wage Act had been in operation for a year the DMA requested, through Wilson, the adoption of 'separate tokens' for payment of 'marra', or workgroup, members – in effect individual piecework. The owners refused this on the grounds that it would 'disrupt continuous working'. The request stemmed from the employers avoiding paying the minimum on the grounds that certain miners were not producing the average output (and thus the whole group lost its right to the basic pay). It is not clear to what extent the rank and file wanted the method suggested by Wilson, but it is evident that the management's understood that work force co-operation benefited them. (Durham *Proceedings*, 1913: 77–8).

The high status of the Durham hewer had consequences throughout the occupational hierarchy. For example, deputies in the North East had much lower status and function because of the autonomous nature of facework. Their job, described as 'partly manual, partly unofficial supervisor' in 1912, consisted of checking timbering, ventilation, lighting and the state of each working in his district, which was to be visited daily (*ibid.*: 32; Bulman and Redmayne, 1951: 73–5). The organisation of work, particularly under bord and pillar working was left entirely to the hewers. Thomas Burt described one such man attempting to distribute men for the back-shift:

He would puzzle and perspire for a few moments. When he had made his final statement, he always had a few men left that he did not know what to do with. All the time . . . we had mentally arranged matters ourselves, and, after we had worried poor Tom sufficiently, and gained a few extra minutes bait-time, we cheerfully resumed the work of the day.

(1924: 166–7)

Partly for statutory, partly for disciplinary reasons, bord and pillar methods required a higher ratio of deputies to men than did longwall: a textbook on mining gives the ratios as 1:11 compared with 1:19 (Bulman and Redmayne, 1951: 228).

Whereas in other areas longwall divided the hewer's role into three (holer, getter, and filler), in Durham this seems to have been resisted. Specifically, there emerged no class of semi-skilled men filling the tubs with coal, since this task was rotated amongst the hewers. Even the introduction of coal-cutters initially failed to break the 'marra' system, since groups simply increased to 16 or even 26, located around one or two machines (Durham *Proceedings*, 1912: 151).

Another factor giving hewers greater influence in union affairs was that haulage, traditionally the other major underground task, was seen as an apprenticeship for face work. The young lad taken at the pit first as a 'trapper' (opening and closing ventilation doors) would graduate (if horses were used) to 'putter's hand', perhaps with the job of anchoring the tubs down an incline or advancing to warn the trappers of their arrival. In hand-putting two or three youths would co-operate until they were strong enough to push a tub each. A visitor to Monkwearmouth Pit near Sunderland in 1853 described a distinct hierarchy:

The term putter includes the specific distinctions of the 'headsman', 'half-marrow' and the 'foal'. Where the full tubs or baskets are to be pushed along the rails from the hewers to the crane the headsmen take the chief part; a half-marrow at the end of the train alternately with another half-marrow, while a foal always precedes the train. Where the inclination is steep there are 'helpers-up' to assist at the worst.

(Leifchild, 1853: 158)

Pay was by the score of tubs moved (sometimes a 'score' would be 22 or 23) and related to the distance from the face. Albert Pallister was paid one shilling per 'score' in 1915 as a putter with ponies. In 1921 he moved to Croxdale as a hand-putter, which he described 40 years later as 'slavery' (DRO MS, D/MRP/II/I.).

After a few years, normally when a man was in his early twenties, the final promotion to hewer would be achieved – a *rite de passage* of community significance (Durham *Proceedings*, 1912: 24). Thomas Burt, later to become leader of the Northumberland Miners, recalled this transition: 'So far as my work was concerned, I now ceased to be a boy and hence forth was a man' (1924: 109). After beginning as a trapper, the 18-year-old Jack Lawson became a putter, and five years later, in 1904, a hewer, '. . . with my own marras and picks', and in the same year he joined the Boldon Independent Labour Party (1933: 102).

As time progressed it seems this type of advancement became less usual, for in 1912 there were 'considerable numbers' of putters over 21. Nevertheless, it is interesting that, according to Wilson of the DMA, 'we still look upon them as youths' (Durham *Proceedings*, 1912: 24). In the words of 'The Putter', in 1897 a local song by the pitman-poet Alexander Barass:

> Aw'm just a smally laddy, hardly owld enough to hew
> But aw've held me awn at puttin wi the best aw ivvor knew.

Putting was also 'training' for piecework since most putters were paid by the number of tubs they shifted from the face to the shaft. When working on the same face it was customary to co-operate (signified by the putters hanging their tokens together), otherwise there would be a mad rush for the available tubs. A putter of persistently 'independent' spirit would soon find mysterious 'accidents' occurring to his tub, or that his tokens for the day were suddenly lost (Lawson, 1933: 59–60). In this way the 'marrowing' system of the hewers was passed on in another form to their putters who, on reaching face-work, became accustomed to co-operative methods.

In summary, the specialised role of the hewer and his *de facto* apprenticeship, combined with the fact that his work was the fulcrum of the pit's operations, gave him a high status in the community and in the life of the local lodge. There are numerous examples of county and lodge officials rising from the position of hewer or checkweighman (undoubtedly an ex-hewer) (Marshall, 1976: App. F).

Because of the two-shift system in Durham, the hewers formed a higher proportion of the colliery work force than in other areas. However, their more specialised role means that this does not show up clearly in national comparisons: the definition of the hewer used in Durham would be quite different from that in South Wales, where he would carry out a number of tasks (Appendix: Table a). This type of information is available in a limited form in the surviving 'cavilling sheets' which list the occupations of all those involved. For example, in 1893 Emma Pit employed about 120 men underground. Adding 20 per cent to this for the total work force, the hewers (70) made up 58 per cent; at Hamsterley Pit in 1912, they made up 54 per cent, and at Lumley in 1900, 50 per cent (DRO NCB 1/SC/566–8; D/MRP 21/2; NCB 2/31). The county average was 42 per cent (Appendix: Table b), but this was, of course, affected by the specialised definition given to the hewer in Durham, as reflected in the high percentage of 'other underground labour'.

As pieceworkers, the hewers and putters set the pace for the rhythm work of the pit, and as such their disputes reverberated throughout the work force. The dense web of conciliation, the fulcrum of which was the Miner's Joint Committee, depended on the co-operation of the face-workers, and in this respect confirmed their leading status. In particular in the North East the practice of cavilling and its effect upon job control and wage determination of face-workers has to be considered in detail.

Cavilling and job control The fact that during the years in question the instruments of production in the mining industry were not revolutionised does not mean the miner was immune to other aspects of 'factory' industrialisation: speed-up, closer supervision, punitive discipline and so on. One response to this by miners of the North was the institution of cavilling, although it originated, as Galloway suggests, in the eighteenth century. He describes it as a mining custom,

peculiar to the north of England ... regulating the distribution of ... working-places among the miners by lot, thus effectively preventing any partiality on the part of the colliery officials.

(1904: 358)

Why then did it not spread to other mining areas? One possible explanation may be that the North East coalfield had no recent history of small petty production. As early as the 1600s the 'Hostmen' coal producers of the Tyne were considerable entrepreneurs, and for over two centuries were able, through close ties with the House of Commons, to avoid both serious taxation and any legal challenge to their monopolist trade with London. This, combined with a policy of organised suppression of competition via the purchase of land and wayleave leases, frustrated the emergence of a class of small colliery owners. When the restrictions were ended in the 1830s the geographical development of the field had passed beyond the simple drift, or bell mine: exploitation required considerable investment (Sweezy, 1938: 9–60).

As a result, the tradition of direct wage-labour (albeit with a yearly bond) established very early among the miners the principle that differences in earnings would have to be solved 'internally', since there was no prospect of future promotion to a small master or a 'butty'. Cavilling can be seen as a response consolidated before the transformation of the industrial market for coal, and which the miners maintained throughout the Industrial Revolution and after. In virtually every other region large scale production emerged only in the period from 1820 to 1840, before which the drift mine was the typical unit (Galloway, 1898: 471–7).

Whatever its origins, cavilling was a very important factor in the miners struggle to retain, collectively, the rhythm of work. Of course, ultimately, the hewer with his piece-rates, for considerable periods tied to the selling price of coal and always subject to revision by the coal owners, was just as subject to the market, as was the spinner or the engineer. However, unlike these latter, the northern miner does not seem to have been imbued with the ethic of work maximisation, perhaps because the unpredictability of the job *ultimately* denied a necessary relation between increased effort and extra reward (independent of any intervention by the market or the management).

The system of rotating work places by a random allocation, whilst benefiting the hewers as a whole, led to sharp changes in income, possibly up 100 per cent every 13 weeks (DRO Fairbridge MS D/MR21/2). Also, the partnership of the hewer and his 'marra' instilled a natural co-operation, often over long periods of time, and was at odds with the *individual* maximisation of wages:

> . . . it was not unusual for some men to be as much as 30% more productive than their partners and remain marras throughout their coal hewing life.
>
> (*ibid.*)

Cavilling agreements are widespread in the records of North East pits. Often written in impenetrable colloquial language, they specify the procedure for integrating 'strangers' into the labour force: how often, which seams and flats were involved, and so on. Although very similar, colliery cavilling rules were not standardised and their negotiation and maintenance gave considerable scope for local leadership. The DMA Executive usually ratified lodge decisions: for example the Boldon Branch refused to let the 'Durham lot' interfere with a cavilling dispute on the grounds that it was based on 'local knowledge' (DRO Minutes MS, DH/Ph71/12).

At each redistribution of working places output inevitably fell as the new team accustomed itself to the new conditions, struck local bargains over the conditions, and investigated the problems that lay ahead. John Simpson, manager of Heworth Colliery, wrote to a client on April 3rd 1879: 'I cannot promise more than 650 tons per day . . . as this is cavilling day and Monday is certain to be a poor day' (DRO NCB IX65). Moreover, on the day lots were drawn (usually a Monday), little work was done, and the Joint Committee minutes give many examples of complaints by owners that the day was treated as a holiday (DMA, 1893: 80, 296). Simpson appealed to the DMA to reconsider his request to have each seam cavilled separately (rather than throughout the pit or colliery):

> . . . the working of the Beacham seam is so totally different from the working of the Hutton and Beaumont seams . . . the new men cavilled into the Beacham seam do not get into the way of working until some weeks after the commencement of each quarter . . .
>
> (DRO NCB IX65)

The lodge used its power in controlling the drawing of cavils as a weapon in collective bargaining: once a new working or 'flat' was opened, the management would wish to start work in it as soon as possible, and this situation could thus be used to the men's advantage. For example, in April 1878 Boldon Committee refused to 'cavil through' until a wages dispute was settled, a tactic also used at South Medomsley in March 1884 (DRO Minutes MS DH/Ph71/12; *Shields Daily News*, March 6th 1884).

Cavilling was also a means of 'democratically' sharing redundancy. Instead of management simply discharging the men in worked-out districts, the miners pressed for the choice to be made by drawing lots, thus at least ensuring that the sackings were not a disguised form of victimisation (Douglass, 1977:235).

To summarise: the 'classic' form of cavilling occurred quarterly, and involved all the hewers and their putters throughout a pit of colliery (occasionally including two or three if they were closely situated) and the flats in each pit. An example is that of Emma Pit, as agreed on June 28th 1893 (DRO NCB I/SC/566–8). However, as might be expected, this procedure was under constant attack from the owners, perhaps before, but definitely following the 1870s when most records begin. The owners wished to cavil pits separately, that is, not throughout the colliery, in order to minimise the disruption of work. From the Joint Committee minutes come the following examples:

Burnhope – this agreed for 2 cavils and then discussed again. Feb. 1877.
Seaham – agreed cavil pits separately. Oct. 1878.
Boldon – separate cavillings. Agreed Feb. 1882.
Deaf Hill and Trimdon – Owners ask these pits to be cavilled separately, as the lessors of Trimdon object to men living in their houses and working at Deaf Hill. Agreed March 1885.

(DMA, 1893)

This last example shows how cavilling could involve pits of different owners, which by tradition had been placed together, possibly because of their proximity combined with the extremes of working conditions found in them. (Clearly it would have been of little advantage to the men if the pits had offered similar advantages and disadvantages.) This did not go unchallenged by the local lodge; the minutes note numerous 'deferments' and 'objections', and several collieries are discussed repeatedly over a number of years. The issue was 'finally' decided by the Cavilling Agreement of July 23rd 1908 which stated:

. . . whether seams should be cavilled separately or together will be decided on the merits of each case and *apart from the customs of each colliery* [My emphasis] . . .

(DMA, 1930)

Another tactic was to press for the cavil to take place less frequently, perhaps only twice or even once a year:

Burnhope – agreed cavil every 6 months. June 1877.
Washington – agreed cavil every 6 months. Dec. 1882.
Victoria Garesfield – cavilling to be every 12 months. Oct. 1886.

(DMA, 1893)

The more management restricted the swapping of work places, the more open was the labour force to manipulation, in the form of incentives and bonuses. This could lead to a loss of job control, as the two following minutes reveal:

Hebburn – That the manager be at liberty to let or cavil for places as he thinks proper . . . Dec. 1877.
Brandon C Pit – The men request if the Secretary be allowed to sit and take a copy of the cavilling sheet . . . Nov. 1888

(*ibid.*)

The loss of the timing of the cavil was not just a formal question; the management could open a new flat and ask for tenders, and the vacant cavil would be filled by 'spare' men of the overseer's choosing. Over a year or six months the integral control of work distribution would gradually be lost, and with it the material interest that the colliers as a group had in sharing the vicissitudes of the pit. This was a common enough occurrence to incite the DMA to issue a circular in 1881 asking whether lodges had managed to get such practices embodied in cavilling rules (Douglass, 1977: 236).

Another weakening of this system occurred as the 'fillers' or 'rippers' (the workers shovelling the 'out' coal into the tubs) were no longer cavilled along with the hewers. Naturally as pieceworkers (which many were, particularly in the bord and pillar system), their earnings were linked to the prosperity of the 'flat', and thus via the cavil to the miners as a whole. Instances of their removal from the cavil appear in the records of Langley Park Pit in 1915, and at Auckland seven years earlier (DRO NCB 4/6; I/CO/141).

Thus, by the early twentieth century cavilling rules were severely curtailed and modified in favour of labour control and discipline. From August 28th 1912 at Langley Park, the Harvey Seam (and all bord and pillar workings) were to be

cavilled separately from all other seams . . . The hewers will be required to marrow themselves in such sets as the Management may desire, and will be required to hand in the names comprised in the set to the Overman three clear days before the cavils are drawn. Should not any man do so they will be marrowed by the Overman at his discretion . . .

(DRO NCB 4/6)

Or, again, from the Cavilling Rules of Heworth Colliery in 1916:

1   All seams to be cavilled as one pit. Each district to be cavilled separately . . .
3   The longwall method – Each place to be cavilled for as a permanent cavil and

to claim it as far as that range of coal goes belonging to that flat . . .
(DRO NCB IX/62)

The whittling away of cavilling procedure over the last quarter of the nineteenth century is difficult to trace accurately, but these fragments are suggestive. They also give some grounds for an assessment of this custom.

An influential view is best summarised by Douglass:

> The cavilling system was the fundamental way in which the Durham miner managed to maintain an equitable system of work and managed to stave off the competitiveness, bullying and injustice of the hated butty system. In essence it was an embryo of workers' control, as can be seen from its ability to handle disputes between sets of workers without recourse to outsiders. It was a little Soviet which had grown up within the capitalist system.
>
> (1977: 239)

However, this view is contradicted to some extent by the above examination which has argued that it was not an alternative to the 'butty' system, since this method of coal extraction was ruled out by the pioneer character of the North East coalfield. But, more importantly, to what extent is Douglass's 'heroic' view of cavilling and job control justified? On the credit side there is the fact that local organisation was required to establish and monitor the cavil – not the least part of which was the election of the cavil leaders (two signatures appear on agreements from the men, and are not usually those of the local lodge officials). This is one area the Joint Committee did not colonise: it is significant that there are only occasional references to cavil customs being used in wage bargaining, for example, Boldon Colliery, April 3rd 1878 (DRO DH/Ph 71/12). However, it was essentially a *defensive* mechanism. Cavilling, for example, *coped* with sackings, rather than being a basis for opposing them: a democratic sharing out of the fluctuations of the market. Its pre-capitalist origins adapted to the 'casualisation' of the labour market, which was mainly contested through the emergence of the County unions, and not by cavilling.

The apportioning of unproductive 'flats' was, as Douglass points out, a way of handling the problem 'without recourse to outsiders', by which he means the managers. But it was also 'without recourse' to the rest of the miners as a national body. When in 1911 the Miners' Federation took up the question of 'abnormal places' (particularly in South Wales) it took the position that a miner,

> . . . working at the coal-face at the fixed tonnage rates [is] to receive full wages, if employed in an abnormal place, the rate to be the average rate of *wages previously earned by the workman* under normal conditions, which shall not be less than the recognised minimum, or county average paid in each district
>
> (Page Arnot, 1967: 59)

In other words, it dealt with the problem by establishing a *minimum* to which *additions* be made.

The North Eastern section of the union had historically been the least enthusiastic advocate of the minimum wage, preferring instead the sliding scale. When at last converted, it found to its embarrassment that the owners' opposition echoed its own arguments in the Federation against the minimum (*ibid.*: 82). It may be fairly summised that cavilling and the sliding scale were linked: *they both accepted the logic of market forces, and their combination in the North East coalfields was not coincidental*. Further acquiescence to market forces is evident in the practice of leaving a pit if a bad cavil was drawn when employment was good. Joe Parks, a Durham miner in the first decade of the century, recalled this (Parks, 1975: 34), and it was a feature of mining life also experienced by the young Thomas Burt in the 1860s and 1870s (Burt, 1924: 20–36).

Finally, it is important to note the reasons for the declining role of the cavil in the present century. As has been seen, the national union had taken responsibility for differences in working places, although that by no means signalled the end of North Eastern customs. Nonetheless it did mean a decline in the cavils function as a fulcrum for rank and file activity which was expressed through movements over wages and discipline (Douglass 1977: 265–281). In comparison with (say) the engineers' shop steward, the cavil-leader's role declined rather than expanded with the growth of 'mature' industrial relations. Insofar as the introduction of coal-cutters reduced both the extremes in output between 'flats', and shortened the time during which a new arrival was unfamiliar with the vagaries of the working, the cavil was diminished in significance as a regulator of work.

The hewers: status and stability. After the interlude to consider the role of the cavil it is useful finally to look briefly at the changes in status and work in the decade up to the War. As has been noted, the supremacy of the North Eastern field was under threat from the 1880s, both domestically and in the export market. Being the oldest field, despite the exploitation of the eastern 'sea' pits in the 1900s, overall it experienced the greatest pressure of diminishing resources and returns. However, the productivity of the Durham underground worker (which was essentially determined by the hewer, whose hours were comparatively short) remained highest until the period from 1905 to 1909. That this was so in a field in which the degree of job control was most refined, the aforementioned pressures notwithstanding, demonstrates how *autonomy was here in fact correlated with high output* (Holbrook-Jones, 1979: 285).

Throughout the negotiations over the Minimum Wage Act in

Durham the owners' comments reflect an appreciation of this fact. Although the introduction of coal-cutting machines increased the co-operative face groups from six or eight to between 16 and 26, nevertheless they persisted with the custom of a collective wage distributed amongst the group. On this question Wilson asserted on behalf of the DMA that the effect of the Act would be to transform this into a simple average and thereby weaken the hewers' position in bargaining for 'consideration' money. Inter-dependence was useful not only for the hewers but also for the management: overall, over a longer period the work would be completed in the best possible manner, and the individual would not be left to scramble to maximise his output on one shift or face to the detriment of the next shift, or to the rational working of the face as a whole. The owners fully agreed to this submission: they, too, wished to impress upon the Chairman the importance of 'collective responsibility', as they termed it. A 'trade-off' is apparent here: the hewers were to retain their right to bargain for the vicissitudes of the work place, whilst the owners were to gain, via the self-discipline of the workgroup in its maintenance of 'internal' control over the method of work (Durham *Proceedings*, 1912: 150–3). In fact the 1912 Agreement was to founder on this very question of averages amongst co-operative groups.

But what of the results of the negotiations over the Act itself? It must be remembered that the backdrop to this Act was the effect of the Eight Hour Act in Durham: from 1909 the vast majority of pits began introducing a three-shift system of working combined with two of transit hands. In introducing intensive shift work this was to the detriment of the hewers in terms of their family life, although not in terms of their hours of work since these were already well below the maximum (Webb, 1912: 70–2). The putters on the other hand gained a clear reduction of two hours per shift. As a 'sop' to the hewers, basic rates for pieceworkers were raised from 3/8d to 4/2d, from which he proportionally gained more (Rowe, 1923: 169). The three-shift system was, nonetheless, very unpopular in union councils – 'the greatest mistake the agents had ever made', according to the Auckland Lodge secretary (*Colliery Guardian*, September 23rd 1910). The Executive's decision not to support strikes against its introduction was overturned on at least two occasions (DMA *Circular*, February 1910; June 1910).

Some reflection of this conflict can be seen in Table 4 i which shows the union demand, the award, and the percentage the latter is of the former. Unlike any other area, here we see an award, in the case of the putters, of a minimum actually *above* the union demand. This is further convincing evidence of the domination of the DMA by the interests of the hewers, a bias sharpened by the effects of the Eight Hour Act. Table 4 ii expresses the awards in terms of differentials. Clearly the putter's status was viewed more highly by the Joint Board than by the DMA, a situation no doubt influenced by the increasingly militant stance taken by this grade of worker in the four years following the Eight Hour Act (*Colliery Guardian*, September 16th 1910).

TABLE 4 i

Grade	(1) *Trade Union demand*	(2) *Award*	(2) *as a percentage of* (1)
Hewers	6/1.25d	5/6d	89
Timber-drawers	6/6.39d	5/8d	86
Fillers	6/5.25d	5/10d	91
Hand-putters	5/1.05d	5/7d	110
Pony-putters	4/9.43d	5/7d	114
Labourers	5/-	4/7d	92

(Durham, *Proceedings* 1912: 2, 6).

TABLE 4 ii

Grades compared	Trade Union demanded (percentage)	Award (percentage)
As between hewers and putters (pony)	23	0
As between hewers and putters (hand)	23	0
As between hewers and labourers	24	19

As has been mentioned the 1912 Agreement was to founder on the question of averages. The DMA called for a renegotiation in 1913 because it claimed that the co-operative work-group method of working created a loop-hole for the employers to avoid the Minimum Wage Act. Wilson argued that it was unfair if all members of a group forfeited the right to the minimum if one member ('a weakling' as he put it) fell below what was considered the 'customary' output for one shift. As was noted earlier, Wilson suggested as a solution the 'separation of tokens' of hewers – in effect individual piecework. It is not clear how far this had been discussed in the Union, certainly the *Circulars* of the time do not mention this specific proposal. Nonetheless, the owners rejected outright what would have been a revolutionary change in the field because in their view it would 'disrupt continuous working' (Durham *Proceeding*, 1913: 71–8,78). Once again the employers recognised that, although the independent work group might be obstructive at the level of the individual pit, its ability, overall, to cope autonomously with the ever changing character of work and to rationally exploit coal reserves outweighed this. Such a view was strengthened by the fact that the Act empowered deputies to decide when the minimum should be forfeited, if he judged the face was not being worked 'right': in a sense this left responsibility with the group but 'rescued' quality control for the management. The DMA vociferously opposed this particular aspect of the Act (since, of course, it mainly affected hewers), and the matter went to arbitration (*ibid*.: 80–5).

As a final example, the debate of 1913 is yet another illustration of the weight of the hewer within the DMA, albeit now challenged. This status flowed implicitly from the organisation of work, not in a technical sense, for as fast as one method became 'normal', a system of rewards and privileges quite separate from work arose around it. This occupational advantage had a 'material' influence upon the control of the lodge, checkweighman and agent, insofar as it became the route to electoral positions in local government.

Cavilling, that unique expression of the hewers occupational solidarity, has to be seen in this context of the struggle to maintain status. Therefore equations, sociological or political, with 'workers' control' are misplaced: whilst conferring advantages for the whole underground work force, its prime concern was the defence of one grade. By cavilling, however, the hewers were forced to confront the problems of the pit as a whole; in particular, the maintenance of the internal hierarchy demanded the organisation of haulage and ancillary labour. The debate over the Minimum Wage nevertheless illustrates how limited this 'spillover' was, as does the general role of the DMA in the Federation at this time.

To emphasise the point: the hewers' sectional interests could to an extent be served only by 'universalistic' policies and strategies. Perhaps this is seen best at the level of community, a feature strengthened by the geographical isolation of mining: in this sphere the hewers sectional outlook was probably altered more than by the changing status at the face. The more the Union became embroiled in national politics the more local political action became a factor – certainly this experience seems to have been important in the development of the socialist left element in the DMA (Douglass, 1977: 283–290; Lawson, 1933: 102–8).

The South and North Midlands Fields
These two inland fields are united in having origins in the internal and local demand for coal in the sixteenth century, and also in their relatively late expansion into areas of national economic importance (Nef, 1932: 56–60, 65–67). In the south (Staffordshire, Cannock Chase and Leicestershire) the principal output was the 'soft' domestic coal, also

used in manufacture and gas production. In the north (Derbyshire, Nottinghamshire and South Yorkshire) the field is divided geologically between the 'soft' seam in the east and the 'hard' or 'Barnsley bed' in the west and south (Rowe, 1923: 26–7; J.E. Williams, 1962: 22).

In contrast to the Northern pits the labour force in the Midlands area was, up to the 1870s, very fluid; seasonal work in agriculture was a common alternative for the miner during depressions (Nef, 1934: 184). As a result work was less specialised, the scale of operations smaller and the surrounding network of distribution, capitalisation and trade less developed. It is therefore interesting that this was one of the last areas for piece-rate payments to become normal, and, perhaps as a consequence, for coerced labour and truck to be eradicated (*ibid*.: 182–3; J.E. Williams, 1962: 28–31). As a result of the underdevelopment of the industrial order, the 'cash nexus' was less well defined; thus in the Midlands fields a plethora of wage-contract forms and working methods existed. Until the early years of the nineteenth century wages often even took the form of a weekly or fortnightly 'subsistence' which did not bear any strict relation to the earnings of the period; at intervals the account of each miner was reckoned and the balance handed over. From this system both employer and employee gained certain advantages: the latter had a type of minimum wage, and the former a method of deferring part of the wages bill until ready cash was available (Ashton, 1928: 322).

The main market for both fields was domestic, and the output diverse. Trade was subject to cyclical and seasonal fluctuations, but generally was more stable than for fields based upon export. An example is seen in Derbyshire and Nottinghamshire, which were in the 1880s producing mainly house and gas coal. In about 1896 a 'top hard' seam traversing both counties was developed, and as a result, by 1913, around 25 per cent of the Derbyshire, and 50 per cent of the Nottinghamshire production was steam coal (Rowe, 1923: 24–5). Another example of the relative flexibility of these fields is the rapid rise of the Yorkshire output to feed the steam engines of the woollen and worsted mills. Between 1870 and 1910 output increased $3\frac{1}{2}$ times, rising to constitute 16.7 per cent of total U.K. production by 1913 (Jevons, 1915: 59; Rowe, 1923: 14). Due to its later development and its even seams, such coal-cutting machines as were available were concentrated in these two areas: 601 were reported in 1912 – about one-quarter of the total for the UK (Jevons, 1915: 69).

Both fields, whilst expanding fastest between 1876 and 1914, did not greatly increase their share of the total output. Staffordshire's and Worcestershire's output increased by an average annual rate of 4.52 per cent from 1854 to 1865; but thereafter up to 1886 only by 0.24 per cent. Derbyshire's output for the same periods increased by 6.06 per cent and 3.14 per cent respectively. From 1886 the latter county had the fastest growth, and by 1913 output was up 50 per cent (J.E. Williams, 1962: 213). By 1913 the South field produced 8.6 per cent and the North field about 19 per cent of the total national output (Rowe, 1923: 14).

According to Jevons, the wages in Yorkshire '. . . are distinctly lower than in the North Eastern, Scottish or South Wales coalfields' (Jevons, 1915: 70). He attributes this to the opportunity for female employment in the mills.

In determining the supply of labour the wages of family are really the effective factor; and where the necessary family maintenance is found partly by women, the men's labour comes to be paid at a lower rate.

(*ibid.*)

This was the case for the South field but not for the North where coal-getting wages were above average. The evidence suggests, if anything, a stronger causal relationship between low wages and agriculture: Somerset, Forest of Dean, Shropshire and Leicestershire had the lowest, and Lancashire (the centre of textiles) wages were about average (1919 XIII: 92). Jevons's general point concerning the role of female labour is however not vitiated.

In Derbyshire by the 1860s mining had become sufficiently stabilised for depressions to cause distress, rather than create an exodus to alternative employment. In addition, the boom of the 1870s further stripped the 'stagnant trades', as mines '. . . spring up like mushrooms, working some cases a few weeks or months at most' (1873 X: 22). The character of labour was said to be 'irregular'; high wages brought universal increases in leisure pursuits, the Derby miner preferring the same income and two days off with his pigeons, rabbits or drink,

. . . indeed in some cases the workmen have preferred improving the conditions under which they work to increasing the amount of their wages in money.

(*ibid.*: 24)

In the late 1860s and 1870s the larger colliery companies began to build the pit villages reminiscent of the North, with the panoply of benefit clubs, schools, churches and other paternalistic symbols. But in no sense did the area become as regionally homogeneous, nor, as in South Wales, were particular areas dominated by huge combines (J.E. Williams, 1962: 74–9).

The butty system and the variety of the wage contract. Virtually the only analysis of this system in print is A.J. Taylor's article of 1960. In it he asserts that it was a product of the early stages of capitalism, and it persisted (largely in Staffordshire) in essentially industrial backwaters. Labour was scarce but was 'undisciplined', that is, not trained to the incentive principle. Management was passed down from the owner of the means of production to a type of 'face foreman' who bargained a price for the coal, and then set about organising the work to make it pay. The decline of the system was due to its inefficiency, rather than to rank and file opposition; in other words, to its irrationality in the face of the all-embracing notion Taylor has of capitalist industrialisation (*ibid.*: 215–34).

In 1844, according to the Mines' Inspector for the area, the unruly state of the miners was largely due to the 'butties'

who furnish part of the capital, and who being only a little raised above the condition of the labouring men are led . . . to exercise their authority harshly . . .

(1844 XVI: 56)

Truck was not principally due to these men but to the 'large employers' of the Wolverhampton area – a point confirmed by the experience of mining in Derbyshire (*ibid.*: 59; J.E. Williams, 1962: 61–6). It was in the Midlands that the notorious trade in pauper children flourished. In May 1842 a circular was sent from the Poor Law Commissioners to the Guardians of the various parishes to enquire how common the practice was. South Staffordshire replied that

. . . such is the demand for this class of children by the butties that there are scarcely any boys in the union workhouses of Walsall, Wolverhampton, Dudley and Stourbridge.

Fifty-nine children were dispensed in this way from 10 workhouses in the area between 1840 and 1842, and bound for up to 12 years with only food and lodging guaranteed (1842 XXXV: 21–35). The Children's Employment Commission provides further details of the inter-relation between butties, truck, and child and female labour – but, as the researches of the Hammonds has shown, such practices were not the preserve of petty producers, but were primarily connected with the enterprises of the large landowners (1928: 172–6).

This then is the traditional Dickensian view of the butty and his world – a sad, but thankfully short, interlude in the progress towards industrialism proper. But in 1873 the system was still flourishing: chartermasters subcontracted seams at a fixed price, and put pikemen in charge at each stall (eight to 10 yards) along the face; these men supervised the extraction process and were on a piece-rate, whilst the stall workers were paid by the day (1873 X: 27–8). By introducing a *further* level of sub-contraction, the system had adapted to the increasing size of the pits.

This process of adaptation of the 'butty' method allowed it to be integrated with a form of sliding scale of wages. In Staffordshire a scale was introduced in 1874 which took account of the two basic different types of seam in the area: the 'thick' and 'thin' beds. Wages were to rise and fall in line with the price of the former. A basic daily allowance called a 'stint' was paid, and actual earnings were one and a quarter to one and three quarters per nominal day. This scale went through several revisions, and in 1884 a Wages Board was introduced to ascertain a fairer price for the coal throughout the area. Up to the 1890s the system still operated smoothly. According to the Chairman of the Owners' Association:

We have had differences requiring modifications, but the wages board somehow have agreed together upon the modifications, and satisfactorily.

(1892 XXXVI: 102)

The crucial point is that these 28 years of the scale had not dislodged sub-contracting. The chartermaster delivered the coal at 'certain prices' and made his own arrangements and engagements of the men, who could number from 40 to 200 miners. The scale did not regulate the price between the owner and the chartermaster,

. . . the chartermaster has a definite price for the work done; and the wages scale is for individual colliers; he has to pay his men on the sliding scale rates.

(*ibid.*)

This man would supply the tubs, picks and other tools, whilst the owner supplied the rails and timber. In such pits customary payments in kind of coal and beer were allowed to the hewers. The hewers also benefited slightly by shorter hours; fillers, loaders and labourers would work the full nine hours, but the face-worker could finish in seven or eight depending on whether 'his place was favourable or unfavourable' (*ibid.*: 102–3). The wage for working 'abnormal places' was adjusted by the collier applying for a reduction in the 'stint' or nominal output he was expected to achieve. Apart from the manager and under-manager, everyone else was employed by the chartermaster.

Following the formation of the Midlands Federation in September 1888, a small section of Staffordshire miners under its guidance agitated against the scale. Partly as a result of this pressure, partly due to increasing technical problems, some of the newer Staffordshire collieries began operating a modified form of sub-contraction in which ultimate authority was vested in a colliery owner's employee – an overman. He engaged small groups of four to five miners to win and load the coal ready for its haulage to the pit shaft. Unlike the chartermaster system these miners were 'on the books' of the colliery, although still paid as a gang (*ibid.*: 104).

It was this variation which persisted into the twentieth century, whilst the chartermaster system divided into two types. Firstly, where the man bought all his own materials and paid the owner a 'royalty'; second, where he was provided with all the gear, and was paid so much

per ton. Of the survivors into the twentieth century 80 per cent continued in the first system and were largely found in the smaller concerns
(1908 XX: 890–4).

The large pits of Staffordshire still used the gang system. Three such
groups would be allocated a section of the face of approximately 12
yards, called a 'stall'.

What we call a stall will contain three of these superior men called stallmen . . .
There is always a leading man to whom we let the stall. That is to say in the
colliery books we recognise one man as being in sole charge of the stall, but he
has with him two men who are equally as good colliers as himself.

(1907 XIV: 87)

The leading men paid their loaders and fillers a daywage: 'they are
really little contractors', numbering two or three, and employing from
four to 12 others (*ibid.*: 101).

The genealogy of the system could be described as the slow permeation of the incentive principle to lower and lower grades of the colliery
work force, and thus, with it, the increase in direct employment. But
the privileges and status of the small contractor was also a bulwark
against the spread of unionism, since that had become synonymous
with universal piecework. The leading hands amongst the stallmen in
one pit constituted 16 per cent of the work force, but generally seem to
have been opinon leaders for the rest (*ibid.*: 87). They were universally
opposed to the eight-hour day whereas, reported a Staffordshire
manager:

The numerical majority of the men would, no doubt, be very pleased to have an
eight hour day, so long as they got enough money from it. They are not the
responsible men.

(*ibid.*: 99)

These face gangs were fairly generic in the distribution of tasks.
These depended on the seam; if, for example, it required 'holing', this
would be the preserve of the 'leading men' under the chartermaster; but
in the '10-yard seam', or thick coal, timbering required the greatest
skill, and thus the occupational hierarchy was organised around this
(Rowe, 1923: 64–5).

A slight variation from the Staffordshire system existed in Cannock
Chase. Here again a sliding scale was introduced in 1872 and lasted up
to 1883, the basis of wages 'regulated by what we call the "holers day"
or "stint", and in all agreements it has been based upon a sum of 3d to
1s.' This customary payment was adjusted in relation to the ease with
which the individual miner could work his 'stint' in his allocated
working place, but no set figures were agreed. These were bargained
with the management. It was this uncertainty that caused disputes and
led finally to the abandonment of a scale system (1892 XXXIV: 346–7).

Two stallmen engaged five to six others per stall; of these men the holers would be expected to undercut nine feet of coal per 'stint' (but in fact, on a normal day, they would do 50 per cent more than this). They could then leave the pit. The timbering and 'cogging' of the face and the under-cut was the responsibility of the stallmen who, along with the loaders and fillers, would work the full 12-hour day. This gang was paid per ton: the holers' pay was determined by the depth of the under-cut and the 'stint' pay for that place; the stallmen's by the current price for coal paid to the owner; and the rest were paid on a day wage (1907 XIV: 75–7).

Finally, in the Forest of Dean, both the form of longwall and the contracting system were unique. In the house-coal pits the face was cut in wavy lines in accordance with some pre-industrial custom, and separated by 'trolley' roads. These ways were very low, and required an extra type of worker known as a 'hod boy' to drag baskets of coal to trams in the higher central roads. The trams held up to 20 or 30 hundredweight, and their size was necessitated by the fact that the shafts were only equipped for single-winding. This in itself encouraged gang work at the face which was universal up to the 1920s (Rowe, 1923: 151). The coal-getters were paid by the ton and employed their own assistants – up to 10 were necessary in some stalls – on a day wage. His contract was to get the coal to the main road where haulage was often also organised through a contractor (1907 XIV: 39–40).

Thus it can be seen that there was no universal development towards one form of wage contract or work organisation in the Midlands fields. Furthermore, these wide divergences co-existed within close proximity and in the same seams, their survival yet more evidence of the inertia deriving from custom. But their survival *also* demonstrates the ability of all sorts of 'irrational' non-capitalist wage forms to continue simply because they 'worked'.

Derbyshire: subcontracting and unionisation This section concentrates on the activities, working methods and union of the miners of this county, although the field in which they worked crossed the boundary into Yorkshire which had, to a degree, its own separate organisations and customs. What all the Midlands areas have in common is that, unlike Durham, there developed no comparative system of a 'county average wage'. Each colliery in Derbyshire had such lists of prices but no machinery existed at a county level for assuring some uniformity (Webb, 1920: 194). A further common factor was the absence of a predominating market or type of coal: there were domestic, steam and anthracite coal, and some exporting was undertaken from the area. In terms of worker organisation, the impetus of an external centralising market or trade feature was therefore lacking. At various times collieries for steam coal were flourishing, whilst those for domestic coal declined, as, for example, during the early 1860s when the former escaped the crushing depression of the 'cotton famine' years (J.E. Williams, 1962: 49). The union, the Derbyshire Miners' Association, established in 1880, was the first of the three compared areas to break with the sliding scale principle and to join the MFGB in 1890. This was a pragmatic rather than principled decision, since none of the Midlands fields had scales extant by the 1880s, although at various times they had been attempted (Page Arnot, 1949: 80–87).

The lack of a standard price list throughout the county had the consequence that the change in cutting-price per ton caused by alterations in the face had to be dealt with pit by pit, that is, the regulation of effort to earnings was individualised and not spread as a collective problem. Clearly here the uncertainty of effort was resolved at the expense of the face gang via the form of sub-contracting.

Longwall was worked through a system of 'little contractors', each stall being 'let out' to two butties who employed six to eight others along a length of 22 to 28 yards; this group was responsible for getting, filling and loading the coal as well as for the maintenance of timber and roads in their area. The two stallmen would average seven to 10 shillings per day, and the fillers and loaders 4/6 to seven shillings, the differential being 'a bargain between them and is not set by the Company' (1892 XXXIV: 386–92). At the Butterley Colliery Company the butty had greater responsibility although he could not engage or dismiss those under him: here two contractors supervised 45 to 60 yards of the face, that is, three to four stalls. The hewers had to be paid a 'minimum' rate per ton for cutting or loading, but of course it was up to the contractor to ensure the degree of effort made his price profitable (*ibid.*: 716). One such contractor was William Kerry of Alfreton in Derbyshire, who, after 10 years as a hewer, had been offered, 'through patronage', the opportunity to tender for a price from 'face to pit bank'. He thus recruited face and haulage workers sufficient for the task, mainly between the ages of 14 and 21 years, and '. . . all I have to do is to superintend them whilst at work' (*ibid.*: 445).

This system had some similarities with the 'marra' group of Durham, insofar as the face gang autonomously decided how each lie of coal should be tackled, its rates of pay, membership and so on. Yet in Derbyshire the 'minor' difference of the *formal* leadership by a sub-contractor led to major differences in the organisation of work and the strength and structure of unionism. The crucial point seems to have been the *casualisation* of the face gang. In Durham, although one hewer would collect and distribute the pay, his colleagues would normally have been longstanding, and often kin; it was also entirely composed of equals with little permanent specialisation, and therefore low differentials. In Derbyshire, due to sub-contracting the reverse was the case: high turnover of membership, a variety of grades included, high differentials, and only the leader paid by results. In contrast to Durham, unionisation emerged despite sub-contractors. Indeed the Derbyshire union refused to send representatives to the Labour Commission on the grounds that the latter had initially invited witnesses, who the former termed 'buttymen against the Union' (J.E. Williams, 1962: 311).

The stallmen were apparently sufficiently well organised to separately resist management attempts to abolish the system, and in at least one case struck successfully on this issue (1892 XXXIV: 702). Their role as 'opinion leaders' in the pits undoubtedly hindered the spread of trade union ideas and principles. An exception, John Burnett, both stallman and unionist, told the Commission that the ballot papers on various issues passed via the checkweighman to the stallman and then to the rank and file, and since the replies were not sealed, he was convinced this process led to intimidation: '. . . they [the loaders and fillers] take the same course as the stallmen suggest to them . . . as a rule I find that' (*ibid.*: 446).

The general effect of sub-contracting in Derbyshire was to resolve the uncertainty of the relation between earnings and effort at the expense of the day-wage face-ganger. The struggle for the *standardisation* of conditions and allowances thus became the basis of trade union policy, and its main recruiting appeal. The stallman, whose percentage depended very much on his own negotiations with the company, could see no advantage in this at all, and in fact had a vested interest in the absence of formal terms and prices. For example the question of 'slack' in the coal was dealt with informally, each ton being in fact several hundredweight over its imperial measure. The coal boom of 1869–73 allowed many miners to press for the election of checkweighmen to replace this system; at the Butterley Colliery it was secured and a 'ton' reduced from 3,000 to 2,800 lbs, and then in 1872 to 2,240 lbs (Griffen, 1967: 22–25).

It is not surprising that, in the late 1880s, the Derbyshire Miners' Union made its priority the standardisation of printed price lists at collieries. Too often higher wages resulting from trade improvements had been 'clawed back' by the management reducing allowances or increasing the fictional 'ton' (J.E. Williams, 1962: 302). As collieries prospered or foundered, so wages fluctuated: one owner claimed that for every pit there was a different selling price, and thus a different rate of pay (1892 XXXIV: 702). The disparate natures of collieries resulted in each having its own Contract Rules which specified *duties* but not prices. For example, the rules of the Blackwell Colliery for 1877 state that:

Every stallman or Labourer may from time to time without notice be removed by the Owners from his pit or stall, or other work, to any other pit or stall . . . he shall not object to any such removal . . . and shall be paid for such work after the current rate of payments established at these mines for such new work at the time of every such removal.

(Griffen, 1967: 14)

By 1892 the Union claimed that the principle of a price list was accepted at every colliery, but this did not mean uniformity. In 1890 a Miners' Federation of Great Britain (MFGB) investigation of 69 Derbyshire collieries showed that hours at the face varied from seven to 10, the decisive factor undoubtedly being the effectiveness of local activity (J.E. Williams, 1962: 305). On average those employed around the face worked 9.28 hours, 7.88 of which were involved in actual coal getting. This was almost exactly the same as in South Wales but 35 per cent longer than in Durham (Munro, 1891: 250). Not surprisingly the Derbyshire Union strongly supported the legal enforcement of the eight-hour-day: with a membership in 1890 of around 12,000 out of 53,396 miners they stood little chance of achieving this through bargaining (J.E. Williams, 1962: 246; 1892 XXXIV: 392). This policy of the Union, was therefore the result of the strengths or weaknesses of local organisation, which was itself determined by the structure of work.

However, during the last 10 years of the century there was a gradual change in attitude and status amongst the stallmen, resulting in their 'colonisation' of the Union. In 1892 they had resolutely opposed a Miners' Federation ballot on the eight-hour day, and achieved its rejection through their influence over the men although they alone stood to lose by its adoption (1892 XXXIV: 446). When this same question was discussed again in 1907 there had occurred a general shift in attitude amongst the stallmen, alongside their rapid absorption into the Union (J.E. Williams, 1962: 385). By the 1900s most of the larger companies in the region had effected a change to a system of 'letting' stalls to gangs *all of whom* were employees. The stallman's responsibilities, differential status and influence, had thus gradually declined (Griffen, 1967: 16). Although still the leader, he could no longer 'hire and fire' or arrange his own level of payments to the holers and fillers. Also, increasingly, haulage had become a specialised and separate task. A change of tactics was not, therefore, surprising: the manipulation, rather than the frustration, of the Union's policies for his own interests. There is, thanks to J.W.F. Rowe's calculations, clear statistical evidence to back up these impressions. Table 4 iii shows a comparison of wages per shift for 1888 and 1914 in Derbyshire and Nottinghamshire (the available records compelled Rowe to consider these as one field). From this a guide to the maintenance of differentials can be constructed. Table 4 iv shows the results expressed as percentages. Despite the rapid rise in unionisation, the shortening of hours and the minimum wage, pieceworking hewers and other skilled workers had increased their differentials vis-à-vis other unskilled workers. This, as will be seen, contrasted with the experience of South Wales where the rupture of the face-workers' control over union policy in 1893 was reflected both in the demands and the actual results of trade unionism. For Derbyshire, this brief investigation of the relationship of the sub-contracting system to union policy coincides with the view that up to 1914, 'the miners' unions of Derbyshire and Nottinghamshire were dominated by the skilled workers during this period' (J.E. Williams, 1962: 440).

TABLE 4 iii

Year	Piecework coal-getters	Haulage	Timberers, rippers	Underground labourers
1888	5/4	4/–	4/8	3/5
1914	9/10	6/8	7/–	5/8

(Rowe, 1923: 72).

TABLE 4 iv

Year	Hewers cf. hauliers	Hewers cf. labourers
1888	35	58
1914	48	75

Finally, Table 4 v examines the figures of the Minimum Wage Board for Derbyshire in 1912. Because of the differing work methods, the comparison uses its own nomenclature. For the most relevant grades the picture is as Table 4 v: the first column the union demand, the second the award, and the third the latter as a percentage of the former. As in Durham the Union's claim was fairly close to the final award, and, unlike South Wales, no one grade did particularly well (although there are no figures here for the various grades earnings under the minimum). Table 4 vi shows that neither loaders nor fillers (assuming fillers to be roughly equivalent to the class of hauliers or putters) was able to press its case in relation to the contractors, and as would be expected, the award reduced the differential by about one-third. As other comparisons, this says nothing about earnings, but reveals the forces of vested interest within the Union and the resultant influence on policy. The earnings 'drift' in terms of differential is seen to almost double this figure by 1914 that is, from 25 to 48 per cent.

TABLE 4 v

Grade	(1) *Trade Union demand*	(2) *Award*	(2) *as a percentage of* (1)
Contractors	7/6	6/8	88
Daymen	7/–	6/–	85
Holers	7/–	5/8	80
Loaders	6/–	5/2	86
Fillers	6/–	5/–	83

(Derbyshire, *Proceedings* 1912: 56).

TABLE 4 vi

Grades compared	Trade Union demanded as a percentage	Award as a percentage
As between contractors and fillers	33	25
As between contrctors and loaders	33	21

Table (c) (Appendix) shows that as late as 1919 nearly one-third of hewers in this area still remained on day wage: in 1912 this figure was 42 per cent (MFGB, 1912: 54). The slow permeation of the incentive principle was related to the degree of sub-contraction and, as stressed elsewhere, this was related to the centralisation of the wage contract and the industrial structure. This brief examination of the Midlands, and Derbyshire in particular, illustrates yet again the lack of linear development, *viz* the ability of sub-contracting to adapt to large-scale enterprises, and the ideological manoeuvrings this caused amongst emerging trade unions.

South Wales
The origins of the exploitation of the South Wales field lie in the history of the iron trade which stimulated much ancillary working in the central area around Tredegar and Merthyr. Initially allied to the fortunes of another trade, working was random and fluctuating; up to 60 per cent of available coal was typically lost, and the amount produced was often too small for steam use (Morris and Williams, 1958: 57–9). It was not until the 1860s' slump in iron prices that, as Jevons points out, the ironmasters turned their attention to the 'sale of coal as a source of profit, a policy which they have ever since continued' (1915: 204). By 1877 output had reached 17 million, by 1897 35 million, and

by 1913, 56 million, and was greater than any other British field (Gibson, 1922: 59). Nonetheless, there remained many small enterprises which emerged as trade quickened:

> . . . much of the extra production was obtained by the multiplication of new units rather than by growth of the older undertakings.
>
> (Morris and Williams, 1958: 134)

The rise of steam coal mining in the 1860s was meteoric, causing a huge migration of labour from the southern agricultural counties of England to the artificially created pit villages: only a few years earlier, in 1856, a chronicler of the coalfields had hardly given South Wales a mention (Leifchild, 1860).

The decline of the iron trade from the 1870s released a good deal of capital and know-how for investment in the new, more lucrative, 'hard' large coal used to fuel the expanding Navy and Merchant Navy fleet. The emergence of the steam coal trade on the foundation of the iron trade led to a greater degree of concentration of ownership than was typical of other fields. Whereas in the 1840s and 1850s, grocers, farmers, clergymen and victuallers could be found frequently amongst the owners of pits, by 1874 four concerns accounted for 35.5 per cent of the field's output, and the next fourteen for 30.2 per cent (Morris and Williams, 1958: 136).

From the 1870s the majority of output went into the export trade, primarily powering the steam engines of the world's ships. The very abundance of the South Wales field meant that diminishing returns and declining productivity were not serious problems. Only one per cent of output was cut by machines in 1913 (the year in which output was at its greatest), less than in any other area.

As A.J. Taylor has noted, productivity in the coal industry rose steadily until the 1880s and thereafter declined (1961–2: passim). South Wales followed this pattern: the annual output per man rose from 224 tons in 1874 to 368 in 1883 – its highest point (Holbrook-Jones, 1979: 285). The ensuing decline has been attributed to an increase in the numbers of ancillary workers (the proportion of hewers to others fell by 5.3 per cent between 1889 and 1914) (Walters, 1975: 281). However, even at its highest point productivity in South Wales was 92 tons below the national average, an average heavily influenced by 'easily' won coal in the smaller pits of the Midlands and Scotland (Clapham, 1938: 63). Furthermore, such comparisons are partially vitiated by the amalgamation of statistics relating to domestic, steam and anthracite coal, the latter two having greater pit-head value per ton. With this qualification, it can be noted that, as in the rest of the coal industry, increased production was largely achieved by *labour recruitment*, wherein lies the significance of the fall in productivity, and not *vice versa*.

It is important to note the divergence of interests between the iron-masters and the colliery proprietors. In the 1870s, as both moved in to exploit the steam coal trade, this was to colour the whole structure and efficacy of the union movement – the iron collieries having already established pools of labour and supply routes, with lower mineral royalties and wages. This advantage was demonstrated in a strike in the Rhondda and Aberdare Valleys in 1871: the iron collieries conceded five per cent, but the sale-coal owners, hoping to close the wages differential, refused. In the event an arbitration award gave the latter $2\frac{1}{2}$ per cent and stipulated that in future sale-coal wage rates should rise or fall *pari passu* with rates at the ironmasters' pits. An inevitable conflict occurred a year later when the iron and coal trade fortunes diverged. The sale-coal masters recognised the Miners' Union and were prepared to match the rise in the selling price of coal. Meanwhile, under the terms of the arbitration award, the recession in the iron trade was supposed to lead to a general reduction in wages. In these pits a strike began in 1873 involving some 70,000 iron-workers of whom 11,000 were colliers. A compromise solution ended the dispute after 12 weeks, and from then until mid-1874 unionism grew rapidly (Evans, 1961: 106).

These events probably contributed to the founding of the first united association of coal producers in 1873, bringing together the existing sale-coal organisation with the ironmasters. This alliance of 85 companies, partnerships and individuals, producing around 80 per cent of the field's total output, was sufficiently organised to win a two-month lock-out in 1885 and force a $12\frac{1}{2}$ per cent wage cut; this event was decisive in obtaining agreement for the first sliding scale (*ibid.*: 104–10).

The sliding scale and unionism The historian of the South Wales miners has argued that due to the scale 'effective trade unionism . . . virtually disappeared, nor did it re-emerge in full vigour for nearly a quarter of a century' (Page Arnot, 1967, 25). The workers' cause was also not aided by the decision to establish an effectively decentralised union structure with the burden of funds and decision-making in the hands of each district, taken by a conference, said to represent 43,000 men, in 1875. This decision, in the context of the emergence of the Joint Sliding Scale Committee (JSSC) and the divergence of interests between sale-coal and iron-work colliers, was to prove very damaging.

The first scale, agreed in 1875, was to last (with only three revisions) until 1902, far longer than any other comparative system. It was administered by a JSSC of six miners and six owners, and during its 27 years, 51 of the former and 28 of the latter served upon it. The first discussions centred upon the legitimacy of profit made by employers and the right of a minimum wage for the miners, which they achieved (Duggett, 1977: 150–6). Unlike Durham's Committee, the JSSC had no umpire or arbitration process, and appears to have interfered more directly in local pit disputes which were outside the rubric of the scale itself (1892 XXXIV: 573). In 1892, a past chairman of the Owners' Association stated that 90 per cent of the cases discussed arose from claims made by the workmen for alterations to their allowances:

> . . . they can scarcely be called coal disputes; they are small claims . . . they are small and trivial and should be settled at home between managers and men . . .
> *(ibid.*: 142)

This undoubtedly reflected the lack of local union organisation, the reasons for which essentially lay in two areas: firstly, miners represented the JSSC in their pit or area, and not, as in Durham, *vice versa*; second, the Committee itself arose out of a defeat of independent unionism after the five-month lock-out in trade conditions not favourable to the miners.

The first scale, agreed in December 1875, coincided with a general price decline and its conditions definitely favoured the owners. Whilst a *de facto* minimum was agreed, the increase in wages of $7\frac{1}{2}$ per cent for every shilling, accruing from rising prices ensured that the major part of the proceeds went to employers. Furthermore, alteration occurred only every six months, and even then if, for example, the price had only risen by 11d, wages were not affected (and *vice versa*) (Evans, 1961: 117–20). This inflexibility reflected the owners' concern for *stable* production costs and output, and the *rationalisation* of competition both between, and in, the different fields. In a statement of 1890 the Owners' Association recalled that before the scale wages had fluctuated by up to 15 to 20 per cent, and, because of frequent strikes it was impossible to get consumers to enter into contracts to take regular supplies' (Gascoyne-Dalziel, 1895: 100).

Over the following three years wages fell by $7\frac{1}{2}$, five and 10 per cent and by 1879 the regional structure of the union had disappeared. The main reason was probably complicity in the wage cuts, but the union was also unable to defend the customs and traditions of working which were increasingly threatened as the owners competed with one another to reduce costs. These practices were not allowed for by the scale, and unlike Durham, local bargaining strength could not maintain them (Evans, 1961: 123).

The structure of the JSSC is significant. The miners' side was elected by delegate meetings of only 30 to 35 persons. Their expenses were met in the main by a 2d per month deduction from each collier's wage by the office, who handed it over to their agent. Under these conditions the delegate became 'very largely the servant of two masters' (Jevons, 1915:

306). He had neither a strong local district, nor the back-up of a well organised regional leadership, independent of the Sliding Scale Committee. As a result the only centralising body of the workers was through their representation on the JSSC, with no parallel union structure. Furthermore, the miners had in 1871, 1873 and 1875, fought long and costly strikes which ended in the financial collapse of the independent Amalgamated Association of Miners in South Wales.

It is worthwhile to examine more closely the state of organisation amongst the miners by the 1890s. In their notes for *Industrial Democracy*, the Webbs collected a large selection of papers, press cuttings and minutes, from which they made the following division into three groups of the South Wales miners. Firstly, the trade unionists proper under the auspices of the Swansea, Neath and Llannelli Miners' Association, plus a small number of Miners' Federation members in Monmouthshire. They had proper lodges, and voluntary contributions, regular meetings and elections, and so forth. They numbered some 13,800 in 1894. Second, the 'quasi-unions' of the House Coal Miners' Association of the Rhondda Valley. They had no lodges, but their 5,000 members paid voluntary contributions to finance delegate meetings where men were elected for the JSSC. Third, there were what would today be called 'company unions' – the Cambrian Association, the Anthracite Miners, and the Aberdare and Merthyr Miners' Associations. They had no lodges, and contributions to the JSSC were deducted at source by the management and then paid to their agents. They numbered some 25,000 miners (Webb Collection: Section A, 26: 156–204). Given that there were at this time some 124,655 miners employed in South Wales and Monmouthshire, then only 35 per cent were in any type of organisation at all, and only 11 per cent in a *bona fide* union.

Perhaps as a result of this weakness, these groups tended to be dominated by a single figure, and above them all stood 'Mabon', William Abraham, MP for Rhondda for over 30 years from 1885. True to Weber's antimony between bureaucratic and charismatic power, Mabon's appeal and direct influence was inversely related to the growth of orthodox unionism. A contemporary recounted:

If any friction arose and pandemonium – so easy to rouse so difficult to quell – Mabon never tried to restore order in any usual way. He promptly struck up a Welsh hymn, or that magical melody, 'Land of my Fathers'. Hardly had he reached the second line, when, with uplifted arms . . . he had the whole audience dropping into their various 'parts' . . .

(Smellie, 1924: 160)

The JSSC itself had a kind of parody of this magical authority in its reverence for the price of coal. Each quarter the chairman would open a sealed envelope containing the ascertained prices over the last three months, and the wages of tens of thousands of men were thus determined. Its simplicity and its inhumanity were its strengths: no one 'was to blame', as it were – the market governed all and its 'holy order' could not be questioned (Duggett, 1977: 189).

To summarise, the main differences from Durham are threefold: in Durham a Joint Committee preceded the adoption of a scale, whereas in South Wales the two coincided. As a result, in the former case trade unionism was recognised, established and independent of, the scale, particularly locally, which was not the case in South Wales. Finally, the regional and trade unity of Durham contributed towards the maintenance of common interest, whereas in South Wales considerable diversity existed in the industry and the conditions under which the men laboured.

It is not surprising, therefore, to find that the surviving miners' agents were, in the main, wholehearted supporters of the scale. The alternative would have appeared to have been no union at all and unrestricted wage reductions (Evans, 1961: 128). Official opinion, such as that of Alfred Onions, secretary of the reformed Miners' Federation, was that, 'The sliding scale is the best way of dividing profits between employed and employer' (1892 XXXIV: 598). It also protected the individual leaders' 'empires' in each region or trade by insulating disputes, and, in particular, the steam coal miners gradually did better out of the scale than the house or anthracite coal miners. The revised 1880 scale was clearly beneficial to them, fuelling the internecine strife. In the face of this, various 'speed-up' changes were made to working methods, such as the introduction of an extra man into the usual two-man stall, and the enforcing of Contract Rules regarding prosecution for hewers who left the face without permission (Duggett, 1977: 186–7; Evans, 1961: 129).

With no grass roots organisation or central leadership it is not surprising that the JSSC dealt with issues of a local nature, rather than simply ratifying or solving disputes already discussed by the colliery owner and his men. Isaac Evans, a supporter of the scale, noted that

many of the officials use the Sliding Scale Committee as a sort of cloak, and consequently send the questions to the Sliding Scale Committee to be dealt with rather than deal with them themselves.

(1892 XXXIV: 573)

Of course, without a lodge structure the local agent had to bypass the individual employer, and this in turn hindered the growth of a local leadership. For example, Evans recounted an instance of an owner refusing to discuss a pay dispute with his own men, saying this was the job of the JSSC: a nine-week strike resulted, ending when two arbiters from each side were appointed. Further examples show how the relationship between the JSSC and the miners produced this combination of sporadic militancy and quietism (*ibid.*: 574–5).

It is important to note that the existence of the JSSC did not mean the recognition of trade unionism, as did that of the Joint Committee in Durham. On the contrary, the owners' attitude was deliberately vague, and both unionists and non-unionists were delegates to the Committee. An exchange took place on this point at the 1892 Labour Commission, where Edward Jones, an owner in the Rhondda Valley, was the respondent:

But you have official relations with the Union? – We have official relations with the representatives of the men as a body or not.

(1892 XXXIV: 140)

Since neither non-unionised nor unionised men seemed able to successfully resist the imposition of the scale, it is not surprising that those unions which did survive were local and apparently dependent on charismatic leaders, such as William Abraham ('Mabon'), Isaac Evans, David Morgan ('Dai o'r Nant') and William Brace.

The union was even denied the focus of organising a relief fund. This was astutely set up by the owners in the 1880s; contributions were 'virtually obligatory' and deducted at source. As such the men were obliged to contract out of the Employers' Liability Act (*ibid.*: 622). A prominent employer considered that 'this is one of the best institutions that has ever been formed among the workmen or our collieries . . .' (1892 XXXVI: 143). As an inducement the owners added 25 per cent to the miners' weekly contribution of 3d per week

. . . with a view of contracting themselves out of the Act and of countenancing and patroning a fund that they [the employers] considered to be of great benefit to the working classes.

(*ibid.*: 153)

Finally, concomitant with the lack of widespread lodge organisation there seems to have been no growth of a parallel informal structure for local agreements, which would have allowed the regional committees to discuss the wider issues. At every point the JSSC was brought into disputes *a priori*, rather than, as in Durham, *a posteriori*, which in turn inhibited the emergence of local regulatory norms. This process determined the operations of the successor of the JSSC, the Conciliation Board, established in April 1903. This body had one singular advantage for the miners: for the first three years its chairman generally accepted their view that wage cuts could not be introduced as a result of cutthroat competition between the owners (Page Arnot, 1967: 98).

The breakdown of 'industrial relations' and the street warfare of the period from 1910 to 1914 cannot simply be related to the traditional

quietism and disorganisation of the Welsh miners between 1875 and
1898. The importance of the lack of a centralising fulcrum of workers'
organisation during these years, and the effect that the Sliding Scale
Committee had in substituting for this role, led to effects which were to
colour the character and structure of militancy in the years leading up to
1914

The organisation of work, unionism and the status of the hewer. In the first
half of the nineteenth century when mining in South Wales was subordinate to the production of iron, much coal was extracted *ad hoc* in
'patches' or by drift mines. Ventilation and pumping techniques were
primitive since the target, house coal, was generally easily available.
Even those mines attached to the larger iron-workings typically employed less than 200 persons, and miners moved between coal-, iron-
working and agriculture as demand fluctuated (1892 XVII: 60–72).
Haulage was undertaken primarily by boys, employed by the face-
workers, who worked in twos in the post and stall (or bord and pillar)
system. If this was badly organised, as much as 60 per cent of the coal
could be left behind as roof supports; and it also encouraged the
production of small coal, useless for steam engines (Galloway, 1904:
238).

Once the capital and technique were available, exploitation of the
steam coal could move ahead. Geologically the hard coal of South Wales
lies midway between the thin seams of Durham and the wide seams of
Derbyshire and the South Midlands. Seams tended to be between four
and nine feet wide, and lay, especially at deeper depths, in natural
layers or 'slips', that is, fairly loosely (1907 XIV: 3). There were,
therefore, no great technical problems in introducing longwall
working. At the Dowlais Collieries this was said to have reduced waste
from 40 to 15 per cent, but, according to the manager speaking in 1868:

> The main obstacle to overcome was clearly the hostility of the men [because of]
> the complications of maintaining a continuous working face when the men were
> so irregular in their attendance.
>
> (Morris and Williams, 1958: 61)

This same crusader of modernisation compared the haulage methods in
use to those used to build the Pyramids (*ibid.*: 69). Whilst improvements were made in the larger steam coal collieries, a more typical
situation is revealed from one miner's report to the Mines' Committee
in 1866: he stated that there were 20 boys under 14 to every 100 adults
in the stalls, whose job it was to 'draw coal back in boxes' to the
tramway. They were usually family groups working in and about the
stall, and the boys worked the same 10 to 11 hours. In steam coal pits
work was casual. If a ship was delayed in arriving, only four hours

would be worked, but if the harbour was busy, 15 or 16 were worked since no stocks at all were held at the pit bank (1866 XIV: 195–6).

Twenty-nine years later an employer's statistician described the method of work in the region in remarkably similar terms.

> The workman and his 'butty' or a boy, as the case may be, having cut the coal, put it into an iron box with their hands. No shovel or other means is used in filling the box. The box when full is pushed, along the ground to a truck, or as it is known a 'tram' and emptied into it. When the tram is filled the workman puts his number on it in chalk figures and it is pushed by him to the siding, whence it is hauled by an engine rope to the bottom of the pit.
>
> (Gascoyne Dalziel, 1895: 109)

It was the geology of the deeper pits and need for a steam coal that determined the *form* longwall took, and, from it, the status and occupational hierarchy of face- and ancillary workers. In the words of a mining engineer:

> The work of a collier in our steam coal pits has been greatly changed of late years, since the sinking of our deep pits and the introduction of the longwall system of working. There is more creep, squeeze or crush now in the deep pits than there was formerly in the shallow ones, and this squeeze loosens the coal making it easier to get, but at the same time it makes the roof more troublesome and dangerous, and though it gives the collier less trouble to get the coal, it no doubt gives him more trouble to keep his roof up . . .
>
> (1892 XXXVI: 155)

As a result, timbering could not be a job apart from face-work, since each attack on the coal, given the wide character of the face, required immediate support.

> The slips are so frequent . . . that a man must always be ready with his post to defend himself and it would not do to wait till somebody else came there and did it for him.
>
> (*ibid.*: 161)

The role of the hewer was thus far less specialised. Each wall was divided into stalls, 12 to 15 yards long, which were divided by a gate from a tramway for the hewn coal. The collier was responsible for all the work within the stall and up to the road (or, as it is termed, 'back to the parting'), hence the need for highly complex price lists to determine his pay (South Wales *Proceedings*, 1912: 21). A mining inspector described how different this collier was from the Durham pitman who continuously hewed the coal:

> . . . with us a man uses a pick for a short time only. By the use of the pick the coal is detached and then he has a lot of other things to do. He had more watching of his roof than a North country pitman has. There is the labour first of all of cutting a little coal and then conveying it to his tram and setting a post, and he has to change the kind of work frequently . . .
>
> (1907 XIV: 3)

One estimate put this non-hewing time at 30 to 40 per cent of the shift of nine hours, during which $7\frac{1}{4}$ were actually spent working at face (the rest taken up by travel and refreshment). This meant that a collier could spend as little as $4\frac{1}{2}$ hours actually hewing, and suggests a partial explanation for the low productivity.

To aid in the principal ancilliary face-task – the 'drawing' and filling of coal into the trams – the colliers typically employed a boy helper, around two-thirds of whom were under 21 years of age. In tighter, more difficult seams, two skilled miners would alternate face-.and loading work, but this was rare by the 1900s (South Wales *Proceedings*, 1912: 24). The helper's status and wage were considerably lower than the hewer's although, paradoxically, as has been implied, the hewer himself did not have the prestige and influence of the specialised colliers. This fact was reflected in the wage differentials between them.

In steam working, the obsessive concern of the collier was the winning of large coal. In most seams, coal interspaced by stone was not separated at the face, except by the 'primitive' method of filling by hand. This resulted in up to 25 per cent of otherwise usable coal being wasted as it was thrown to the side of the face to form side supports along with the stone (1903 XVI: 182, 159). The commissioners could not hide their amazement that a quarter of the nation's steam coal reserves were being deliberately wasted as policy of the coal owners:

25 per cent of the small coal is wasted? – No, 25 per cent of the whole. Do you really mean of the whole? – Yes.

(*ibid.*: 161)

As the market for house coal improved some pits introduced different wagons to take small lumps. Until the 1900s wagons had sides which were not closed but made of bars so that only lumps could be carried; elsewhere the tram was used, 'a low, flat vehicle, and the coal is piled up. It is not suitable for small coal' (*ibid.*: 161, 185). The pressure on the face-worker for this type of coal increased the danger: a quick but unstable method of loosening large coal was to allow the 'squeeze and creep' to progress, that is, timbering in a way designed to pressure the face itself. In Monmouthshire this technique was particularly widespread since it removed the time-consuming job of holing under the face. Longwall working in these geological conditions increased the likelihood of roof falls, but such practices were encouraged by the wage structure, which in the main allowed no pay for small coal. (South Wales *Proceedings*, 1912: 62). Managers claimed they had no power to curtail this.

I beg to differ from you when you say the management would have full control of the face in all cases, because I think the men control to considerable extent. We have tried a number of times to get men to pull out timber, and notwithstanding that, they will not pull it out. There is nothing that spoils the face more than leaving of the back timber, which throws the weight upon the face and crushes the coal.

(1903 XVI: 244)

Throughout South Wales the collier generally used three times more timber per ton of coal than in any other field (1892 XXXVI: 172). The implication is that the owners had little incentive to reduce the use of coal for packing since the timber was a direct charge on unit costs and thus profits. The labour of setting the timber as supports was about 130 per cent of the price of the material, and was not paid as well as coal output: thus both management and miners, through the pressure of the market, had an investment in an irrational method of extraction (1903 XVI: 203).

The 'skill' of the collier in this situation therefore lay in the recognition of the 'slips and cleavages' in the coal face and the judicious use of the pick to 'hole' under them, thereby loosening coal (in large lumps) to be dragged to the transport. In this procedure there had to be a fine balance between the loosening and the timbering of the face, and productivity was directly related to safety. This fact, combined with the large influx of inexperienced agricultural labour in the 1880s and 1890s, produced the highest death and accident rate in the country. In 1897 South Wales contained 18.6 per cent of the total mining population but incurred 24.6 per cent of the accidents (1892 XXXIV: 172–3; 1899 CVII: 136).

The system of working and the lay of the coal required a considerable back up of ancillary labour. The hewer was not as dominant numerically, nor was his role as that of an 'aristocrat' of an occupational hierarchy. In a hypothetical colliery of 1,000 an employer gave a ratio of 500 face-workers to 500 officials, hauliers, labourers, repairers, and so on, adding that the majority of recruits to a mine went to the face, nominally under supervision (although union agents claimed this was frequently disregarded) (1892 XXXIV: 169).

As the pits were deeper and the size of coal crucial, hauliers formed a definite occupational group apart from the hewers. There was next to no handwork; ponies or engines were used, and the job had marked *esprit de corps* and was not merely a preparatory role for face-work as in Durham (South Wales *Proceedings*, 1912: 31). The repair work on the roads was done by timberers mostly paid by piecework, each of whom had an assistant to whom he paid a day wage. The colliers' helpers became too expensive for the face-worker to pay when they reached the age of 19 or 20, and so, if the latter did not graduate to the face, they were replaced. Nationality and family influences were important in South Wales: nearly all hewers were Welsh and graduation to the skilled jobs was dependent on family connections (*ibid.*: 22, 43).

By the 1890s direct wage contracts were the norm, although, as has been seen, this was symbiotic to a series of individual sub-contracts in all grades. Chartermasters were by no means extinct, however. In 1892, the agent for the Miners' Federation reported that there were

contractors at some of the collieries who are not only contractors in the mine but they keep grocers shops and drapers shops and public houses . . .

(1892 XXXIV: 619)

As elsewhere, they compensated miners for irregular work and low pay by liberal quantities of free beer during the shifts (*ibid.*).

In the great majority of cases the face-worker was paid by the piece, but his wage, because of the generic role he was called upon to do, was not only calculated on the tonnage produced at the pit-top. In 1919 an estimate suggested that up to 26 per cent of the South Wales collier's wage accrued from work other than coal-getting and filling (1919 XIII: 206). His less specialist position is highlighted by the relatively low ratio of this class to the haulage class (Appendix: Table d). Unlike virtually every other region, the hauliers were paid a day wage which fluctuated with the price of the coal they were moving, in accordance with the principles of the sliding scale. Therefore, unlike the colliers, they could not compensate for a fall in this price (and their wage) by working faster. Whereas in Durham the incentive principle tied these two groups together, here it served to divide their interests, and in the process created tensions in the development of unionism.

As with Derbyshire, it is not as easy to link the organisation of work in South Wales to the structure of unionism as it is in the more homogeneous Durham. But there are several obvious points arising from the period of the scale and the JSSC. Firstly, the division of the field geographically and by product (house, steam, anthracite and iron collieries) found almost exact reflection in the fragmented union or quasi-union organisation. The miners' representatives were elected from within these market boundaries, and much of the representatives' struggle on the Committee seems to have been directed towards obtaining the best deal for their respective constituencies, rather than for the miners as a whole. The Webbs' discussion of the hauliers' strike of 1893 illustrates a more general point.

The position of the South Wales coalminers is even more striking. Not a third of the 120,000 men are even professionally members of any Trade Union, or in any way represented in the negotiations, and of the organised workmen a considerable proportion, forming three separate unions, and each covering a distinct district, expressly refused to agree to the 1893 Sliding Scale, and withdrew their representatives from the joint committee. Nevertheless, the whole of the 120,000 men, with infinitesimal special exceptions, find their wages each payday automatically determined by the accountant's award. In this the associated employers, in alliance with a minority of the workmen, enforce, upon an apathetic or dissentient majority . . . a method of remuneration and rates of payment which are fiercely resented by many of them.

(1920: 209–10)

During the period from 1870 to 1890 the Sliding Scale Committee had gradually become dominated by the steam-coal interest and the scale had been revised accordingly (Duggett, 1977: 186–7). But with the hauliers' strike the stage was set for the first steps toward a fully regional independent union. In January 1893 a committee was formed, based in the Rhondda Valley, to press the case for a 20 per cent rise in wages for the hauliers, who had suffered a series of eight quarterly reductions under the provisions of the 1890 scale. As day workers whose wages were tied to this, they were both the most numerous and the most autonomous class of workers, and yet the least able to counteract the scale's influence (compared to piece workers) (Gascoyne-Dalziel, 1895: 181). The hauliers' protestations were not merely rejected, but were ignored by the Committee: the miners' representatives issued a statement to the press that the hauliers action was in violation of agreed procedure; and the rank and file colliers' support was patchy:

. . . whereas in Glamorganshire the strike was entirely due to the action of the hauliers, in Monmouthshire the hauliers were distinctly supported by the colliers.

(*ibid.*: 182)

The figure of Isaac Evans came to the fore in this dispute. He was a JSSC member, but an opponent of its workings, and a bitter personal and political foe of the South Wales traditional leader William Abraham. His influence was to channel the hauliers' militancy towards the newly formed Miners' Federation of Great Britain. According to the Webbs' notes, the MFGB probably had no more than 3–4,000 adherents in 1890; at the height of the hauliers' action, a resolution was passed calling upon all the 40,000 involved to join the South Wales section of the Federation. This was a portent of rather than an initiative towards unionisation, but it did signal the first significant challenge to the scale principle; it led directly to the later formation of the 'Hauliers and Wagemen of South Wales' Association'. The organisation's members joined the Sliding Scale Associations as individuals in order to propagandise for the Miners' Federation against the Scale, after failing to maintain the momentum of lodges affiliating to it *en bloc* (Page Arnot, 1967: 32–4). The significance of the whole affair was the *independent spirit* shown by the hauliers in the face of opposition from employers and the JSSC agents, and with only partial support from the face-workers. Although this class of labour was involved in separate disputes in Derbyshire and Durham in neither area was this involvement to the extent shown in South Wales. The individual class identity and *form of the wage contract* constituted the material basis of the hauliers' ability to take autonomous action.

The reverberations of this action went further. In response to the surge of support for the MFGB, in April 1893 the sliding scale unions drew up a scheme designed to bring their organisational structure closer to that of a *bona fide* union: lodges were to be established, a 2d contribution standardised, a central fund inaugurated, and a joint committee of the regional unions to co-ordinate policy formed (N. Edwards, 1938: 6). Much of this was, however, cosmetic; the majority of pit-lodge branches were not formed until after they had joined the MFGB in 1898. The extent of this transitional organisation's commitment to genuine independence may be gauged by its initiation of a scheme in 1896 to unite owners and miners in a policy of output restriction (Duggett, 1977: 329). However, it would be wrong to dismiss or ignore the rising propaganda influence of Federation ideas as expressed through the person of William Brace, leader of the Monmouth miners who were the first adherents to the Federation in South Wales. This influence was reflected in the form taken by the demand of September 1897 for a revised scale which called for a minimum wage by stipulating: 'the minimum price of coal to determine wages to be ten shillings per ton' (N. Edwards, 1938: 9).

The reorganisation of the miners following the failure of the 1898 strike to abolish the sliding scale was uneven. 'Mabon', who arrived at the MFGB conference 'as a penitent Welshman' with his affiliation fee of £60 (£10 per 10,000 members), was still ideologically committed to the scale; throughout the strike his views in print had been constantly to this effect. To Parliament he stated:

Though we gave notice to terminate the sliding scale, it was not we who gave notice to terminate the contract. We should not have left work but for the fact that the employers gave notice to terminate the contract . . .

(*Hansard*, 24.6.1898)

Of the first four officers of the South Wales Miners' Federation (SWMF), three (William Abraham, Alfred Onions and Thomas Richards) remained committed to the scale principle; however, those elected to the new JSSC were all adherents of the MFGB, thus, in effect, giving full recognition to this one body as a negotiator for the miners as a whole (Page Arnot, 1967: 60).

Up until the formation of SWMF, the majority of miners had organised through branch groups based on villages, *irrespective of their pit*. The effectiveness of these bodies was largely determined by the rhythm of activity of the JSSC, and, with a few exceptions, their officers were firmly in the pockets of the local colliery owner (N. Edwards, 1938:

164). In contradistinction, the new union demanded a pit-lodge structure, that is, one lodge for one pit. The unit of work became the unit of trade-union organisation, and consequently introduced a number of organisational possibilities: a lodge could directly challenge a specific owner's decision and muster the indigenous support to press its claim; the lodge meeting could now become the ground for a discussion of the conditions which applied to all those attending – each of whom was aware of the issues and had a personal interest in them – and the lodge was therefore also a potential *collective instrument for their realisation*. However, as Page Arnot points out, irrespective of the developments at individual pits, the 20 districts which formed the SWMF each retained an exceptional degree of autonomy, and real power lay with the miners' agent. Each district corresponded almost precisely to a geographically isolated valley with its own traditions and 'tribal' loyalties, and although district presidents, secretaries and treasurers were subject to elections (the agent, once successful, was not), in 1932 Noah Ablett was to speak of these men as 'little chieftains' (Page Arnot, 1967: 74–5).

The fact remains, however, that in the early years of the Federation tremendous gains were made in membership. In 1898 only 46 per cent of miners were unionised, but in 1900 the figure was 77 per cent, and in 1903, 79 per cent. In numerical terms this represented more than a doubling of union strength during five years (N. Edwards, 1938: 20; Gibson, 1922: 59). But the numbers of those employed increased rapidly, and by 1908 the percentage of unionised miners had fallen by seven from that of 1903. Nonetheless, in formal terms it remained a huge advance.

It is hard to believe that such a movement could just have been instigated from 'above', in particular since the Executive, although less powerful than elsewhere, was for the first time made up of men elected from the pit-lodge-district system. This had dual, even contradictory effects: on the one hand it allowed the leadership to be influenced by the rising temper and militancy of the lodge organisation, while, on the other, the system of election and structure of organisation strengthened the parochialism of the valley 'tribes'.

In the establishment of the SWMF infra-structure, the first step was often the election of a regular checkweighman; before the existence of the Federation, the sliding scale representative had often performed this role (1892 XXXIV: 574). Employers universally refused to deduct Federation dues at the office (unlike the JSSC moneys), and this encouraged the election of lodge officers. Alongside the usual president, secretary and treasurer, the pit committee consisted of delegates from each grade of worker in the pit. However, unlike their North-Eastern colleagues, the South Wales miners had no system similar to cavilling to ensure the random distribution of work places, but had to rely on bargaining an allowance for a bad place. The owners used this advantage to the full, and lodge officials would find themselves allocated to the least profitable work places. In one example of a strike led by a haulier over the payment of overtime, the manager first tried to buy him off:

'Drat thee eyes mun; why doesn't thy leave this thing alone? I've got a good heading for thee . . . I've summat good for thee . . .'
I took no notice and walked away. We met him as a deputation, and made him sign his hand to an agreement over this overtime.

(N. Edwards, 1938: 19)

Since the method of work made the hewers' task less specialised and skilful, this category of labour became less proportionally important (Appendix: Tables a and d). There is some evidence to suggest that concomitantly, they played a less crucial role in the councils of the SWMF, and, certainly, in policy debates there seems to have been much less division between the face-worker and the rest than there was in the North. In practical terms there was much less difference between the colliers' working time and the ancillary workers': around 10 hours 'bank to bank', that is, approximately eight hours getting the coal. This implies that there was a general relationship operating: the more specialised the hewer's role, the less time spent at the face (Munro, 1891: 250). The checkweighman's position (normally the preserve of hewers) was counter-balanced within the union by the agent (rather than a lodge deputation) whose role it was to advise the Executive, for example, on the payment of strike pay (SWMF *Rules*, 1902: para. 30). Furthermore, certain lodge customary procedures were the preserve of hauliers: generally it was the oldest of this group who would be in charge of the beer at annual general meetings of the lodge, and of stewarding the proceedings (N. Edwards, 1938: 18).

The hauliers and hewers: The Eight Hour Act and the minimum wage The intial struggle of the hauliers in 1893, which led to the first movement towards the SWMF, also had an effect, indirectly, on the whole character of industrial conflict up to the First World War. For it was the joining of the miners into one national body that transformed a 20-year-old rhetorical clarion call – the eight-hour day – into a practical possibility. This fusion, occurring at an industrial level, also coincided with the Liberal Party's drive to incorporate sections of the trade unions under their wing before the Labour Party could transform its tenuous organisational links into a political voting lobby (McKibbon, 1974). South Wales was the key for two reasons. Firstly, the issue of 'abnormal places' had assumed national importance through a legal decision of January 1909 which held that a collier at the Ocean Coal Company in the Rhondda could not claim allowances for an 'abnormal place' unless it was specified in the colliery price list. Since, overwhelmingly, such provisions were customary rather than contractual, the precedent opened up an avenue for the cutting of costs by management. Second, partly as a consequence, the coal owners of South Wales had claimed that the Eight Hour Act would ruin them since it would result in a greater reduction in hours relative to other fields:

I say distinctly that in Monmouthshire it is going to affect us and reduce the output to the extent of 20 per cent. Elsewhere I would estimate 15 per cent as a minimum.

(1907 XIV: 39)

This view was based on the assumption that output was at its optimum already – even if it were to increase in a shorter working day existing colliery equipment would not have been able to deal with it. In a frank, if somewhat naive admission, of responsibility for the excessive hours of toil of the colliers, an owner stated that

. . . if the men could fill more coal we should not be able to deal with it . . . The narrow neck of the bottle is the mechanical equipment of the collieries? – Yes.

(*ibid.*: 35)

In South Wales, after July 1909 the reduced hours under the Eight Hour Act reinforced the drive by the owners to recoup their losses by cutting allowances for 'abnormal places', as they were now legally entitled to do. It was this issue that sparked off the Cambrian Combine dispute – the bitterest and most violent regional strike in mining since the 1840s. As Page Arnot stated, this strike

'came to be inextricably mingled in the outlook of the strikers with the question of abnormal places and the minimum wage' (1967: 241).

This feeling was expressed by the SWMF and eventually prodded the whole Federation into action. At the Annual Conference in 1911 a resolution was passed for an 'individual district minimum wage' – a *principle* which was conceded after a national stoppage from March to

TABLE 4 vii

Grade	Percentage below the minimum wage agreed	
Coal-getters on piecework	34	
Hauliers	75	
Timberers	32	
Rippers	20	
Timberers and rippers assistants	39	
Labourers	91	(1919 XIII: 306).

TABLE 4 viii

Grade	(1) Trade Union demand	(2) Award	(2) as a percentage of (1)
Colliers	8/–	4/7	57
Timberers & Rippers	8/–	4/7	57
Assistants of above	6/6	3/4	48
Hauliers	7/–	3/11	57
Labourers	5/–	3/4	68

South Wales, *Proceedings* 1912: 3, 9).

mid-April (Page Arnot, 1953: 101–10). The Eight Hour Act had established Joint Boards to decide on the district minimums for each grade; in South Wales, figures covering around half the work force were presented to the Sankey Commission and show how many of each grade of worker were earning *below* the minimum wage once this had been established in April 1912. Table 4 vii shows the results expressed as percentages. They are revealing in a number of ways. Firstly, from the point of view of bargaining power it suggests that the timberers and rippers were better able to defend their positions than were the coal-getters. Second, it highlights the severe degree to which the hauliers were suffering under the offensive against allowances.

Table 4 viii shows the union's minimum wage demand for various grades, the award, and the percentage the latter is of the former. Comparing Tables 4 vii and viii, the actual monetary gain of each grade under the award can be seen. Obviously, the labourers did best, followed by the hauliers. But examined in terms of differentials, as shown in Table 4 ix, the picture changes. Clearly the hauliers were able to press their case very strongly in relation to the colliers, and the differential awarded actually *increased* the gap. In contrast, the labourers, as would be expected, did best in closing the differential, not through the union but through the Joint Board. In terms of real income the increase was about the same for the colliers and hauliers, and greatest for the labourers, that is, the minimum increased the average wage of each grade by 14, 14 and 21 per cent respectively (South Wales *Proceedings*, 1912: 78).

TABLE 4 ix

Grades compared	Trade union demanded as a percentage	Award as a percentage
As between colliers and hauliers	14	21
As between colliers and labourers	60	35

These figures underline the fact that, after 1893, the hauliers were able to break the rigidities of the wage hierarchy because of the generic role of the hewers, the increasing importance of haulage as pits became larger, and the consequent ability to act independently. This illustrates the general point that the relations established by the organisation of work are not socio-technical. On the contrary, although perhaps originating as a reflection of the organisational problem of work they have to be sustained by the groups themselves. In this case the hewers could not maintain their differential with the hauliers in the face of their decline in status. Elsewhere, as will be shown, in contrast to this a leading grade's technical or skill basis disappeared, but they nonetheless maintained their position.

Comparisons and Conclusions

Coal is an industry not subject to the usual methods of social investigation employed by labour historians: union histories, output statistics, technological change, politics, and so on. Certainly, in the period discussed there was no such things as *the* miners. The survey of work experience shows how little the hewer in his isolated Durham community would have had in common with the stallmen of metropolitan Derbyshire, or with the indigenous South Wales collier. History 'from above', either in the form of organisational genealogy or economic formalism, is particularly irrelevant, precisely because of this chronic regionalism. But the pressures of the gradual concentration of ownership (followed sluggishly by employers' associations and even more hesitantly by miners' unions), impose upon the investigator the need to go one step, but only one step, beyond the localism and parochialism of the historical subjects. For the same reason, that most valuable of historical material, the participant account, has to be balanced by the available 'objective' evidence. For example, in considering the Minimum Wage Act figures, the submissions by the Union side and the discussions about them have combined here to produce the best 'quantitative' view of such a 'qualitative' subject as the occupational hierarchy.

Although the specialist hewer of Durham maintained his differential, unlike the similarly privileged stallman of the Midlands, he was forced to organise the work force as a whole. In South Wales the face-worker's task was neither as unique, nor his social role as dominant, as were those of other grades, particularly the hauliers, who were for this reason able to change significantly the balance of influence within their organisation. This ability to defend status had reverberations throughout all grades. One final statistical illustration: Table 4 x shows the percentage increase in wages from 1886 to 1914 of piece-working coal-getters and labourers in the three 'sample' areas.

TABLE 4 x

Area	Percentage increase 1886–1914	
	skilled	*unskilled*
Durham	80	54
Nottinghamshire and Derbyshire	84	66
South Wales	93	103

(Rowe, 1923: 85).

The ascendency of the Durham hewer in this 'league table' of differentials is all the more apparent given that these figures do not show the non-monetary 'perks' he had negotiated, such as free housing, coal, and so on. Alongside this, and partly as a result, was the control he had of the DMA – a *universalistic* union thus dominated by a *sectional* group.

In the Midlands, over the period from 1890 to 1914, the stallmen 'colonised' their union and turned its policies to their advantage. It is significant that this process was accompanied by a reorganisation of sub-contraction to produce a system more closely approximating direct labour, and thus the invasion (and acceptance) of the incentive principle throughout the face-gang. But figures have shown how the stallmen were able by 1914 to earn around half as much again as their hauliers, and three-quarters more than their labourers. To an extent it can be surmised from this that the form of 'full' sub-contraction extant in the 1880s limited differentials to a degree, insofar as it restricted those who could be paid on piece-rates: that is, *incentive replaced authority as the 'prime mover' of the rhythm of work, just as differentials replaced the group bargain as the focus of the wage contract*. 'Individualisation' of the wage form seems to have been closely connected with collective bargaining and action.

In this context it is not surprising that the once worst organised areas became champions of universalistic policies such as the eight-hour day and the minimum wage. As has been seen, the form of longwall working reduced both the status and the autonomy of the face-worker, since his labour was proportionately less, and the hauliers' more, of the unit cost of production, compared with the other areas (Appendix: Table b).

To summarise: this investigation of the three areas in terms of their work organisation, occupational hierarchy, union structure and policy, demonstrates the fluidity of the form of wage contract: In particular in mining the issue of *certainty* was common to all. In general the strategy of a privileged layer within a wider work force was likely to be characterised by the maximisation of *uncertainty* at the 'front-line' of the organisation, and its minimisation at the centre. Local conditions determined whether this involved the adoption of universalistic tactics. Where this leading layer were able to resolve this uncertainty to those subordinate to them (sub-contraction), there will be no incentive, whilst their high status and differential remain, to confront the management on this issue. Equally they will have little motivation to adopt universal tactics, whatever local conditions prevailed. If the organisation of work created no clear leading layer, the initial stage of organisation will be hindered by the lack of specificity in the appeal of unionism, and its development will be characterised by an antinomy between charismatic forms and egalitarian universalism.

Appendix
Tables a, b, c and d are derived from figures in the Sankey Commission on the Coal Industry, Third Report, 1919 XIII.

TABLE a   The Ratio of classes of labour in three areas[1]

Area	Ratio of underground workers to hewers	Ratio of hewers to other face workers
Durham	2:1	2:8
Monmouthshire and S. Wales	2:2	4:1
S. and N. Midlands[2]	2:2	3:5

NOTE: 1 Derived from Table 8a, p. 119.
    2 Defined here as Nottinghamshire, Derbyshire, and South Yorkshire.

TABLE b   The proportion of workers in various occupations in three areas, 1918 (adult males only)[1]

Occupation	Percentage of occupation as total		
	Durham: 207 *pits of 53 collieries*	*Notts., Derby, S. Yorks:* 101 *pits of 85 collieries*	*Mon., S. Wales:* 363 *pits of 114 collieries*
Coal-getters	42	45	38
Putters, fillers, hauliers	10	12	14
Timbermen, stonemen, brushers	10	8	11
Other underground labour	19	12	18
Surface labour	15.5	17.8	16

NOTE: 1 Derived from Tables 5–1 to 5–13, pp. 93–6.

TABLE c   The percentage of coal-getters on day and piece-wage in three areas, 1919[1]

Area	Day	Peice
Durham	0.01	99.9
Nottinghamshire, Derbyshire, S. Yorkshire	22.9	77.1
Monmouthshire and S. Wales	7.6	92.4

NOTE: 1 Derived from Tables 5–1 and 5–2, pp. 92–3.

TABLE d   The ratio of hewers to the total of putters, hauliers and trammers in three areas, 1914[1]

Area	Ratio
Durham	4.1 to 1
Derbyshire and Nottinghamshire	3.9 to 1
S. Wales and Monmouthshire	2.7 to 1

NOTE: 1 Derived from Tables 4–6, p. 100.

5 Spinners: The Modern Plebeians

Mechanisation and Politics before the Self-actor
Throughout labour historiography the history of the textile workers, and the spinners especially, is regarded as the first example of the creation of an occupational class of wage earners, living in urban areas, and with a 'factorised' industry – in short, the progenital proletariat'. Cotton manufacture has also been pivotal to accounts by economic historians of the Industrial Revolution: its demand for markets, its innovatory form of socio-economic organisation, its technical progress and capitalisation, all reverberated throughout English society. Whilst this latter aspect has received continuing and thorough attention, the textile workers and their unions remain only partly researched. Yet these workers and their organisations were unique prodigies of industrialism: they were machine minders and servers, whose craft tradition cannot be said to have been destroyed, since in a sense it never existed.

A 'journeyman cotton spinner' described, in the radical paper, *Black Dwarf*, the exploitative process as it appeared to him in 1818:

When the spinning of cotton was in its infancy, and before those terrible machines for superseding the necessity of human labour, called steam engines came into use, there was a great number of what were called *little masters;* men who with a small capital, could procure a few machines and employ a few hands, men and boys (say twenty to thirty), the produce of whose labour was all taken to Manchester . . .

Raw cotton had been prepared by the spinners' wives in their homes so that they could 'cook and attend to their families', but now that this process was mechanised, and the little master ruined,

. . . the overgrown capitalists triumphed in their fall; for they were the only obstacle that stood between them and the complete control of the workmen.

(Thompson, 1968: 221)

It must be remembered that this account pre-dated the self-acting mule: the author identifies the *factory* and its effect on family life. The use of a prime mover is cited as the agent of exploitation and not the jenny itself, which, although hand-driven, required little skill in the craft sense. It is the tyranny of large scale organisation, impersonal in its authority, distant in its rhythm of production.

This concern with the primacy of authority relations stemmed from a heritage of petty mechanical production and found an echo in the character of the spinners' activity and politics throughout the period of the Combination Laws. Clubs and benefit societies existed amongst them from at least 1792. Their purpose 'was to keep up the price of labour to its statute'. They were wholly regional and parochial in outlook, often with separate associations for jenny and water-frame spinners (1824 V: 408–10). Although illegal they managed to maintain a shadowy existence, perhaps not continuous, but certainly strong enough for them to flower into proto-unions during disputes, when they paid benefits, sent delegates to solicit support, and so on (Aspinall, 1949: 251–80).

The years up to the 1840s are usually considered to be the 'revolutionary' stage of the textile workers' development and are contrasted with their accommodating stance in the second half of the century (Webbs, 1950: 114–118). But the earlier period deserves closer observation. The spinners were only a very small percentage of the work force; an estimate of 1841 put this at $9\frac{1}{4}$ for spinning only firms, and four in those which combined this with weaving (1841 XXII: 27). Even in the days before the self-actor the figure was not much higher, mainly averaging around 13 per cent (1824 V: 558, 576). Occupationally their position was analogous with that of the engineer: they were a small group within a factory population, at the top of the vocational ladder. In terms of skill and tradition, however, the comparison does not hold and, as will be seen, organisationally and ideologically the spinner was closer to the North Eastern hewer.

Under the Combination Acts the textile workers were often at the centre of industrial action, yet despite their best endeavours Home Office spies were able to detect little political motivation in their strikes, a fact confirmed by later historians (Aspinall, 1949: 251–80; Thompson, 1968: 211–12; Hobsbawm, 1976: Chapter II). What contemporary reports *do* show, in contrast to the Luddite- and Radical-influenced tendencies, is a scale of organisation and stability which had greatly surprised the reporters, so used to labelling all proletarian dissent as 'mob rule'. A Home Office letter of July 1818 noted that in Manchester,

the spinners have adopted the practice of assembling in large bodies of two or three thousand each and parading through some of the streets of the town almost daily, certainly still without committing any breach of the peace . . . The system of support from one trade to another is carried on to an amazing extent, and they regularly sent delegates out to the different towns who are in work to receive their subscriptions.

(Aspinall, 1949: 254)

In Bolton seven years later a prosecution under the Acts revealed 'irrefutable proof of the existence of a combination . . . of Journeymen cotton spinners' since at least 1811, who were able to pay strike pay, organise subscriptions, membership cards and so forth (*ibid.*: 368).

It will be noted that these accounts speak only of the associations of spinners. Their corporate nature is revealed in a fragmentary but clear way; unlike the still extant craftsmen whose organisational structures tended to be built across trades, the spinners' situation within both the factory and the labour movement pushed them inwards. Their position as 'internal aristocrats' of a factory was not maintained by skill but by experience and insularity; the factory working class, on the other hand, was, up to the 1840s, still a minority of the proletariat and neither politically nor sociologically homogeneous enough to encourage national movements. This dualistic or 'plebeian' position was demonstrated in several ways.

Primarily, there is much to suggest that co-operation between spinners and weavers in the urban centres was very limited. In the 1818 generalised action of textile workers in the North West, the spinners in Stockport ended their strike two days before 'a general turn out' of Manchester weavers for a wages advance (*ibid.*: 280–1). A year later in Leeds there was a similar dislocation of effort, described in Joseph Oates's evidence to the Select Committee of 1824. Here, where no power-looms were as yet used, the weavers 'as a body' stopped work in response to a price cut by the masters, but the spinners, although eventually laid off, did not act in concert. The reverse had occurred in Dewsbury a year earlier, and Oates recounts how, in response to these and other *débâcles*, 'a general union of weavers and spinners' was formed in December 1822 of upwards of 5,000 members. However, despite its name it remained largely a union of the hand-loom weavers (1824 V: 534–40).

In individual struggles with employers the spinners were not lacking in militancy; and, similarly particularly against blacklegs, where they revealed a paranoia perhaps sharpened by a realisation that their vocational superiority relied almost exclusively upon corporate unity. In Glasgow in 1818 imported spinners received threatening letters signed by the 'Captain of the Blood-red Knights'. Further, their general policy was 'not [to] allow women or boys to work as spinners; nor will they allow a man from a neighbouring county to enter a Glasgow mill . . .' (*ibid.*: 479).

At this time the weavers were still largely outworkers, in urban areas, grouped in sheds and, although subject to some forms of elementary factory discipline, they were still entirely hand-workers. Their position hindered any unification which would have allowed them to act forcibly when their bargaining position was best (S.J. Chapman, 1904: 23–30). This combination of circumstances was expressed exactly in an exchange before the 1824 Committee:

> Do you not understand that combination to a much greater degree, and has been carried with much greater violence among the spinners, whose wages are high, than among the weavers, whose wages are comparatively low? – Certainly.
> Are not the spinners collected together in one manufactory, whilst the weavers are out in different houses? – Yes.
> May not that influence a good deal the facility of combination? – It does.
>
> (1824 V: 561)

As wage-labourers *en bloc*, the spinners, earning up to twice that of the weavers, were able to identify more precisely when to act for better terms or conditions: 'when they have got most, then they turn out, not otherwise' (*ibid.*). From such a position they were able to initiate 'modern' tactics of industrial action such as the 'rolling strike', which was first used in 1810 to obtain parity with Manchester by the spinners of Staley Bridge, Preston and Oldham. Selective stoppages in key mills gradually impressed upon the employers the force of organisation opposed to them, but, as in 1818,

> . . . the spinners were the only persons relieved by their combination.
> . . . only those connected with the spinners received the 14s per week relief . . .
>
> (*ibid.*: 573, 558)

The Self-actor and Trade-union Action 1830–50

The spinners' trade policy was then characterised essentially by three features: they desired to maintain their status by occupational hierarchy; they were opportunistic and self-reliant insofar as strikes were calculated attempts to exploit favourable turns of trade or local circumstances; they were insular in organisational form and modern in tactics: aggressive or offensive, but always corporate, and intended to establish standards in the developing process of 'factorisation'. The weavers showed contrasting behaviour: essentially a defensive and unco-ordinated policy determined by forces external to the occupation (Turner, 1962).

The original Jenny invented by Hargreaves had replaced the human hand by rollers revolving at unequal speeds which reproduced the effect of the stretch of the individual spinner's arm. The carriage still had to be pushed to and fro by the left hand whilst the right turned a wheel causing the spindles to revolve, and thus the roving became yarn (Baines, 1835: 157). Arkwright's water-frame replaced human effort by water power but was, for technical reasons, confined to the production of warps. In 1775 these methods had been combined by Samuel Crompton to form the mule.

The distinguishing feature of the mule is, that the spindles, instead of being stationary as in both other machines are placed on a moveable carriage which is wheeled out to the distance of fifty-four to fifty-six inches from the rollerbeam, in order to stretch and twist the thread, and wheeled in again to wind it onto spindles.

(*ibid*.: 198)

Until the mid-1820s and the introduction of the self-actor, the movement of the carriage was entirely by hand, as was the regulation of winding. Up to this time the number of spindles on the carriage was limited by the power of the spinner's arm to propel it back and forth, and was about 40 to 50. Power had been applied to this process and had enlarged it somewhat, but it still required the attention of an experienced hand (S.J. Chapman, 1904: 68).

The self-actor removed the need for human labour in either thrust of the carriage, and also automated the winding and the speed of the revolving spindles: apparently, in one technological step, the need for an adult male experienced machine-controller had disappeared. However, the introduction of this machine was slow and the hand mule still remained important for three decades following the invention of the automated version in 1825.

The automated mule was just *one* aspect of the general speed-up of work; power meant that the spinner could attend to more than one machine. Leonard Horner reported in 1841 that, 'where manual labour is still necessary it is done by children and young persons instead of adults . . .' The intensity of work had, however, increased for all, since the spinner was subject to the

. . . lengthening of the mules of carriages, so as to make them carry a greater number of spindles; by making one man work four instead of two of these carriages, by a process technically called 'double-decking'; and by the introduction of self-acting mules.

(1841 XXII: 26)

The significance of the self-actor, above and beyond its ability to increase output, was its crystallisation of an already emerging hierarchical work-group consisting of the spinner, big piecer and little piecer. These latter two did the manual work, principally, as the name suggests, the 'piecing' of broken threads whilst the carriage was in motion. They were employed and paid by the spinner on a day wage, whilst the spinner himself earned a piece-rate: a wage contract that remained basically unchanged until 1933 (Jewkes and Gray, 1935: 7, 185). The self-actor, by gradually removing the last element of skill from the spinner's task, made this relationship entirely one of economic subservience, and quite unlike the apprenticeship system in other occupations. It is important to stress that the self-actor confirmed, not created, this relationship of dependency: the latter was not the outcome of a paradigmatic revolution of the 'socio-technical' system of work. Table 5 i, derived from the wages book of a 'large Manchester mill', demonstrates this point. It shows wages paid before the introduction of the self-actor and afterwards.

TABLE 5 i

	£ s d
In 1836 wages paid to the spinner for 2 mules, average of 10 weeks:	3 5 –
Deduct his payment to piecers:	1 6 –
Leaving to the spinner net earnings of:	1 19 –
In 1841 wages paid to the spinner for 4 mules, average of 10 weeks:	4 14 –
Deduct his payment to piecers:	2 8 –
Leaving to the spinner net earnings of:	2 6 –

(1841 XXII: 27).

In 1841 the spinner's workload had doubled that of 1837 (although with less mechanical requirements from the mules), but his wage had risen by only 29 per cent. The *overall* wages to the piecers had risen by 45 per cent, (but represented a closing of the differential with the spinner of only 10 per cent. Thus, in financial terms, the essential structural system of subordination had not changed. Table 5 ii shows the differential between spinners' and piecers' wages from 1814 to 1906.

TABLE 5 ii[1]

Year	(1) Average spinner's wage	(2) Average piecer's wage	(2) expressed as a percentage of (1)
1814	26/–	6/6	25
1833	25/10	6/–	24
1849	21/10	7/–	30
1874	33/1	11/3	37
1886	31/1	11/9	40
1906	41/5	15/–	36

NOTE: 1 Derived from Wood, 1910: Tables 6 and 7.

The consistency of the differential is remarkable, especially after the formation of piecers' unions in the 1890s. Of course, whilst only the spinner was paid by the piece, he alone benefited from faster speed of work and union organisation. One result was wide variations in the earnings of piecers; in 1906 the big piecer in Oldham earned 46.3 per cent of his spinner's wage, but his counterpart in Leigh, only 31.7 per cent (Jewkes and Gray, 1935: 32). Generally the finer the count being spun, the greater the differential, since fine counts were constantly worked to a greater extent on hand mules (Wood, 1910: 63). This then was the structure of work which the spinners maintained throughout the nineteenth century, a system which was only tenuously based upon skill with the hand-mule, and not at all upon that with the self-actor.

According to the Webbs, local setbacks in the late 1820s convinced the spinners of the need for a centrally led organisation. The involvement of John Doherty has perhaps led historians to identify this as a 'universalistic' strategy; certainly the spinners did intend to organise piecers (Webbs, 1950: 117–18). But the adopted *Rules* of the 'Grand Central Union of all the Operative Spinners of the United Kingdom' specified:

14   That no spinner shall allow a piecer to spin of any account whatever after the 5th of April 1830 except such as may hereafter be provided for . . .

18   That no person or persons be learned or allowed to spin after the 5th April 1830 except the son, brother or orphan nephew of spinners, and the poor relations of the proprietors of the mills, and those only when they have attained the full age 15 years . . .

24   That female spinners be urged to become members of an association formed exclusively for themselves . . .

(Cole and Filson, 1967: 249–50)

Clearly then the structure of unionism was designed to reinforce the spinners' hegemony of the work process.

At this time the employers were not prepared to allow such a move to be consolidated, since they saw it as a first step towards the unification of price lists operating within the mills (Hammonds, 1919: 132). Accordingly, they moved to force a full-scale confrontation to circumvent the Union's policy on wages. This policy was described by an employer as

. . . ordering the Hands in only limited numbers of mills to turn out at a time in order that, until these shall have gained their point, they may be supported by the Funds of the Union. When they have got their wages increased to the extent of their demands, another set of Mills are turned out, and so on, so that a constant state of irritation is kept up.

(*ibid.*)

On the penalty of £500, 52 firms bound themselves to reduce wages, whereupon, in December 1830, 23,000 textile workers were locked-out in Manchester and the North West. The weakness of the 'Grand Central Union' was immediately exposed: Scottish and Irish workers refused to respond to a general strike call, and even those in Preston, Stockport and Bolton gave only half-hearted support. By March the men returned on the masters' terms; throughout neither piecers nor labourers had received any strike pay (*ibid*.: 134–5).

From this date until the 1870s, spinners' unions remained local associations, nonetheless retaining, at least in the large centres, a continuity and strength matched only by the engineers. Several examples of disputes during this period illustrate the developing ideology of localism in the spinners. In Preston in 1836, a local union of 250 to 300 members (about half the town's spinners) had survived the 1830 *débâcle*, and began to agitate for parity with Bolton whose prices rose and fell with the state of trade. Interest in the union grew, and by the time the men made their claim a virtual closed shop had been achieved. The employers offered a 10 per cent rise on condition that their association was disbanded (a move reflecting their anxiety over the spinners' potential 'internal' power in the mill), 8,500 persons were affected by the ensuing strike (or lock-out depending on which account you accept), only eight per cent of whom were spinners, and 15 per cent piecers, the other 77 per cent being weavers, labourers, engineers, overlookers and card-room hands for whom the dispute could have had no possible pecuniary benefit, and who received no strike pay (Ashworth 1837: 3–8). After three months the spinners' strike-pay dried up and the strike collapsed; in a few mills the self-actor was introduced, it was to take another dispute in 1853 for it to become wide-spread; in the next five years six reductions in prices were introduced and the union reduced to a shell (Banks, 1888: 2).

The regionalism of industrial relations meant that neither victories nor defeats were passed on from one area to another: in Manchester in 1838, only 75 per cent of spinners were said to be organised, whilst in Glasgow, 90 per cent of spinners were organised and a well organised system of monitoring wage differences existed (1838 LX: 280, 31). Admission was £1, weekly subscription, two shillings, and funeral and emigration benefits were available (*ibid*.: 44). (Both entrance fees and contributions were generally double that of the Engineers' Society for example.)

The spinners' history up to the 1850s consistently shows an opportunistic and exclusive trade policy, essentially insular in outlook and politically conservative by the radical standards of other contemporary working-class movements. However, the hand-mule was disappearing, albeit slowly, and with it the spinners' last claim of being a skilled trade. Even so the progress of machinery in textiles was not linear, and there were many instances of power creating 'hand' tasks. The next section reviews this confused technological context of the spinners up to the 1900s.

Technical change in spinning

In contrast to the demise of the hand-loom weavers, the demise of the independent spinners was much less spectacular and complete. Mechanisation of spinning proceeded over decades, stage by stage, even with its transfer to a factory setting. The spinning jenny merely increased the quantitative capability of the individual spinner by reproducing his or her hand motions on a greater scale, the 'subjective' division of labour. The productivity of the jenny still depended on the skill and effort of the spinner, even though now the action of the spinners's drawing arm, now produced many, rather than one, thread (S.J. Chapman, 1904: 53). The water-frame was the real qualitative innovation, but not used widely on cotton, particularly since it required a prime mover and thus a greater outlay of capital. The prevalence of jenny-spinning contributed to the small size of mills: since skill was at a premium, supervision of the work force was of fundamental importance (*ibid.*: 57).

Similarly, the Crompton mule, established in 1810–20, still required to be pushed by hand and winding the yarn was a separate operation. The control the operative therefore had over the process of production seems to have been a major incentive in the introduction of the self-actor. Now the pace of the carriage was determined by a central motive power, its traverse was lengthened, spindleage per frame raised, and the operative was put in charge of four machines by 'double-decking' (1842 XXII: 26–8).

The adoption of these machines was however patchy, and the 'marvels of ingenuity' described by chroniclers such as Ure, Baines, and Smiles were, up to the 1860s, a minority. To begin with, the self-actor was labour, rather than capital saving, and thus there was no incentive outside the well-organised trade union centres such as Oldham and Bolton. Furthermore, outside the Lancashire textile machinery area it would have been hard to obtain and well-nigh impossible to service. Although recent research suggests cotton machinery prices as a whole were steady, or even falling slightly from 1840 to 1866, contemporary observers cited the high cost of self-actors as the reason for their unpopularity. Speaking of the 1850s, the secretary of the Oldham Master Spinners considered self-actors to have been 'the exception' (S.J. Chapman, 1904: 68); most mills, such as those at New Lanark in 1851, would have had a mixture of machinery, since at that time only the hand-mules could cope with fine counts (Clapham, 1932: 30). According to Ure these innovations were designed to 'restore order' amongst the workers, yet nonetheless required much tuning and adjusting and became very much the preserve of the individual spinner (Catling, 1970: 149). Whilst dispensing with the effort required in drawing the carriage, the self-actor required continual cleaning (undertaken by children while the machine was still in motion – a task previously done by the spinner).

In 1833 it was estimated that the self-actor was installed in only 100 mills, but by 1873 it was said to be 'universal except for fine spinning' (1873 LV: 812). The progress of the next paradigmatic step in spinning technique, the ring-frame was, however, less complete. This invention allowed the same grade of yarn (spun at the same speed) to be produced in one-third less time than the mule. Crucially, it also required much less attention: it put much less strain on the yarn during spinning, thereby causing fewer breakages, and its simplicity reduced the 'tuning' required for different counts of yarn. It, therefore, only needed unskilled light labour, undifferentiated by experience (Copeland, 1917: 69–71). Yet by 1907 only 16 per cent of the total spindleage in England was of this type. There has been much debate on the reasons for this, but the concern of this discussion is the extent to which the policy of the spinners avoided potential technological displacement: i.e. the degree to which the occupational hierarchy established in the first mills of the 1800s remained essentially undisturbed through over 100 years of industrialisation and development in the textile sector.

Trade Union Tactics and the Emergence of Wage Lists

Unlike the miners or the engineers, the spinners were subject to the constant improvement of techniques and methods throughout the last half of the nineteenth century. As a piece worker leading a datally paid work group, the spinner had little choice in the adoption of strategy. The usefulness of limiting output, and indeed the potential to do this, was severely curtailed by the process of production. Since spinning was basically a non-craft occupation, the control of the labour market was impossible; the only alternative was for the spinners to embrace the piece-rate system and attempt to manipulate it to their advantage. What 'lever' or bargaining strength were they able to marshall against the management? Clearly the strike was a particularly dangerous weapon: the spinners were subject to substitution not only by alternative human labour but also by improved machinery, or the adoption of more and more automated machines – hence the tremendous violence against 'blackleg' labour in the early disputes of the 1820s and 30s. By the 1850s it was clear that such a blunt instrument as strike action was ineffective.

The other side to these spectacular and well-reported conflicts, was an emergent factory-by-factory approach to trade union policy. The bedrock of local spinners' unions was the maintenance of similar prices for equal work throughout 'their' town (S.J. Chapman, 1899: 594–5). In the 1830s in Glasgow, the 'main purpose' of the union was to send deputations to employers paying below the 'standard of the trade'. The final sanction was a strike, but this was preceded by at least three approaches by the spinners' committee, who were no doubt well aware of the state of trade and of the order book of that particular mill. The use of fines was gradually eradicated by demanding that the 'offender' be dismissed, and 'the consequence was, that up to this period we have heard very little of fines' (1838 VIII: 31, 33). In both cases the strategy was to 'up the stakes' of a dispute by locating a factory issue in a regional context. The embryonic form of this action was seen in Bolton and Preston strikes, but general lists were not universal and in some cases firms refused to issue even their own lists, preferring to negotiate day-by-day. It is significant that it was the larger establishments that favoured the system: it was, for example, the claim that their benefiting unduly vis-à-vis the smaller concerns had caused the demise of the Manchester Standard List in 1831 (*ibid*.: 270).

Throughout the 1850s and 1860s lists appeared sporadically: Bolton in 1844, Blackburn in 1852, Preston in 1859. Burnley, Bury and Stockport had lists in 1867, while Oldham and Hyde waited until 1872. At Oldham it remained customary for each master to make a separate bargain with his labour force, as had been the case at Preston until the 1859 strike. As late as 1875, however, many places were still without lists, and many firms disregarded them and used their own (S.J. Chapman, 1904: 266; 1886 XXI: 170). It must be remembered that all the lists, of this and the later period, referred solely to the operatives on jennies or mules – though in turn they indirectly affected the wages of their 'employees'. Lists were in fact a peculiar form of individual piecework, insofar as they were concerned to establish a relationship between effort and earnings which, as it were, 'by accident' also determined the rhythm of work for the piecers, and, by implication, for the whole factory. As with all such systems, it was not method so much as the industrial context which determined the effect. The effort/earning coefficient is meaningless unless the basic rate of pay at which the worker is being paid is known. The work of the spinner varied in intensity (and his product in quantity) according to the number of the spindles which he had to attend and the speed at which the machinery ran – conditions over which the operative had no control. Accordingly, spinners' officials regarded piecework remuneration as the only defence their trade had against 'sweating': since once in effect, piecework automatically penalised the employer for the 'speeding-up' of work, since it raised his direct costs (1886 XXI: 170–6).

In the 1870s two basic lists appeared after the disparate and unco-ordinated struggle of the 50s and 60s, and as a consequence, as it were, of the 'survival of the fittest'. These two principal types, based in Oldham and Bolton, differed in one crucial respect: the former determined prices by reference to the *speed* of the machinery, whereas the latter adjusted its prices according to the *character* of the product (which, of course, in part determined the speed of the mule) (Jewkes and Gray, 1935: 56–7). The recognition of these two standards in 1869 and 1887, respectively, represented a considerable step forward for the spinners' unions within their own frame of reference; they saw their job as *centralising* piecework systems in order that rate changes would be trade or regional, but not factory issues (Mawdsley, 1885: 136).

Between 1850 and 1870 the spinners were subject to a constant influx of new working methods – the adoption of the self-actor, and the various improvements to it and the preparatory stages of work. In 1873 a report produced figures for the workload in fine spinning:

In 1833, 148 spinners and 595 piecers worked with 112 spindles per hand.
After improvements, 73 spinners and 545 piecers worked with 152 spindles per hand.
In 1873, 26 spinners and 50 piecers worked with 517 spindles per hand.

(1873 LV: 813)

Such dramatic transformations were not typical of the middle and coarser counts where the self-actor's progress did not alter the structure of work so considerably since the labour cost was lower.

The proliferation of techniques was the prime reason for the multiplication of lists. Whilst employers had a vested interest in the lack of a standard list, certainty in factory prices was not to their advantage. The industry was still expanding, albeit in fits and starts, and the demand for labour was generally high. Nonetheless, the lion's share of this period of prosperity benefited the employers. Labour's financial reward from output fell to a nadir of 50 per cent in 1867, compared with 95 per cent in 1834 (Blaug, 1960–61: 360, 379). In as much as this suggests post-1870 developments tended to capital saving, it does not tell us why and what implications this had for the organisation of work.

The spinner's experience can be seen as very much a creation of the factory system. Of course, by the second half of the century his was by no means the only occupation subject to this process. But the significance of the mill, and of the textile industry in general, was that its productive system was geared to *continuity*, unlike those of the other principal 'factorised' trades such as shipbuilding, engineering, and rail and steam-engine makers. Long runs of standardised production, which themselves were repeated at routine intervals, had given rise to a very early detailed division of labour, with a highly differentiated, and historically stable, occupational structure. It was this – the incessant discipline of the working system — which impressed the contemporary apologists of capitalism, and there are several accounts of the extent to which employers would go to achieve this (Pollard, 1968: 213–226). A spinner of the 1820s recalled that: 'A rope hung up in every wheel-house, for what purpose we will leave you to judge' (Banks, 1888: 1). An employer used the following analogy:

A mill is as much organised as a regiment; there is a hierarchy of Overlookers, and each particular branch is under one Overlooker who has inferior Over-lookers under him, who manage some of them a room and some of them, a small part of a room.

(1856 XIII: 113)

Where long runs were typical and competition fierce the character of output centred the attention of both employers and operatives on market prices, or, more precisely, on the 'margin', that is, the differ-ence between the raw material cost and the selling price of the product. Lower raw material costs simply increased internecine rivalry and placed pressure on internal factory prices; in consequence, spinners' strikes were traditionally *defensive* actions (Smith, 1954: 400–3). In the mind of the leadership of the early spinners' union the *fact* of a strike was a defeat for its power, and emphasised that strength lay in the factory (Mawdsley, 1885: 134). What then enabled the spinners to maintian their privileged work role, achieve a very powerful union, and retain control over the piecers, in a period, from 1873 to 1896, when raw cotton and yarn prices fell by almost 50 per cent (Smith, 1954: 83)?

An answer is suggested by the contemporary accounts of the English textile workers in the 1880s and 1890s. In contrast to earlier com-parisons of punitive 'external' controls used by employers, now the different degrees of supervision required of English and German spinners was compared. Whereas in the latter's mills, 'tyranny and bridled force' remained supreme, in Lancashire overlookers were less numerous, less well paid and largely ex-spinners of near retirement age – that is, symbols, rather than agents, of control (Schulze-Gaevernitz, 1895: 99–101). Elsewhere, the relation of labour to capital in England was characterised 'as organised discipline' (*ibid.* 1893: 146). It was this ability to sustain continuous intensive labour that has been acknow-ledged as 'saving' the English textile industry from its self-imposed technological isolation (Copeland, 1917: 300).

As has been suggested, the position of the spinner in the occupational hierarchy made the use of the piecework system essential to his trade union tactics, and there is much evidence to suggest that they did exactly this, if with a degree of ambivalence. It was only logical that, when organised, the spinners' unions attempted to penalise employers who failed to introduce new machinery (Webbs, 1920: 413). The more competitive the employer became, the less he was able to resist threats to disrupt continuous working, and thus the more he relied on the spinner as the 'linkman' in the productive process. James Mawdsley told the 1886 Royal Commission that:

The new and improved machinery brought in is an advantage to those who work upon it in respect to their earnings as compared with what they would have gained working on old machinery.

(1886 XXI: 176)

When such innovations were introduced the management would, until the machine was 'tuned', pay a day rate for, say, three months, and

at the end of the third month the men are put on piecework, and we find a great leap in production, showing that the men have done a great deal more than they did when on time.

(*ibid.*: 174)

It is interesting that the master spinners questioned were unanimous in agreement that wage rates were not the cause of the Depression:

Do you consider the Depression is attributable at all to the current rate of wages . . .? – No.
. . . may I ask you further, supposing rates were lowered do you think business would revive? – Not by that means only.

(*ibid.*: 198)

In the context of orthodox economic thinking this attitude is quite extraordinary. On both sides it is, in fact, 'modern': the worker accepted and encouraged technological improvement, and realised that the more capital intensive the production process the less crucial the *quantity* of wages became in comparison with the *effort* required from the workers; concomitantly, the employers understood this, and therefore proposed solutions to the 'crisis' at the level of trade – in the words of one textile manufacturer, 'either entire free trade or tariffs' (*ibid.*: 286).

In the context of international competition in an industry which exported over 70 per cent of its output, the 'plebeian' position of the spinner would appear to have been highly *functional* in maintaining labour discipline. Given a wages system based on an ever-changing relation between the yarn quality, mule speed and the type of product, the spinner aristocrat ensured the smooth transition from job to job, and rate to rate, and, what is more, was responsible for these decisions from within the work force itself. In the words of one veteran union activist from Preston:

The good spinner's machine never stopped running during his shift . . . from this both he and his piecer ultimately benefited and thereby the trade as a whole.

(Banks, 1888: 15)

Productivity, Conciliation and Spinners' Unions
There is overwhelming evidence that the spinner was subject to a

continuing increase in the rhythm of work in the last quarter of the century, which reflected the exhaustion of *labour*-saving innovations. This took an 'intensive' form and hours of work fell during the period (at least formally). Despite the technical interregnum, labour unit cost fell by 25 per cent from 1860 to 1890, another indication of the pressure on customary working rhythms. There was also constant pressure on the *hours* of labour: $56\frac{1}{2}$ was legal, but 'recourse to crib time' could push the average two hours above this if, during a trade decline, the union could not prevent it (1886 XXI: 72). The spinner was particularly susceptible to 'speed-up': mule speeds increased from 5,000 revolutions per minute in 1839, to 11,000 by 1890; and numbers of spindles per operative from 109 in 1850, to 234 by 1890 (Farnie, 1953: 478, 41).

These increases were evidently less a result of adding more capital to each worker, and more a consequence of using existing techniques more intensively. There was thus less financial commitment by the employer relative to the expected return. It can be seen that the spinners themselves encouraged this by their enthusiasm for payment by results, since piece-rates, and not time-rates, provide the motivation for *labour*-saving innovations. But, during the last quarter of the century when the price of yarn and of piece-goods fell faster than the price of imported cotton, labour costs as a proportion of all costs probably fell. Thus the pressure on unit costs for the individual proprietor expressed itself as a relation between his capital investment and profits, rather than, as in former times, as a relation between the market prices and wages (Blaug 1960–61: 368; Smith, 1954: 202; Farnie, 1953: 401). The effect of this was that the work force as a whole produced an increase of approximately 40 per cent in output per unit of labour between the years 1885 and 1914 (Sandberg, 1974: 108–9).

This analysis, together with an understanding of the significance of the spinner's 'plebeian' role, clarifies the relation between the emergence of unionism, conciliation and the list system of wage contracts. In effect, the employers had to reach a *détente* with the operatives in an effort to win their co-operation in overcoming overseas competition: the technological stagnation in *labour utilising* methods after the 1870s meant that the major contribution to greater efficiency had to be provided by the efforts of the workers themselves.

The two most important spinners' unions were formed in Oldham in 1870 and in Bolton in 1871. In the latter case the central executive was composed of mill delegates elected by proportional representation. Each mill had the right to nominate candidates to this body in which one seat became vacant every two months. In contrast, the Oldham leadership came from districts whose representatives were appointed from above, and who with the president and secretary, formed a sub-committee which investigated all minor cases and ran any strikes (which could only be called by ballot) (S.J. Chapman, 1904: 246–8). The two areas were dominated by coarse and fine spinning respectively, which in turn governed the content of the list adopted.

Bolton fine spinning had a totally piece-price list, that is, it laid down a price for each count of yarn and each length of mule, from which the weekly wage was computed. Differences in machinery therefore affected the employer and not the operative, since the labour cost was a rate per pound of yarn and remained the same whatever the time taken. As a result,

The Bolton List . . . makes for a measure of equality in labour costs between mills of varying efficiency, but inequality in operatives' weekly earnings.
(Jewkes and Gray, 1935: 58)

In contrast, the Oldham List introduced an element of the time-wage system by stipulating that all operatives working on mules of a given length should earn roughly the same wage. The weekly output of such mules was calculated, by reference to their known speed, and a piece-price determined. The effect of this system was to encourage the employer to lower his labour costs to the minimum, since for each length of mule a standard wage was payable. This list, therefore, equalised wages whilst varying labour costs between mills. The element of time-wage was related to the higher degree of automation amongst the larger Oldham mills producing coarse yarn: ring-spinning, an innovation that removed much of the labour of piecing, became largely an occupation for female operatives, and it was here, where automation was at its zenith and organisation lowest that the time-wage reasserted itself in textiles. The operative was now totally subservient to the pace of the 'automaton' (1909 LXXX: xxvii).

The differences between Oldham and Bolton are important since, as will be seen, they produced differing union characteristics and policy, particularly in relation to the piecers. This is especially clear when considering the first quasi-universal union, the Amalgamated Association of Operative Cotton Spinners formed in 1870; Oldham being the most important constituent part. A considerable simplified historiography of the lists and of unionisation is as follows: in 1887, nine lists governed the wages of 18,500 spinners, and in 1909 there remained 148 unions in the cotton industry (Porter 1967–8: 50; Copeland, 1917: 291).

In 1884 The Amalgamation reorganised along centralised lines, and appointed full-time officials (decided by competitive examination) to deal with the complexities of the lists. As the Webbs noted, the modernisation of trade union forms and the wage contract were related:

> . . . the Bolton Spinning List, for instance, comprising eighty-five pages closely filled with figures – the intricacy of the calculations is such as to be beyond the comprehension of the ordinary operative or manufacturer, or even of the investigating mathematician without a very minute knowledge of the technical detail.
>
> (1950: 308)

At first only six local districts, including Oldham and Bolton were wealthy enough to appoint such officials, but this permanent cabinet came to dominate the Amalgamation (Turner, 1962: 137). Yet Oldham and Bolton remained separate worlds: by 1891 the Amalgamation had 18,926 members, equivalent to 93.3 per cent of all spinners employed, and whilst but in Oldham only 77 per cent were organised, Bolton recorded a virtual closed shop, 99 per cent membership (Smith, 1954: 332, 328, 330).

Oldham was much more affected by overseas competition, since its industrial organisation was more modern than Bolton's and the resultant list less favourable to the operatives. For example, actual wages of the average mule spinner increased about 18 per cent more than can be explained by the wage lists, and this increase must therefore be due to improvements in output per man. Under the Oldham List such a rise reflected a probable increase in productivity of 30 per cent per worker (Jewkes and Gray, 1935: 18–20, 197–8). The Oldham spinners had agreed to the first list in 1876 (after a six weeks stoppage in 1875) on condition that grievances were to be, in the first instance, dealt with in the mill. If no agreement at that stage materialised, the employers and union secretaries would investigate the complaint. James Mawdsley claimed that 99 per cent of cases were dealt with in this way (1892 XXXV: 27).

However these procedures do not fit the facts of the first 10 to 15 years of the lists. Their whole structure was designed to remove responsibility for disputes further and further from the 'front-line' operative, and 'vertically' up the parallel lines of organisation between the employers and union. The structure of the list allowed less individual compensation by work groups for changes in speeds or counts: within three years, four wage cuts were imposed via the list, and this achievement would undoubtedly have posed the employers insurmountable difficulties on a plant-by-plant basis. In each case the spinners' leadership played an indispensable role in diffusing opposition (Smith, 1954: 523, 411–13, 414–15). A trade recovery in 1880–81 enabled the spinners to retrieve one-half of the reductions sustained in 1876–79.

Some years later the Oldham masters proposed a 10 per cent reduction in list prices to come into effect in April 1885. In a fascinating example of corporate trade union action, the spinners instead proposed short-time working to combat the over-production, which was caused, they argued, by the 'reckless investment' of capital in the industry (*ibid*.: 415–16; 1886 XXI: 178). Sixty-four companies actually implemented the alternative plan for two months. However, under pressure from the limited liability firms, a general lock-out was instituted in July, although some private companies stayed open on the same terms, or on the basis of only a five per cent reduction. After 14 weeks an overall compromise was reached, and the 5 per cent cut instituted (Smith, 1954: 438). It must be stressed that, whilst only 4,000 spinners were actually 'in dispute', the lock-out affected 24,000, with roughly one-third of these as piecers under the tutelage of their work-leaders.

Thus, between 1876 and 1891 there were under the Oldham list five reductions of five per cent each between 1887 and 1881, followed by four advances of the same amount between 1880 and 1891. The essential significance of the lists for industrial relations was that they provided a method for dealing with 'quick speed' or 'bad work' disputes, so that, in 1892, Mawdsley could claim that 'there is now not the slightest friction between employed and employers' (1892 XXXV: 27). Yet this appears to be contradicted by the answer provided by his own union to the Commission's survey of strikes and lock-outs during the previous 10 years: 'Hundreds of them, too numerous to hunt up' (1892 XXXVI: 253).

What Mawdsley referred to was *general confrontations* of the 1885 type, while continuing uninterrupted was a series of 'front-line' disputes concerning the quality, or the speed, of output. The list system's success was not in conciliation but in concealment – an assertion well supported by the answer of the Oldham branch of the Master Cotton Spinners' Association to the same Commission:

Settle in an equitable way any small disputes that may arise at individual firms, and so prevent growing discontent; but even this does not altogether prevent strikes as we have found by experience. We are now trying to preserve peace by preparing for war, viz., building up a strong fund to support individual firms attacked unjustly by trade union officials.

(*ibid*.: 818)

In fact during the period from 1883 to 1893 some 3,000 disputes were recorded by the Oldham Spinners' Union, most of them relatively short (Smith, 1954: 325).

Despite the 1885 defeat there is much evidence that the rank and file spinners were able to maintain their position by accepting higher workloads; one estimate put real earnings for the piece-workers as rising 20 per cent from 1880 to 1887 (Porter, 1970: 398). This put considerable strain on the Oldham companies who, with their heavy fixed charges and capital investment, were most susceptible to unofficial disputes. As margins declined their structure encouraged them to maximise output and improve productivity to remain competitive – leading to union complaints of 'over-production'. Whilst the spinners' real income improved, the financial position of their mills worsened dramatically during the 1880s (Smith, 1954: 219). This encouraged the employers to buy inferior grades of raw material which, since it reduced the spinner's income, caused disputes on the shop-floor. These, in turn, hit at the margins of profit, which encouraged further 'economies' such as enforced overtime. The spinner objected to this, and the cycle of disputes continued.

Bolton, the centre of fine spinning, differed from Oldham both in the sense of industrial character and in trade union organisation. Cotton firms were predominantly family concerns, and an employer's relations were often used, as an extension of central authority, when establishing a new mill (Thorpe, 1969: 174–90). From the 1820s Bolton fine spinners had regarded themselves as somewhat apart from their coarse- and medium-count colleagues; strikes during the period from 1821 to 1823 were specifically motivated by them to retain their differential with other districts (Turner, 1962: 76). By 1886, 99.3 per cent of mulespinners in Bolton were unionised and they had approximately 20 per cent better wages than their colleagues in Oldham (Thorpe, 1969: 117; Wood, 1910: 28, 63).

The coincidence of family firm and such high trade union density is not accidental. Bolton was the originator of a unique form of trade union structure – the 'shop-club'. Spinners' unions were organised geographically, so that, formally, employees in many different mills could be in the same branch. But where price lists were historically unique to each mill, as they were in Bolton, (and even when integrated into an area list subject to numerous mill customs and practices) there existed a material basis for a sub-layer of the branch centred upon the mill. The shop-club arose on these foundations, the spinners paid to it a separate levy beyond their union subscription, and it had its own rules and procedure (including progressive fines for non-attendance and for speaking 'out of turn'). To some extent this spread throughout the Spinners' Amalgamation: under the Oldham Rules the shop-club officers dealt with mill disputes in the first instance and had direct access to the area executive (Thorpe, 1969: 250–2; Turner, 1962: 283–4).

This combination of family ownership and highly organised but localist trade unions produced a notably stable history of industrial relations. The employers remained outside the militant Federation of Master Cotton Spinners' Association until 1905, whilst the Bolton Spinners produced three leaders between 1884 and 1907, whose influence, for example, in the years 1897 to 1906, resulted in only *four* strikes, despite the average of 136 disputes per year being notified to the local executive (Thorpe, 1969: 32). Thus, although Bolton was not without its crop of day-to-day issues, endemic to an industry in which there was a constant flow of potential pay disputes, what is clear is that here the family firm and shop club were symbiotic in their effect of localising these disruptions. The wage issue, given the complexity and peculiarities of the list, was often solvable at mill level, and the shop club provided the organising force for deputations and 'memorials' to the master. The two combined to insulate conflict and thereby hinder general confrontations. Apart from the atomised shop clubs, the Bolton Federation was divided again into 10 branches, whose area leadership met infrequently but which each had its own full-time official who collected its own subscriptions. (*ibid.*: 249).

Not surprisingly Bolton had a reputation amongst Lancashire mill towns as a 'haven of the industrious and provident', qualities shared by 'all sections of the manufacturing community' (*Cotton Factory Times*, 15.7.1887). In 1894 the spinners launched an ambitious superannuation scheme designed to provide up to 10 years' pension for the fully contributed. Their secretary, A.H. Gill wrote in the 1905 *Report* 'The public ought to be thankful that trade unionists take this action as their contribution to the rates are thus materially reduced.'

The Bolton spinners were fully aware that their relative privileges depended to an extent on the retention of family control in mills, and they issued frequent statements against the 'Oldham Limiteds' and the joint-stock principle as a whole, and in this they were often co-signatories with the Bolton and Preston employers (*Cotton Factory Times*, 12.10.1886; 1892 XXXV: 85).

The 'Formalisation' of Conciliation

In different forms there existed considerable 'informal' avenues of negotiation, unwritten codes of procedure which employers generally conformed to. In the case of Oldham they did so perhaps reluctantly, in Bolton, with more enthusiasm; in both cases (and throughout the rest of the trade) it was localised to a mill, or group of mills, and not structured through an organisation such as a 'Joint Committee'.

The differences between fine and coarse spinning areas became accentuated in the 1890s as the latter came under severe overseas competition. The Oldham employers were particularly concerned at the growth of unionism in the late 1880s, which they blamed for the loss of foreign markets (Smith, 1954: 277). This concern was reflected in the reformation of an employers' combination in 1888 under the somewhat misleading title of the 'United Cotton Spinners' Association'. This was governed by a General Committee whose members were elected in proportion to the number of spindles they controlled (*ibid.*: 280–1). This inevitably gave the Oldham Limiteds control, and thus potentially involved fine yarn centres in conflicts in which they had no interest and little representation upon the employers' negotiating body. At the first attempt to implement a common policy – an agreement by 450 firms to work short time in July/August 1889 – these divergent interests parted and the Association collapsed.

Its successor, the Federation of Master Cotton Spinners, formed during 1891–2 included only the coarse-yarn centres, principally the Oldham and Ashton employers. It was notably more militant. The division of employers into trade or regional enclaves had probably operated, whilst the industry was generally expanding, to the spinners' advantage. However, the Federation was now able to act in a united fashion. Its determination was founded on a dramatic fall in profits: in 1890 the leading 90 Oldham companies had made £376,041, and in 1891 this was reduced to a mere £10,764 (Smith, 1954: 179). Rather than force a head-on collision, the Federation responded by buying in cheaper cotton. This was much harder to spin correctly, thereby causing a fall in the spinner's income. There followed a series of running disputes; eventually, the Stalybridge Mill Company refused a request by the Union for a five per cent addition to the wages as compensation for the low quality raw material, and a strike ensued. The Federation responded by a lock-out involving some 60 per cent of the members of the Spinners' Amalgamation. The Oldham branch believed that the 'final test' had come (Porter, 1967–8: 52). In fact, some manufacturers were agitating for

a general stoppage all over the country, of manufacturers as well as spinners, so that the organisation of the men in both departments of the trade can be broken down.

(1894 CVII: 10–11)

In the event the union leaders forestalled a generalised confrontation, abandoning their Stalybridge branch by allowing that the quality of the raw cotton should be investigated *after* the mills were back at work. Clause 5 of the settlement embodied a further compromise: strike-breakers were allowed to continue at work whilst about 50 per cent of the card-room operatives failed to get their jobs back (Smith, 1954: 476–8).

This comprehensive victory set the scene for a full-scale confrontation in September 1892. When the spinners refused to accept a five per cent wage-cut, some 40–50,000 operatives were locked-out, 20,000 of whom were card-room workers, 16,000, piecers, and 7,000, spinners, the rest being ancillary workers (*ibid.*: 487–8). Thus, again, only a small percentage (14) of the strikers were in direct dispute, only their funds lasted the entire 20 weeks, and it was their officials who negotiated the famous 'Brooklands Agreement' which brought the affair to a close.

From March 1893 to 1913 this Agreement became the basis of all relations between employers and employed in the spinning industry. It stated that all new wages would stand for six months, and alterations could only be plus or minus five per cent of the current rate. However, historically the Agreement is remembered primarily for the elaborate grievance procedure it established which was regarded by the Webbs as 'approaching the ideal' (1920: 203). The exact details are less well known, but they are intrinsically interesting since they 'formalised' the already extant process of mill-by-mill, 'vertical' conciliation. In essence four stages were created through which each dispute had to pass: (1) the issue was submitted in writing to the local secretaries of the trade union and the employers; (2) it was then investigated (within seven days) by these, or by a committee of three representatives nominated by each side; (3) failing a local settlement, the matter was considered by a Joint Committee in Manchester of four members of the Spinners' Amalgamation and the Employers' Federation, the decision again to be made within seven days; (4) this Committee could, in specified circumstances, extend this deadline indefinitely (1894 CVII 288–90).

In practice it was the first two stages that played the decisive role: between 1904 and 1912 on average only seven per cent of cases overall reached the Joint Committee, and only three per cent of those particular to the spinner (Porter, 1967–8: after Table 11). In other words, in the absence of a decisive change in work organisation, the 'Brooklands Agreement' represented, not some paradigmatic shift in the organisation of industrial relations, but the formalisation of existing procedures with the addition of a central, but largely symbolic body. The running conflict within the mills continued unabated: some 4,000 voluntary agreements were made in the period from 1904 to 1912 largely over 'bad spinning', that is, poor raw cotton (from the spinners' viewpoint). This was cushioned by the rising earnings resulting from the acceptance of 'speed-up' in the first nine years of the Agreement (*ibid.*: 57; Wood, 1901: 155n).

Why did the Agreement alter the character of industrial relations only marginally? The answer to this will also explain the extraordinary stability of the structure of work, and the hegemony of the spinners over the entire cotton textile labour force. In effect what occurred was a 'trade-off' between the militant employers and the 'militant', that is, exclusive, workers: each area of authority was defined, as were their mutual interests and enemies. Important here is the fact, already noted, that the slow closing of differentials between spinners and piecers stopped in the 1890s and actually increased slightly up to 1906. The spinners' 'plebeian' position was strengthened by the absence of provisions for the piecers in the 'definitive' statement of negotiation procedure: the 'formalisation' in stages (1) and (2) of the Agreement consolidated the leading role of spinners and further distanced the piecers from the collective bargaining process. In this sense the spinner's position, previously recognised informally as the intermediary between employer and work force, was brought into the formal conciliation machinery.

We are witnessing the recognition of the spinners' duties as well as his rights . . . Responsible leaders in the Amalgamation can only welcome this, as will responsible employers. The public can now hopefully look forward to an era of prosperity in the industry, and social improvement amongst the operatives.

(*Cotton Factory Times*, 12.5.1893)

Thus, although the Agreement in no way disturbed the internal hierarchy of work, it did represent a new climate of economic and industrial circumstances. Speaking to the Manchester Statistical Society in 1905, A.H. Gill, the Bolton Providence secretary, bemoaned the passing of an age:

The old system of master and servant, where the private employer knew his individual workmen and often treated them generously is rapidly giving way. In its place the limited company, with its shareholders is largely in evidence . . . Sentiment has largely gone out of business.

(1905: 84)

Balancing this were the complexity and number of lists still surviving. In the wake of Brooklands, as a next logical step, the *Cotton Factory Times* advocated the adoption of a universal list, but also recognised that,

labour segregates according to its delicacy, skill and versatility . . . to force a universal list might require complete reversal of trade union policy.

(1.2.1898)

In short, conciliation 'from above' characterised the 20 years up to the First World War; the 'real' history of the spinners shows that this was in many respects a continuation of their work experience, rather than a watershed. The key factor which ensured this stability was the hierarchy of work with the role of the spinner at the 'industrial fulcrum' of the process of production.

Spinners: the Modern Plebeians

The spinners' role like the industry, was a creation of technology which transformed the occupation from the minor part-time task of agricultural workers to a major factory system within three decades. The spinners' position as wage labourers was not 'encumbered' with the pre-industrial heritage – the potential was open for a rapid elimination of what Marx called the 'subjective' division of labour (1976: 501).

For the cotton entrepreneur the disjunction between mechanisation of spinning and weaving allowed capital investment in spinning to occur under particularly favourable circumstances. He could shift the main burden of adjustment to technical change to the domestically based weavers, and whilst the latter were ultimately to become a hindrance to textile expansion, during the 'take-off' period their declining wages ensured rapid capital accumulation (and in turn lowered the initial outlay needed to enter the spinning industry). Within the factory, however, the rational organisation of production around the machine depended on the 'socialising' of the work force.

The labour brought into the cotton factories was, in one sense, the 'first' working class within the orthodox factory structure, on a mass scale, the majority of whom were unskilled or semi-skilled. Only 25 per cent were adult males (and thus eligible for union membership), half were women, and the rest male piecers and children (around 10 per cent each). These proportions remained remarkably stable throughout the nineteenth century, the only significant change being the gradual rise in the number of women (Wood, 1910: 607).

The picture conjured is of a heterogeneous labour force with neither tradition of craft, nor experience of organisation. The employer had simultaneously to discipline and pace this diverse group. Thus a factory hierarchy evolved in contradiction to what was in technical terms a meritocratic structure of production. This is demonstrated by the evidence of James Mawdsley to the Royal Commission on Labour of 1892. He revealed that, of every three piecers who had served their six years 'time' and become qualified as spinners, only one was selected by the employer, and 'the others drift into miscellaneous occupations . . . and then a certain proportion remain piecers all their lives' (1892 XXXV: 801).

The trained spinners thus realised no extra surplus value (in the Marxist sense) and their eventual exit from the industry lends further support to the proposition that the spinners' role was a creation of the industrial system and functional in the creation of a suitable wage/effort relationship. Given the complexity of the piece system created by the contradiction between the advanced state of mechanisation and the 'unsocialised' labour force, the continued existence of the spinner's role testified to the essential simplicity of the supervisory tasks involved in the work process. Yet it was precisely the increasing complexity of the production cycle in other industries that led to the replacement of the piecemaster by a professional non-manual management (A.J. Taylor, 1960: 234).

Thus it can be seen that the function of the spinner was to resolve the contradiction of capitalist production *within the work force itself*, by the policing of a wage bargain that exactly mirrored the changing relation of labour to capital in the cotton industry. It would be too simple to present this as entirely advantageous to the employer: the spinners limited the number of mules under their supervision, for example. However, the effect of the spinners' enforcement of a job hierarchy advantageous to themselves was to lower the wage bill overall. Had not the spinners fulfilled this role,

. . . the conditions of work might have resulted in virtual apprenticeship, ending in a moderate wage, perhaps again to increase moderately; but the policy of the spinners necessitated a system of long apprenticeship with a higher wage ultimately.

(S.J. Chapman, 1910: 469)

Spinners' unionism corresponded to this – piecers' unions were held in a subordinate role. As Mawdsley explained to the Labour Commission:

Do you control the piecers at all by Society? – Yes, our local districts have largely organised in that direction, and if we come out on strike the piecers are brought out as well, and paid.

(1892 XXXV: 29)

However, this strike pay depended on the issue.

If they wanted to better their position at the expense of the spinners, we might object, but if they wanted to better their position at the expense of the employers we are quite willing they should do so.

(*ibid.*)

A contemporary observer summed up the piecers' dilemma.

The piecers all hope to become spinners soon, and find it hard to fight against their own future bread and butter.

(S.J. Chapman, 1910: 470)

Whilst the organisation of work remained hierarchical, despite its meritocratic technical form, those at the top had no need to artificially limit entry to the occupation. This puzzled the Webbs who identified apprenticeship with strong unionism – yet the cotton spinners undoubtedly had the latter without the former.

Yet no part of the strength and success of this Trade Union can be attributed to a limitation of apprentices, or to any monopoly features whatsoever . . . the cotton spinners positively encourage as many as two [piecers] to each spinner, a ratio which is approximately ten times as great as is required to recruit to the trade.

(Webbs 1920: 474)

Of course, as has been noted, the 'monopoly' was an already established form of *work*, rather than a manipulation of the labour market.

In a working life of approximately 30 years a spinner would employ about four or five big piecers and five or six little piecers, but in an industry of constant size, only one piecer would graduate to the top position (Jewkes and Gray, 1935: 173). Up to 1914 the industry was still growing sufficiently to allow the graduation of about one in three. In the aftermath of the Brooklands Agreement the spinners were able to pass on the loss to their group over 'bad spinning' to the piecers, whose workload increased as more breakages occurred in the cotton whilst output as a whole fell. Many unofficial strikes of the 1890s were piecers' strikes, as much against the spinners' deductions, as against the employer's use of inferior raw material (Burgess, 1975: 289).

Local control in the mill became more, rather than less, important. It could take up to 20 years for a little piecer to become a spinner. The graduations of seniority were strictly limited in each mill. If a place became vacant it was obligatory for it to be filled from the 'inside' on the decision of the shop club, not of the management. The piecer had to be 'shopped', that is, accepted by the shop club, before being recognised as a spinner. In this way 'strangers' were effectively excluded. Elaborate local procedures existed for the 'minding' of carriages if a spinner was ill or the place not yet permanently filled (Thorpe, 1969: 253). Examples of disputes from both 'sides' appeared regularly in the trade press.

Work was temporarily stopped at the Eclipse Mill of Messrs. Jackson and Co. at Bolton over the minders' [spinners] insistence that their nominee take on a vacant pair of mules . . .

(Cotton Factory Times, 3.4.1896)

Considerable efforts must be made to bring more equity to the position of the piecer otherwise the rash of strikes and stoppages by them over promotion will continue . . . The experienced minder is due his worth, but this must not be at the expense of those below him . . .

(Cotton Factory Times, 1.2.1901)

In fact in Oldham the spinners were obliged to pay a minimum to their helpers, despite protests over 'management interference'. However, being in a position to control the division of labour, they 'managed to retain all the extras for themselves, and so leave the piecers in much the same position as before' (S.J. Chapman, 1889: 598–7).

This organisation of work, born in the water-driven factories of the 1790s, survived over 140 years virtually undisturbed. The self-actor, mechanisation of preparatory and ancillary processes, the emergence of the alternative to the mule (the ring-frame), and finally the independent organisation of the subordinate workers themselves, all failed to effect any major change. The failure of the American ring-frame to take over from the mule deserves closer observation. It undoubtedly had technical superiority, yet, 'Instead of warmly receiving the ring-frame the English manufacturers bent their energies to the perfection of the mule' (Copeland, 1917: 71). The explanatory factors are numerous, but it seems to have been the policy of the spinners' unions that was overwhelmingly important. This was *a policy facilitated by the organisation of work*. In the 1890s the Webbs noted that, if an employer wished to introduce the ring-frame,

he was offered . . . a revision of the piecework lists so arranged to stimulate him to augment the rapidity and complexity of the mule, in order that the mulespinners, increasing in dexterity, might simultaneously enlarge the output per machine and raise their own earnings.

(1920: 425)

This conclusion is confirmed by a recent extensive econometric investigation (Sandsberg, 1974: 63–5).

Both express this opinion in terms of the flexible, non-militant union policy – but, of course everything we have analysed so far points to the fact that this in turn relied on the organisation of work. The 'flexiblity' of the spinners was based on their ability to pass on the necessary speed-up to the piecers, and the way the latter were hamstrung in their response. Thus the role and authority of the spinners was to their employer's advantage in the short term: there was a mutuality of interest not simply in ideological terms, but reflecting the actual relations of production inside the mill.

On several occasions the piecers attempted to form their own independent union. In 1890 in Bolton such a union was founded, but the spinners' reaction was immediate. They enforced a closed-shop against any rebel members supporting the movement by making it obligatory for them to collect the subscriptions to the spinners' own 'Piecers' Union'. A similar fate awaited other ventures in 1908 and 1919, although on each occasion the piecers gained more say within the Spinners' Amalgamation, albeit still as second-class members (Turner, 1962: 142; Jewkes and Gray, 1935: 168–9). The essence of the piecers' status was defined by the spinners' original motivation in organising them at all. This motivation was outlined in the annual report of the Oldham Province for 1878:

For several years the Amalgamation has been labouring under a disadvantage both in general and individual strikes in having to pay piecers, creelers and scavengers, strike pay although they never paid anything to the funds of the District . . . This system was felt to be a great drain on the resources of the Amalgamation and it was resolved to form, in connection with the Amalgamation, a Piecers' Association.

(*ibid.*: 167)

Further proof of the subordination of the piecers is demonstrated by the fact that the degree of organisation was strongly correlated to the strength of the local Spinners' Province. Bolton, for example, had traditionally 100 per cent membership of their auxiliary Piecers' Association.

The essential function of the work group was machine-tending, minding and servicing. The spinners were increasingly, in the latter half of the century, referred to as 'senior minders', while the nomenclature of the piecer (mending broken threads) and scavenger (cleaning and preparatory work) also reflected the machine-based character of their tasks. To the extent that the spinners were co-ordinators and organisers of the spinning process, an essential feature of their role (embodied in the fact that they were the only pieceworkers) was to ensure that the machine was inactive for the least possible time. There were at least four possible factors continually present in the labour process which could lead to interruptions. Firstly, the quality of the yarn: with coarse yarn the work rhythm is faster and the cops need to be replenished more often since the carriage moves faster and the cops hold less yarn; cleaning is also heavier because coarse yarns throw off more impurity than the fine. Second, the speed of the machine decides how fast the operatives have to travel (on average an Oldham minder covered 13 miles daily in his supervision of the carriage). Third, the length of the mule and thus the number of spindles determines the extent of the duties described above. Finally, the quality of the raw material: inferior cotton or faulty preparation increases the frequency of thread breakages, and stoppages cumulatively become unavoidable.

It will be noticed that, without exception, the work group had no immediate control over these disruptive elements in their work situation. If all had been equal, say on collective piecework, there would have been constant pressure towards conflict, and a natural tendency to act together to raise prices in compensation. Groups would have evolved norms and 'horizontal' affiliations with similar groups on the other mules. In short, the essential division would have been membership or non-membership of the group (as with the 'marra' system in the North Eastern coal pits). In fact, the actual divide was created *within* the work group: there were numerous isolated conflicts, where the subordinates were involved in an atomised dispute with 'their' minder instead of with system as a whole. As a form of sub-contraction the system remained unique, for although very common in the nineteenth century, it was the only one of this kind contained within a factory trade (Schloss, 1907: 180–204).

The essence of sub-contraction and its rationale in the industrial order is the mediation of *control* from the centre to the periphery of a production process. Nominally it would, therefore, appear to have been unnecessary in spinning where the employer clearly had 'formal' and 'real' control by virtue of the complete subsumption of labour to capital. But, in fact, the greater the fixed capital costs, the greater the cost to the capitalist when this is not producing – a pressure intensified by the continually competitive nature of the industry.

The payment system and hierarchical work group are one answer to this: building into the organisation of work the 'labour of superintendence and management'. As such it is interesting to note the unanimity of contemporaries in observing the 'self-discipline' of the English spinners: 'the English spinner does not require overlooking the same as the German'. Whereas the latter apparently needed one supervisor to 10–20,000 spindles, the English spinner required only one to 60–80,000 (Schulze-Gaervernitz, 1895: 99). Similar favourable comparisons were made with American textile workers, who, it was said, were 'unruly and disorganised' in comparison with their English colleagues (Copeland, 1917: 290). A paper given to the British Association for the Advancement of Science declared:

In the cotton trade I believe that we have at the present time the most effecious (*sic*) labour in the world. It is not only bred and trained, but it is fitted and disciplined to its work and under the present lists with the present improved machinery you may always rely on its performing its duty with the exactitude of a clock. (1887: 51)

Furthermore, in contrast to the transient and largely immigrant labour of Continental and American mills respectively, in Lancashire the intense geographical concentration produced . . . 'a new type of man . . . the industrial worker, born and educated for the machine' (Schulze-Gaevernitz, 1895: 53). As a result of this 'psychological adaptation',

the highest class of cotton operatives – the mule spinners – are really the aristocracy of England's labour, as well as, in general, that of Europe.

(*ibid.*: 150)

A Craft Union?

The spinners constituted an 'aristocracy of labour' through their collective exclusion of other workers from a grade *of* an occupation, not from the trade as a whole. They had, therefore, no need for apprenticeship 'monopolies' or cumbersome trade policies based on the 'right to a trade'. In fact, on the contrary, their benefit rules seem frequently to have been designed to get unemployed members out of the occupational labour market altogether. The Oldham Rules, for instance, withdrew unemployment pay from a member incapable of work through illness, and 'friendly' benefits were usually modest lump sums (in Bolton linked to emigration and alternative work). A spinner out of work for a year automatically lost his union card, and if he had exhausted his unemployment entitlement by the time he restarted work he was transferred to a Piecers' Association and had to await the availability of a minder's position. Equally, superannuation was remarkably generous and, in one case in Bolton, payable at as early an age as 52 years (*Cotton Factory Times*, 1.12.1901; Gill, 1905: 71).

'Mutual insurance' was only necessary to the spinners' unions as a mitigation of the ultimate consequences of their own customary labour controls, whereas with the 'traditional' craft unions it constituted an indication of their relative position in society. These provisions reflected the ultimate expression of insular instrumentalism – the outlook, in fact, of the 'modern' twentieth-century worker found in recent sociological theory (Goldthorpe, 1968–9).

The structure of trade unionism in the textile industry was, by the turn of the century, extraordinarily polarised. One hundred and forty-eight unions organised 271,124 members, but no less than 19 per cent of these were in the Amalgamated Association of Operative Cotton Spinners. This Association at that time included 96 per cent of the mule-spinners in Lancashire (1909 LXXX: 24), and with a membership of 50,349 (including piecers) it was nearly three times larger than the next largest, the Burnley and District Weavers, Winders and Beamers. By the standards of the time, its branch sizes were huge, averaging 839 members, and clearly, therefore, including at least three mills. The branches demonstrated the combination of centralism and localism, since it is clear that the real basis of activity was the shop-club. Yet at the 'top', as the Webbs noted, the Amalgamation was run as a 'fully-equipped democratic state of the modern form' with a leadership elected for their technical ability by a delegate meeting of only 100; it was a 'permanent civil service' (1902: 40–41). This was not at odds with localist, *de facto*, 'primitive' organisation, but was completely symbiotic with it in the context of an exclusive, occupationally aristocratic, trade activity.

The bedrock of the Amalgamation was not its well publicised leaders with their examinations, offices and political influence, but the increasing number of local full-timers employed by the provinces, whose power lay with their unique knowledge of the labyrinth of customs, rates and practices particular to their areas. J.T. Fielding, secretary of the Bolton Spinners in the 1880s, was fond of announcing that he alone understood the complexities of the Bolton List with all its constantly changing mill circumstances (Thorpe, 1969: 259). At Province level, also, there was a combination of localist and centralised features in industrial relations: a constitutional form based on the Province with considerable power and autonomy, yet having a structure of collective bargaining governed from the 'centre'. Such a system was formalised by the Brooklands Agreement but had been in existence since the 1870s (Webbs, 1920: 195–7). It contrasts strikingly with that of the engineers who had a centralised constitution, but local bargaining governed by no central plan or executive (Jeffries, 1945: 159).

Of course, the geographical concentration of both employers and the employed facilitated large-scale collective bargaining, but similar conditions in the typographical and shoe-making industries did not have the same effect (Musson, 1954: 201–24; Fox, 1958: 130–40). Whilst the ambivalent organisational position of the spinners produced a stalemate in industrial relations – any systematic attempt to raise their wages inevitably provoked systematic resistance from the employers – the employers unlike, for example, the coal owners, had high fixed costs which constrained their industrial tactics. The federalist structure of the Amalgamation made it particularly organisationally unsuitable for general confrontations – in addition to the technocratic characters of its leaders and their political conservatism. Yet the fundamental basis of the wage contract remained the complex regional lists, rather than 'standard minimum'. In short, different pressures upon employer and employee, and not the character of their relationship, produced the same desire for collective bargaining over the procedure for dealing with breakdown in the local determination of the wage/effort relation.

The spinners' occupational history mirrors the evolution of piece-work in the industrial system. But in embracing this form of payment they were unable to construct the traditional craft defences against the 'chiselling' of prices. The stability of their position depended solely on their role as organisers and supervisors of the labour process – if they earned less they had less incentive to ensure the continuity of production. The entry and exit of labour to and from their *grade* were their concern, not the problems of the trade as a whole. This insular conservatism also led them to seek industrial peace agreed 'at the top' which allowed them to maintain their distance from both the employer above and the subordinate workers below.

6 The Significance of the Incentive Principle

From the three examples discussed, it can be seen that there was no simple linear development of one form of the wage contract commensurate with the growth of capitalism. In fact the growth of capitalism, and the technical structure of work has been subordinate to the creation and reinforcement of a medium of authority and a nexus of control. In terms of the discussion in chapter one, it can be concluded that capitalism contains not a rationalising, but a perpetuating force: universal is its ubiquity. Having only teleological purpose, capitalism as an *economic* system can only be defined as 'arational'; as a *political* system, however, it is thoroughly consistent.

In industries susceptible to improvements in productivity which result from increases in the organic composition of capital – engineering and cotton spinning are examples – technical changes depended upon the structuring of the work force to the machine and upon the elimination of restrictive practices, both in the shop and at the level of labour recruitment. Marx has shown clearly how the contradictory and halting emergence of what he called 'machino-facture' from the social and industrial structure of the first 50 years of the Industrial Revolution retained many of the elements of 'manufacturing' authority relations. In 'machino-facture', 'The worker has been appropriated by the process; but the process has been previously adapted to the worker' (Marx, 1976: 501).

However, in the technologically evolving sectors this was soon superseded. The 'subjective' division of labour was overthrown by the 'objective' structuring of the work process to the needs of efficient authority. In turn this could only occur when the revolutionary technological basis of the process was freed from the limitations of reliance upon skill. Only when the initiative for the further de-skilling of labour within a branch of industry became monopolised by the capitalist and his control of knowledge, could craft control be completely eliminated.

Large scale industry therefore had to take over the machine itself, its own characteristic instrument of production, and to produce machines by means of machines. It was not until it did this that it could create for itself an adequate technical foundation, and stand on its own feet.

(ibid.,: 506)

In industries where, historically, wages formed a declining share of the unit cost of production, and where vestiges of craft control existed side by side with the genesis of machine production, payment by results became the transitory method of structuring the work force. Thus the employer was able to tie the most capital-intensive sectors of production to that form of wage-relation most easily susceptible to the intensification of labour. The gradation of the labour force into those whose effort is assumed to increase with incentive, and those whose wage remains fixed, provides a reflection, important ideologically, within the wage structure, of those who have learnt, and those who are only learning, the 'rules of the game'. In this respect the differential of, particularly, the cotton spinner, can be viewed as a reward for becoming an agent of the incentive principle within the work force, rather than representing a reward for any realisation of extra surplus value.

Piecework would seem to be a direct contradiction to trade unionism since it removes the deciding factor in the wage received by the worker to each individual, rather than to a collectivity. However, it was the specific conditions of British industrial development which, generally, did not allow this to occur. The lack of overseas competition allowed both the cotton and engineering industries to meander through the last half of the century without systematically making the transition to machine production. In neither case did technological improvements penetrate sufficiently to allow standardisation of the work process, and it was in the complex resultant situation that the foundation of the piecemaster system lay.

Where the structuring of wages to effort remained negotiable, and therefore each production process in part unique, the division of labour remained to a degree subjective. How this operated within each industry was in turn largely related to labour traditions and the degree of task dilution. In the engineering industry it can be argued that the comparative lack of a supervisory caste, and the hostility (rather than reverence) felt towards them, were products on the one hand, of the widespread acceptance of a piecework ideology in the larger shops and, on the other, of the lack of a material basis for such a system in the smaller specialised sectors. Marx pointed out that the reduction of the capital/labour relation to the wage contract was the foundation of the illusion that capitalist society was a system of freely negotiating individuals. The piece-wage, therefore, whether inside or outside the factory system, represents an extension of this 'illusion' to the individual worker or group (1976: 683–6; 692–4).

In this fact lies the essential contradiction between piecework and craft traditions. For, in engineering, the latter did not simply obstruct the rationalisation of the wage relation within each factory, but also interfered with flexible recruitment and structuring of labour into that branch of industry. That this conflict took the form of a war of attrition was the result of the dearth of capital re-equipment at the end of the railway building mania in the 1860s: increasingly, the engineering industry became concerned with maintenance and repair (Jeffries, 1945: 199).

It is also important to recall the doggedness of local non-recognition of piecework in the engineering shops and the relationship of this attitude to the 'density' of trade-union affiliation. To the ASE as a craft union, which was *also* exclusive (as opposed to simply an exclusive one), such shibboleths were materially important for the survival of a certain *form* of association. The ideological legacy of the millwright had not been erased by the formal subsumption of labour to capital in engineering; it continued into the twentieth century. The struggle against it had to be localised (given the formal defeat of 1851–2), but this merely served to reinforce the actual organisational strengths of the ASE, strengths which were manifest in the 'informal' side of a union's bargaining which never surfaces into written history.

In the development of the mining industry there was a close relation between the increase in capital and the decline of sub-contracting in its original sense. As Pollard says,

. . . it survived into the factory age, to become, if not a method of management, at least a method of avoiding management.

(1968: 52)

However, whilst the sub-contractor declined as a minor partner within the enterprise, the natural system of the work group in the industry ensured the maintenance of a similar grade in the hierarchical structure in many cases, albeit with the uniform status of wage labourer. One consequence of the low mechanisation of the coal-getting process was the retention, by hewers, of control over the pace and intensity of labour. Thus, precisely at periods when the motivation of the capitalist to mechanise was high (that is when demand was buoyant), so also was the ability of the work force to resist the necessary reorganisation strong. The North East hewer whose status remained high was best able either to resist the progress of change or to adapt it to his own advantage. As Marx indicated, the inability of the capitalist to 'capture' the whole of the production cycle for the machine hindered the free development of production. This was of course not entirely a result of technical difficulties inherent in the process. By 1913, whereas only eight per cent of British coal was mechanically conveyed from the face, the figure for the USA was 72 per cent. An undoubted reason for this widespread low mechanisation was the multiplicity of concerns with a tradition of fierce local competition, but even more important was the functional role of traditional labour hierarchies in controlling a potentially explosive 'unsocialised' work force.

This goes a long way to explaining the favourable attitude of the miners towards piecework. Whilst the hewer maintained control over the pace of work, his major concern was inevitably to ensure the *price* of the product (in the checkweighman system). In turn, paying piece wages rather than increasing the intensity of labour at the face, was the only way the employer could attempt to regulate effort. Herein lay the basis for the system of sliding scales where the sole concern was to link effort to the market price. With the demise of the sliding scale the incentive principle was no longer regulated by an 'external' factor (the market), but by the management whose essential task became the matching of output to market fluctuations. In attempting to achieve this a Derbyshire colliery owner complained to the 1892 Commission that, 'The percentage of absenteeism rises whenever the wages improve' (1892 XXXIV: 39). The 1919 Commission also drew attention to this, which was, it said, particularly prevalent in Durham (1919 XIII: 42).

The impossibility of complete managerial supervision and the non-existence of any 'internal' work-group hierarchy suitable to the construction of a role of 'pacesetter', was, as the Webbs understood in 1897, the fundamental basis of the mineworkers' insistence on piece-rates (1920: 290). The discipline and pacing of the work process remained a function of the individual effort, and, as long as this was the case, the 'control' of effort remained with the workers themselves. In such circumstances the 'socialising' of the work force to increase effort in response to wage incentives was bound to be slower than when the pace of work was governed by machine production. The introduction of the longwall system, to capitalise on better methods of transportation from the face to the shaft, basically did not change the position:

the average standard of job control remained very high, but now it was exercised by a team of hewers, advancing shoulder to shoulder against the face, rather than by lonely pairs of marras

(Douglass, 1977: 250)

The cavilling system is a further indication of the miners' realisation of the importance of effort autonomy. The randomisation and rotation of working places ensured that some of the uncertainty of piecework rebounded back on management: every three or six months, whether trade was good or bad, seam prices had to be negotiated. In other areas, particularly those under a sliding scale, the relationship between prices and union power acted as a further disincentive to capital investment and the rational exploitation of resources (Jevons, 1915: 290).

The vast increase in the supply of labour in the last two decades of the century in South Wales undoubtedly aided the rapid rise of a 'minimum wage' movement in that area (*ibid.*: 286; Page Arnot, 1967). With the ending of sliding scale agreements, wages were consequently determined solely by bargaining between employer and employed, without taking account of the vicissitudes of market forces, and it is interesting to note the emergence of complex and lengthy piece-rate tables similar to those of the spinners.

The wages of each individual hewer are often composed of many items and subject to many deductions that clerical work in calculating the wages for payment must occupy several days.

(Jevons, 1915: 344)

For the employer to retain some control over the relationship of wages to effort required, cost accounting had to be introduced, and, with it, the expansion of supervisory and technical staff. In particular, the allowance made for 'dead work' (removing stone, securing the face, and so on) was under constant pressure:

The custom was adopted by one after another of the bigger companies of keeping detailed cost accounts of each district of a mine, and thus putting different overmen and undermanagers in competition for the lowest costs on dead work. Success meant a substantial cash prize . . .

(*ibid.*: 528)

In this way trade depressions, whilst not automatically reducing wages, still remained periods of intensive conflict over rates and tonnages. The situation was to remain thus whilst wages constituted 60 per cent of production costs.

In engineering, Sidney Webb argued (in a series of lectures delivered to works managers in 1916–17) that it was really the arrival of piece-work and bonus systems which demanded the presence of supervisors, time sheets, and so on. But this argument confused cause and effect; it was the conditions which allowed the atomisation of tasks that also broke down the 'internal' control of the work group. Although Webb was correct in linking the two elements, his basic message was that the role of the works manager was to devise and implement a piecework system amenable to collective bargaining, by which 'the innate industrial Toryism that is characteristic of the manual worker will be overcome' (1917: 107). J.A. Hobson was, however, nearer the mark with his perceptive comment that 'the consideration of incentives involves the question of industrial control' (1922: 6).

In the first half of the nineteenth century 'quality control' was undoubtedly in the hands of the skilled workers, and was crystallised through the apprentice system. At the Labour Commission it was, however, said, that the *all round* skilled man, 'The old millwright, the most useful class of man almost that existed, has almost absolutely disappeared' (1893, XXXII: 337). A crucial factor in this development was the decline in the importance of the pattern shop: as design and technique were separated, less initiative remained with the workshop.

Nothing in the recent history of engineering is more illustrative of the changes which are taking place than the removal of practically the whole of the design of the product to be manufactured in the shop, that is, from the men who are doing the actual physical work on the material . . .

(*Engineering*, February 1907: 173)

The precursor of individual piecework was the piecemaster system, whereby a leading hand contracted with the firm for a job and paid his group according to the improvements that could be made on the original price. This system was prevalent in the period from 1860 to 1880 particularly in the larger shops, such as railway sheds, castings and forges. The ASE checkmated it by introducing a rule which stipulated that the 'excess' or premium on each job was to be shared in proportion to the established differentials of pay. The rule was enforced by fines at branch level (1888 XXI: 530). W. Glennie of the ASE confidently asserted that attempts to restore personal motivation in work (lost because of specialisation) through the taskmaster, 'whose duty is to flog the men up to the highest pitch', were simply evaded for the men knew their work, and their own capabilities to pursue it (1893 XXXII: 178).

Certainly the size of the firm and the complexity of product do seem to have been determinants of the degree of specialisation and thus the form of the payment system. At the turn of the century, W.F. Watson's chequered career through a variety of firms led him to experience the extremes of scientific efficiency and casual traditionalism (1935: *passim*). Where the union did not exist the piecemaster was an effective agent of the employer, operating in a manner similar to that of the 'poundage' system in the weaving sheds (Schloss, 1907: 167). Such a person could earn £10–12 a week in 1900, and Watson, along with his fellow non-union underhands, received his pay at the local pub, some of whom inevitably fell into debt with this man and received credit (with his permission) at certain shops.

The control of work, once the element of skill was declining, no longer corresponded to the hierarchy of experience, or simply to 'respect', within the work force. The transition to repetitive task-work, involving as it did the weakening of internal group norms, as a consequence also removed the ladder of promotion from within the group itself: in this case from apprentice to leading hand. To be sure, the latter was still a servant of the employer and an agent of his instructions, but his *modus operandi* in order to achieve discipline was different from that of the externally trained and appointed supervisor (A. Williams, 1915: 75–8).

Pacesetters and Pacemakers

As *pacesetters* in the labour process the spinner and hewer had, for different reasons, a common commitment to payment by results. The former saw it as an 'automatic' defence against over-work: as long as prices remained stable, faster machinery would mean some financial benefit for them without a trade struggle. For the hewer, on the other hand, who saw himself as a producer of a specified amount of coal, piecework was an *extension* of his autonomy. In 1917 the MFGB passed a conference resolution in favour of abolishing piecework. However, a vigorous minority, led by the Durham Miners insisted that its abolition would mean much more irksome supervision: 'you would probably see a "doggy" or a deputy in every stall to see that the men are working their hardest,' claimed a Northumberland delegate (MFGB, 1917: 208). In short, the spinner (whose total subservience to capital was obvious) saw in piecework the opportunity both to collectively deal with, and to respond to, his objective position; while the hewer viewed it as a confirmation of his individual freedom.

Although the spinners and hewers were widely separated in situation, their pacesetters role demanded a common strategy towards payment by results and collective bargaining – namely, the consolidation of prices into a formal agreement at a national or county trade level (either as a 'list' or a 'scale'). Such a policy required a particular organisational structure: *representatives* were necessary to establish and monitor its running. Industrial relations, in both industries, thus tended towards long periods of calm, interrupted by centrally-led, stage-managed disputes.

In their attitude towards subordinate workers, spinners and hewers were different. The spinners *organisationally* isolated their piecers into separate surrogate 'unions'. The hewers, however, recruited the 'underclass' of haulage and surface workers, but where this latter group had a particular corporate unity (such as in Durham), a *de facto* isolation took place through the monopoly of trade-union positions, and thereby policy. This apparently 'universalistic' approach can be seen as covert exclusionism, since only by recruitment could the non-face workers be stewarded.

The engineer, however, was a *pacemaker*: his rhythm of work was not governed by the need to set the pace for the rest of the factory (like spinners), nor seen as an extension of his fundamental autonomy (like miners). As a craft-worker, the material roots of his exclusive activity were 'inside' the trade, and not a response to the 'external' pressures of capitalist socio-economic organisation on his position. This governed his response to the incentive principle and thereby the organisational structure of his union. Opposition to piecework formed the bedrock of local branch activity, as part of the struggle to control the labour market and thus obtain the 'craftsman's due'. The cornerstone of this policy, the local shop vigilantes, reported infringements to the branch, who then approached the employer. This procedure meant that the Society was structured as a federation (whose branches each had widely differing estimates of the craft rate) despite its famous centralised 'New Model' constitutional form. As a consequence, until the piecework system became generalised (the formal transition occurring rather neatly in the period of the post-1897 lock-out reorganisation) the *delegate* remained the central organising principal of the Society's activity. The piecework system established in real terms the dominance of the central Executive; its numbers were increased, whilst some of the customary powers of the district committtees were removed. This process was symbolised by the signing, in 1902, of the 'Carlisle Agreement': a formal statute between the ASE national leaders and the majority of employers. The residual power of localism was by no means overcome by this pact, and underlay the survival of the 'pacemaker ideology/localist organisational structure' relation.

Pacesetters and pacemakers both had (albeit with differing ideological results) the ability to control the 'external' vagaries of the labour market and the 'internal' power of the employer by occupational self-discipline. This form conflictual collaboration between capital and labour was fertile ground for the emergence of a symbolic mutual ideology: concern for the 'margin' (spinners), the 'state of trade' (engineers), and 'supply and demand' (miners). The creation of a common trade jargon served to reinforce the separation of *representatives* from workers' organisations, since the former shared a common language and understanding of the intricacies of collective bargaining rituals with employers' functionaries. Workers' *delegates*, on the other hand, still inhabited the cultural and social world of the rank and file, and because of this relative continuity they often acted as the bearers of custom and tradition.

Pacesetter and pacemakers are in essence different types of social closure, empirically resting on very differing foundations. But viewed as modes of occupational action their common goal is clear – the exclusion of both management and subordinate workers from an area of organisational territory. This was a *collective* exclusion involving the maintenance of group and union solidarity: a type of 'cultural capital' successfully passed on to the next generation of privileged workers.

In this discussion of work experience wage incentives have fallen into three basic types: firstly, a haphazard, ill-defined, lump-sum payment following a task or working period, and often associated with sub-contraction; second, a specific extra amount per unit completed, but not standardised throughout the industry, and typically, *both* employers and workers try to 'play' the system to their advantage; finally, scientific piecework, where the inducement is an arithmetic calculation usually related to complex regional or national bargaining procedures, and conflict tends to result from the *enforcement* of one interpretation of the agreement. The adoption of each type appears to have been determined by a need to mediate efficient authority, and from this perspective the 'survival' of more primitive forms is quite consistent with the capitalist system.

The role of piecework has been characterised here as an 'ideological discipliner', for it is one of the ways in which 'rational' working-class action created internal differentiation of labour, which was distinct from the divisive effects of the labour process. The involvement in the mediation of authority, as with the spinners, was one obvious example, but the fragmentation of collective working-class consciousness by the exposure to incentives was much more subtle and widespread (Melling, 1980). In a sense this is more significant than technological stratification, because, in time, it becomes a vehicle for the *active* participation of workers in their own subjection. The more the authority of the capitalist is sub-contracted to the 'front line' of the enterprise, the less it is likely to be perceived as authority (Nichols and Beynon, 1977). In fighting for its interests on the terms established by incentive systems, labour sub-divided itself into atomised strata, facilitating the de-skilling of work and the attendant redistribution of power. Utilisation of the existing capital/labour relations to sell their labour power more effectively, both mobilised the workers into unity over immediate goals, and created relations of supremacy and subordination within their own ranks.

This process is far more profound than that implied by the concept of 'economism': it is not simply the reduction of struggle to the economic terrain, but the restructuring of the labour movement within suitable sectoralist boundaries (crystallised by their own organisations). The relations of supremacy and subordination that this engendered hastened the formation of national corporate unions, and, in the wider community, caused further sub-divisions along racial, sexual, ethnic and regional lines.

7 Summary and conclusions

This discussion began by interpreting Marx's understanding of class as a form of *activity*, albeit limited by the social structure which it has in the past created. As such, all forms of enquiry into the meaning of class for the historical protagonists are necessarily oblique and one-dimensional. In order to have 'history' at all, human beings have to be able to live: 'the first historical act is thus the production of the means to satisfy these needs' but, in producing this, a new 'need' is created, and, in this way, individuals 'daily remake their own life' (Marx. 1970a: 48–9).

The historian can, thus, outline the fundamental or 'abstract' conditions of the emergence of class society – the 'dichotomous model' of the *Communist Manifesto*. This is an indispensable first step, but only such; it leads, correctly, to the framework of considering the working class as a *productive* force, discovered in the process of production, and all other classes as refractions of this. But if 'class' is only formed in action, it is obvious that this is not limited to 'action' at the productive level; there are also the levels of property and juridical relations, of political superstructure (the state) and of ideological forms (Lefebvre, 1972: 104–122). Finally, there is the specific *application* of these forms to a particular historical event, their combination and inter-relation being determined by the object of study, and not by the enquirer.

In this case, the 'object of study' is work experience, and the 'peculiarity' of English development for this purpose is the fact that the emergence of occupational interests pre-figured the creation of the working class itself. Therefore, following Marx's method, it is necessary to modify this method, that is, to construct a theory of class formation concurrent with the actual struggle for immediate goals by sectional interests. In other words, a 'dichotomous' theory of class *action*.

To remain entirely faithful to the original premises of this dicussion, 'peculiarities' at levels other than those affecting the working class should have been considered, since class consciousness is forged *in* the struggle *between* classes, not by the activity of one class. The boundaries of such a task would, however, have been: an analysis of the legacy of two parties of the ruling class, the Tories and the Liberals, and the latter's attempts to restore its shrinking electoral base amongst the working class; the geographical and political localism of the major unions in coal and cotton, and the potential for a reformist electoral and industrial symbiosis of interests; the consequences for the social composition of the bourgeoisie of the relative lack of inter-penetration between finance and industrial capital; and, finally, biographical and ethnographic studies of the careers of trade-union and Labour Party leaders *at a local level*, in the early years of the labour movement.

In Marx the 'other half' of this equation appears as the decline of the polarisation thesis. The implications of this have been examined in the light of the labour aristocracy theory, the account of which, whilst critical, assumes that it puts the right questions to history. It has been concluded that the industrial *élite* are an uneven layer of variegated character, and thus *have an equally non-uniform ideological impact upon the working class*. Put in this theoretical framework, 'social closure' could help to activate this argument into historical enquiry, that is, direct attention to the internal manufacturing relationships of capitalism.

As regards politics, generalisations have to be made with particular caution. Within the mining industry there were clear historical and geographical differences, to which the organisation of work contributed. Durham was the initiator of 'Lib-Lab' electoral arrangements after the 1885 Third Reform Act, a pattern which changed little during the next 20 years (Gregory, 1968: 67). John Wilson's unopposed reign over the mid-Durham constituency from 1886 to 1910 was the public manifestation of a political alliance that was built on the loyalties of the active hewer and checkweighman in the DMA lodges. The bedrock of this relationship was not, in fact, the occasional election, but through the increasing role of miners in county and parish councils, only a very few of which were not Liberal-backed (Marshall, 1967: 133–5). So it was that in South Wales, with its less defined internal hierarchy of work but equally concentrated mining vote, the break with Liberalism was both earlier and more complete. Whereas the Labour *Party* in Durham never developed anything like as strongly as its vote would suggest, in South Wales there occurred a clear ideological and organisational rupture with the Liberals, and the concomitant development of various socialist and syndicalist groupings (Woodhouse, 1970: 10).

The opportunist political strategy of the spinners, which involved support of both Liberal and Conservative MPs (especially the latter), was justified by their trade paper, since 'cotton operatives have done a great deal by judiciously squeezing the present MPs representing the manufacturing districts' (*Cotton Factory Times*, 27.6.1890). Local interests determined party affiliation: Lancashire spinners had historic links with the Tories since the first Factory Acts, and because of their stronger line on opening Indian and Oriental markets for textiles. By 1903 the United Textile Factory Workers' Association had joined the Labour Representation Committee, although a strong case has been made for this representing as much a *Liberal* incursion into emerging Labourism as a break with past political loyalties (Clarke, 1971: 396–8).

Socialist influence amongst the engineers coincided almost exactly with the advancing threat of technology to their hard-won advantages – London and Newcastle were centres of the 'new mood', both former strongholds of the all-round skilled man (Clegg, 1964: 297). The ASE had members in the famous Taff Vale unofficial dispute, after which punitive legislation followed, and their secretary warned the membership of the need both for a more centralised union, and for, in future, the putting of 'politics in its proper place, Parliament not industry' (ASE *Journal*, May 1902).

The Hierarchy of Work
A recurring issue of work experience in the early labour movement was certainty in the wage contract. The three occupations considered each struggled to resolve this to their advantage, but each produced a different combination. If the collective bargaining system is defined as a continuum of 'centre' to 'periphery', and the wage contract's perimeters as 'certainty' and 'uncertainty', a diagrammatic comparison of the resolution of these tensions within each occupation can be evolved (Table 7 i). The miners strove to maximise uncertainty at the periphery, the spinners to minimise it: yet as pacesetters they did so by a common form of social action – the 'corporate inclusion' of subordinate workers. The engineers, on the other hand, in order to retain

TABLE 7 i

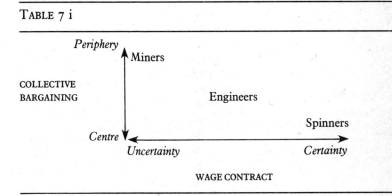

autonomy *and* to resist incentives, did so by the 'independent exclusion' of the semi-skilled and the absorption of de-skilled tasks into their territory. As each occupation fought to optimise this relationship it fulfilled a functional purpose in the social relations of the firm: the maintenance of labour discipline. As a result, the construction of an internal working-class hierarchy based, not on the creation of surplus value, but on the creation of the work ethic, can be identified.

TABLE 7 ii

Form of exploitation	Objective	Objective and subjective
Absolute surplus value	1780s – 1820s (1)	1820s – 1850s (2)
Relative surplus value	1850s – 1890s (3)	1890s —— (4)

In chapter 1, Table 1 represented how this process was related to the exploitative relationship between, on the one side capital and labour and, on the other the form of control of the factors of production. Table 7 ii repeats the pattern, applying it to an occupational example, the engineers. The stages can be roughly described as follows:

1   The transition from all-round wood- and iron-worker to iron-worker based in workshops, making textile machinery. Standard day wage.
2   Use of the first machine tools, but pre-slide rest, factory production, for example, the railways. Bonus payments added to day wage.
3   Slide rest but not the turret lathe in use, pattern-making becoming specialised. Factories specialising in textiles, armaments, and so on. Piecework, but with locally enforced minimums.
4   Consolidation of the fitter/turner division based on long runs of machine production. Amalgamations of engineering firms into corporate bodies. Scientific piecework.

The dates are used to illustrate the predominant form of work experience in a period; they do not imply a linear progression. In fact, we know a consequence of the stage (4) factories was the re-birth of firms in the ancillary trades, more typical of stages (1) and (2) (Allen, 1929).

It may be objected that to argue that the main body of engineers were not under 'real subsumption' until the 1890s is to suggest that the industry was not capitalist until then – clearly a ludicrous suggestion. However, as Marx noted, 'real subsumption' is a social, not a technical, relationship, and is thus defined by 'the direct *subordination of the labour process to capital*, irrespective of the state of its technological development' (1976: 1034). 'Non-capitalist' forms of labour management are not simply possible, but absolutely essential, to the capitalist mode of production. Just as the modern rational capitalism of the West is based on the suppression of similar forms in the Third World, so the diverse manifestations of capitalist hegemony in nineteenth-century industry were created by the logic of perpetuation. This argument follows on from the earlier definition given here of the labour process as a refraction of labour discipline: the relative autonomy of the craft engineer survived only so long as it was functional to the 'real subsumption' of labour to capital. The employers' direct control was, for a time, traded in return for industrial harmony, and although this was organisationally irrational within the individual firm, it was logical to the continuity and conquest of capital.

Finally, the position of the three occupational groups can be summarised in the context of the contention that what constituted a 'craft' union was the strategy of social action it adopted to defend its interests. This contention allows a much more flexible application of the 'labour aristocracy' theory. Here the 'craft union' is defined by its *action* rather than, sociologically, by the fact that it is a 'leading' layer of an organisational situation.

The engineers' opposition to piecework was formally broken in the 1851–2 lock-out, but the lack of basic technological change and the men's own rearguard struggle delayed the standardisation process upon which payment by results depends. Hence, the division of labour remained subjective, and the subsumption of labour only 'formal' until well into the 1890s. In other words, to the degree that the engineers were able to resolve the contradictions of the capitalist work process, in this period, at the expense of the employers *and* the unskilled. Their tactics – restriction, apprenticeship, district rates, retention of a day wage – consolidated a superior status which had a material basis in the realisation of surplus value. The ASE was not simply an agent of discipline and authority of the capitalist, but had a separate pre-capitalist tradition of craft customs and identity. This tradition was 'universalised' throughout all the working situations of its members, as principles which were applied under local guidance, but which would be a common language to all the Society.

By way of contrast, there was no such thing as 'the miners'. Their working situation had similarities – wages as two-thirds of costs, uncertainty of the effort/remuneration relationship, punitive discipline – but the response to this varied widely. The North Eastern hewer by his own activity constructed a complex of procedures and committees designed both to reinforce his position and to entangle the employer in a web of formality. Elsewhere, where no one layer emerged as clearly, trade unionism was at once potentially more militant (in the long term) whilst numerically weaker. This cannot be entirely accounted for by geological differences. Much more important were the social origins of capital and labour, the structure of the market for the product; and the different ways in which these combined. The control over the instruments of production opened up the possibility of considerable autonomy and job control as a response to the fundamentally random character of the work process, but the extent to which this was exploited was a matter decided by conflict between the contending parties.

The spinners present a contrast to both the engineers and the miners. Theirs was a factory occupation, but its claim to any skill was gone by the 1840s. Yet they were a leading layer of about 25 per cent of the spinning work force. Apart from a considerable differential, their superiority was embodied in: (1) the right to hire and fire assistants; (2) the payment of a time-wage to these; (3) their role as supervisors and pacesetters. They were undoubtedly under 'real subsumption' of labour to capital, yet for reasons of *control* and *discipline* this was transformed into an internal organisational bargaining strength for them. Thus their position was not based on the realisation of extra surplus value as contributors to the work process, but as agents of 'machino-facture' – a plebeian layer in the hierarchy of industrial authority.

This study of work experience reveals in microcosm the working out of the processes described abstractly in chapter one. It demonstrates the importance of the study of the structure of work in understanding corporate responses to capitalist industrialisation, which are the real 'material basis' of reformism in the working class. It has shown that ideology is formed in the struggle *between* social groups or classes, always as a two-way process, and, consequently, the subservient class or group is actively involved in its own submissive role. Finally, it has suggested that a crucial link in the chain of social control is the form of the work process, and thus investigation of it the location of fundamental social change.

Sources

Parliamentary Papers Consulted

1824 V, 'Select Committee on Artisans and Manchinery'.

1825 V, 'Select Committee on the Export of Machinery and Artisans'.

1830 VIII, 'Select Committee on the Coal Trade'.

1834 X, 'Select Committee to examine the Petitions . . . of Handloom Weavers'.

1834 XV, 'Select Committee on Mills and Factories'.

1838 LX (First Report), 'Select Committee to investigate the Condition of the Handloom Weavers'.

1838 VIII, 'Select Committee into the Combinations of Workmen'.

1840 XXII, 'Select Committee on the Act for the Regulation of Mills and Factories'.

1841 VII, 'Select Committee on the Laws affecting the Export of Machinery and Artisans'.

1842 XXXV, 'Letters from Poor Law Guardians concerning the use of apprentice children in Mines from the Workhouse'.

1844 XXXV, 'Correspondence of the Poor Law Unions of Halifax, Oldham and Preston, with the Poor Law Commission'.

1844 XVI, 'Report of the Inspector of Mines'.

1856 XIII, 'Select Committee to enquire into the expediency of establishing equitable tribunals . . . between Masters and Men'.

1857 LVII, 'Report of the Committee into the advance of Machinery used in Textiles'.

1866 XIV, 'Select Committee on the Regulation and Inspection of Mines'.

1867-8 XXXII, 'Royal Commission on the Trade Unions: Reports, minutes and evidence'.

1871 LXII, 'Return of Factories and Other Manufacturing Establishments'.

1873 X, 'Select Committee to enquire into the present Dearness and Scarcity of Coal'.

1873 LV, 'Report on the Proposed Changes in Hours and Ages of Employees in Textile Factories'.

1886 XXI (Vol. I), XXII (Vol. II), XXIII (Vol. III), 'Royal Commission on the Depression of Trade'.

1887 XIV, 'Select Committee on the Manufacturing Departments of the Army'.

1888 XXI (Second Report), 'Select Committee on the Sweating System'.

1892-4, 'Reports, Evidence and Minutes of the Royal Commission on Labour' (Volume numbers given in the text).

1894 CVII, 'Report of Strikes and Lock-Outs in 1892'.

1895-6 IX (Third Report), 'Select Committee on the Distress caused from Want of Employment'.

1895 LXXX, 'Report on Gain-sharing and other systems of Bonus of Production'.

1903 XVI (First Report), 'Royal Commission on the Coal Supplies'.

1907 XIV, 'Royal Commission on the Coal Trade'.
1907 XIV; 1908 XX, 'Miners Eight Hour Day Committee: Reports One and Two'.
1909 LXXX (First Report), 'Report on the Hours of Labour in the Textile Industry'.
1911 LXXVII (Part Four), 'Census of Production, 1907'.
1918 XIII, 'Report on the Engineering Trades after the War'.
1919 XIII (Third Report), 'Royal Commission on the Coal Industry'.
1925 XIV, 'Royal Commission on the Coal Industry'.
Factory Inspectorate Reports for years ending:
    1842 XXII; 1857 XIV; 1862 LV; 1866 CV; 1869 XIV; 1878 XVI.
Census of Population:
    1851 XIV, 'The Ages and Occupations of the People'.
    1893–4 CVI, 'The Ages and Occupations of the People'.
Mining Statistics:
    1842 XVII, 'Report of the Commissioner of Mines'.
    1846 XV, 'Report of the Commissioner of Mines'.
    1852 XXI, 'Report of the Commissioner of Mines'.
    1869 XIV, 'Report of the Commissioner of Mines'.
    1878–9 XVIII, 'Report of the Commissioner of Mines'.
    1884 XVI, 'Report of the Inspector of Mines'.
    1888 LXXXIV, 'Mining Statistics'.
    1897 CVII, 'Mining Statistics'.
    1889 LXXXIV, 'Summary of Mining Statistics for 1888'.
    1899 CVII, 'Mines and Quarries, General Statistics, 1897'.
Government Publications:
    Statistical Abstracts, Volumes 31–33, HMSO.

Trade Union Journals

Amalgamated Society of Engineers, *Journal* and Monthly *Record*.
Bolton Spinners' Providence, Annual *Report*.
Durham Miners' Association, Monthly *Circular*.
Miners' Federation of Great Britain, *Conference Resolutions and Minutes*.
Oldham Spinners' Annual *Report*.

Trade Union Publications

Durham Miners' Association (1893), 'Joint Committee Decisions from 1875 to 1892'.
Durham Miners' Association (1930), 'Acts of Parliament and County and National Agreement'.
Joint District Board for the District of Derbyshire (1912) *Proceedings*.
Joint District Board for the District of Durham (1912) and (1913) *Proceedings*.
Joint District Board for the District of South Wales (1912) *Proceedings*.
Miners' Federation of Great Britain (1898, 1912, 1913, 1917) 'Report of Conference Resolutions and Policy'.
South Wales Miners' Federation (1902) Rules.

Newspapers

Durham Chronicle, Durham Record Office.
The Economist, Liverpool University.
Newcastle Daily Chronicle, Durham Record Office.
Newcastle Weekly Chronicle, Durham Record Office.
Northern Mail, Durham Record Office.
Shields Daily Gazette, Durham Record Office.
Shields Daily News, Durham Record Office.
The Socialist, microfilm.
The Times, microfilm.

Trade papers

Colliery Guardian, Newcastle University.
The Engineer, Newcastle University.
Engineering, Newcastle University.
The Ironmonger, Manchester University.

Manuscripts and papers

Private paper

Allen, Robert, MSS. Held by Mr. J. Clarke, Newcastle Polytechnic.
The Webb Collection, London School of Economics.

Durham Record Office (DRO)

Boldon Colliery Minutes MS.
Fairbridge MS.
Kell MS.
Londonderry Collection.
National Coal Board (NCB) Collection.
Pallister MS.

Books, Theses, Pamphlets

(Place of publication London unless otherwise stated)

Allen, G.C. (1929), *The Industrial Development of Birmingham and the Black Country*.

Allen, V.L. (1962), 'A methodological critique of the Webbs as Trade Union Historians', *Labour History Society Bulletin*, No. 4 (Spring).

Anderson, P. (1964), 'Origins of the Present Crisis', *New Left Review*, No. 23.

Anthony, P.D. (1977), *The Ideology of Work*.

Page Arnot, R., (1949) *The Miners*, Vol. I; (1953), Vol. II.

Page Arnot, R., (1955), *A History of Scottish Miners*.

Page Arnot, R., (1967), *The South Wales Miners 1898–1914*.

Ashton, T.S., (1977), *An Economic History of England: the Eighteenth Century*.

Ashton, T.S. (1928), 'Coalminers of the 18th Century', *Economic History Review*.

Ashworth, H. (1842), 'Statisitics of the Present Trade in Bolton', *Statistical Journal*, Vol. V.

Ashworth, H. (1837), 'An Inquiry into the Origins, Progress and Results of the Strike by Operative Spinners of Preston from October 1836 to February 1837', *British Association*.

Ashworth, W. (1972), *An Economic History of England 1870–1939*.

Aspinall, A., (1949), *The Early English Trade Unions*.

Baines, H. (1835), *The History of Cotton Manufacture in Great Britain*, Reprinted 1966.

Banks, T. (1888), *A Short Sketch of the Cotton Trade of Preston for the last 67 Years*, Oldham.

Barr J. and Stroud, R., (1902), *Notes on the Premium-Bonus System of Wage Earning*, Manchester.

Bauman, Z. (1972), *Between Class and Elite: the evolution of the British Labour Movement*.

Beynon, H. (1973), *Working for Ford*.

Blackburn, R. (1976), 'Marx and Politics', *New Left Review*, No. 97, June-July.

Blaug, M. (1960–61), 'The productivity of capital in the Lancashire Cotton Industry', *Economic History Review*, 2nd Series, XIII.

Blewett, N. (1972), *The Peers, the Parties and the People*.

Booth, C. (1903), *Life and Labour of London People*, Vols. I-V.

Braverman, H. (1974), *Labour and Monopoly Capitalism*, New York.

British Association (1887), *On the Regulation of Wages by Means of Lists in the Cotton Industry*, Manchester.

Stonewell-Brown, H. (1887), *An Autobiography*.

Bulman, H.F. and Redmayne, R.A. (1951), *Colliery Management and Practice*.

Burgess, K. (1969), 'Technological Change and the 1852 Lock-out in the British Engineering Industry', *International Review of Social History*, XIV.

Burgess, K. (1970), 'The Influence of Technical Change on the Social Attitudes and Trade Union policies of workers in the British Engineering Industry 1760–1866', Ph.D. Leeds.

Burgess, K. (1972), 'Trade Union Policy and the 1852 Lock-out in the Engineering Industry', *International Review of Social History*, XVII.

Burgess, K. (1975), *The Origins of British Industrial Relations*.

Burgess, K. (1980), *The Challenge of Labour*.

Burnett, J. (ed.) (1977), *Useful Toil*.

Burt, T. (1924), *From Pitman to Privy Councillor*.

Burton, F.G. (1899), *Commercial Management in Engineering Works*, Manchester.

Butterworth, E. (1847/1848), *Historical Sketches of Oldham*. Reprinted 1856, Manchester.

Catling, H. (1970), *The Spinning Jenny*, Newton Abbot.

Chadwick, D. (1859), 'The State of Trade in the Engineering Centres of Lancashire and the North', *Journal of the Royal Statistical Society*, XXIII.

Chadwick, D. (1860), 'Rates of Wages in Manchester and Salford 1839–1859', *Journal of the Royal Statistical Society*, XXIII.

Challinor, R. (1967–8), 'Alexander MacDonald and the Miners', *CPGB History Pamphlet* No. 48 (Winter).

Chaplin, S. (1978), 'Durham Mining Villages' in M. Bulmer (ed.), *Mining and Social Change*.

Chapman, S.D. (1972), *The Cotton Industry in the Industrial Revolution*.

Chapman, S.J. (1899), 'The Regulation of Wages by Lists in the Spinning Industry', *Economic Journal*, IX.

Chapman, S.J. (1904), *The Lancashire Cotton Industry*, Manchester.

Chapman, S.J. (1910), 'Some Policies of the Cotton Spinners', *Economic Journal*, X.

Chapman, S.J. and Ashton T.S. (1913–1914), 'The sizes of Businesses, mainly in the Textile Industries', *Journal of the Royal Statistical Society*, LXXVII.

Chapman, S.J. and Marquis, F.J. (1911–1912), 'The recruitment of the employing classes from the ranks of wage-earners in the cotton industry', *Journal of the Royal Statistical Society*, LXXV.

Charity Organisation Society (1908), 'Report of Special Committee on Unskilled Labour. Available at the LSE, London.

Church, R.A. (1975), *The Great Victorian Boom 1850–73*.

Clapham, J.H. (1915), 'Some Factory Statistics of 1815–16', *Economic Journal*, XXV.

Clapham, J.H. *An Economic History of Modern Britain* (1926), Vol. I; (1932), Vol. II; (1938), Vol. III.

Clarke, P.F. (1971), *Lancashire and the New Liberalism*, Cambridge.

Clegg, H., et al, (1964), A History of British Trade Unions since 1889, Vol. 1.

Clements, R.V. (1961), 'British Trade Unions and Popular Political Economy 1850–75', *Economic History Review*, 2nd Series, XIV.

Collier, F. (1930–33), 'An early factory community', *Economic History Review*, Vol. II.

Cole, G.D.H. (1928), *History of the Labour Party*.

Cole, G.D.H. (1962), 'Some Notes on British Trade Unionism in the Third Quarter of the Nineteenth Century' in E.M. Carus-Wilson (ed.), *Essays in Economic History*, Vol. III.

Cole, G.D.H. and Filson, A.W. (1967), *British Working Class Movements: Select Documents 1789–1875*.

Conference of Socialist Economists (1977), *Capital and Class*, Vol. 1, No. 1.

Cooper, T., (1873), *The Life of Thomas Cooper, written by Himself*, Leeds.

Copeland, M. (1917), *The Cotton Manufacturing Industry in Britain and the USA*. Reprinted, New York, 1966.

Croucher, R. (1971), 'The Amalgamated Society and Local Autonomy 1898–1914', M.A., Warwick.

Gascoyne-Dalziel, W. (ed.) (1895), *Records of Several Coal Owners' Associations of Monmouthshire and South Wales from 1864 to 1895*, Cardiff.

Day, C. (1927), *The Distribution of Industrial Occupations in Britain 1841–61*, New Haven, USA.

Deane, P. (1968), 'New Estimates of the GNP of the UK 1830–1914', *Review of Income and Wealth*, XIV.

Deane, P. and Cole, W.A. (1969), *British Economic Growth 1688–1959*, Cambridge.

Dobb, M. (1972), *Studies in the Development of Capitalism*.

Douglass, D. (1977), 'The Durham Pitman' in R. Samuel (ed.), *Miners, Quarrymen and Saltworkers*.

Duggett, M.J. (1977), 'Sliding Scales in the South Wales and Durham Coalfields 1875–1900', Ph.D., University of Wales.

Edwards, E. (1961), *The South Wales Miners 1893–1914*, Cardiff.

Edwards, N. (1938), *The History of the South Wales Miners*.

Elbaum, B. *et al.* (1979), 'Symposium: The labour process, market structure and Marxist theory', *Cambridge Journal of Economics*, No. 3.

Ellison, T. (1886), *The Cotton Trade of Great Britain*.

Engels, F. (1950), *The Condition of the English Working Class in 1844*.

Fairbairn, Sir W. (1861), *Useful Information for Engineers*, 2nd Series.

Fairbairn, Sir W. (1908), 'His Autobiography' in S. Smiles, *Lives of Engineers*.

Farnie, D. (1953), 'The English Cotton Industry 1850–1896', M.A. Thesis, Manchester.

Fay, C.R. (1920), *Life and Labour in Nineteenth Century Britain*, Cambridge.

Felkin, H. (1867), *A History of Wrought Hosiery and Lace Machinery*.

Fernbach, D. (ed.) (1973), *Surveys from Exile: Marx's Political Writings*, Vol. II.

Fitton, R.S. and Wadsworth, A.P. (1958), *The Strutts and the Arkwrights*, Manchester.

Floud, R. (1976), *History of the Machine Tool Industry*.

Fong, H.D. (1930), *The Rise of the Factory System*, Tienstin.

Foster, J. (1976), 'British Imperialism and the Labour Aristocracy' in J. Skelley (ed.), *The General Strike 1926*.

Foster, J. (1977), *Class Struggle and the Industrial Revolution*.

Fox, A. (1958), *A History of the National Union of Boot and Shoe Operatives 1874–1957*, Oxford University Press.

Sharpe-France, R. (1953), 'The diary of John Ward of Clitheroe, Weaver 1860–4', *Transactions of the Lancashire and Cheshire Antiquarian Society*, Vol. 105.

Fraser, R. (ed) (1969), *Work*, Vols. 1 and 2.

Von Schulze-Gaevernitz, G. (1895), *The Cotton Trade in England and on the Continent*.

Von Schulze-Gaevernitz, G. (1893), *Social Peace*.

Galloway, R. (1898), *Annals of the Coalmining Trade*, Vol. I. Reprinted 1969.

Galloway, R. (1904), *Annals of the Coalmining Trade*, Vol. II. Reprinted 1971.

Galton, F. (1895), *Workers on their Industries*.

Gibson, F.A. (1922), *The Coal Industry in the United Kingdom*, Cardiff.

Giddens, A. (1973), *The Class Structure of the Advanced Societies*.

Gill, A.H. (1905), 'The Cotton Trade in 1905', *Manchester Statistical Society*, February.

Goldthorpe, J.H. (1972), 'Class, Status and Party in Modern Britain', *Archives of European Sociology*, XIII.

Goldthorpe, J.H. *et al.* (1968–69), *The Affluent Worker*, Four Volumes, Cambridge University Press.

Goodrich, C. (1920), *The Frontier of Control*. Reprinted 1975.

Gorz, A. (ed.) (1978), *The Division of Labour*.

Gouldner, A. (1971), *The Coming Crisis of Western Sociology*.

Gramsci, A. (1973), *The Prison Notebooks*.

Gray, R.Q. (1975), *The Labour Aristocracy in Victorian Edinburgh*.

Gregory, R. (1968), *The Miners and British Politics 1906–14*, Cambridge.

Griffen, A.R. (1955), *The Miners of Nottinghamshire*, Notts.

Griffen, A.R. (1967), 'Contract Rules in the Nottingham and Derbyshire Coalfield', *Society for Study of Labour History Bulletin*, No. 15.

Guttsman, W. (1964), *The British Political Elite*.

Habakkuk, H.J. (1962), *American and British Technology in the Nineteenth Century*, Cambridge.

Halevy, E. (1929), *A History of the English People*, Vol. V.

Hall, W.S. (1929), *A History of the Durham Colliery Mechanics Associations 1879–1929*, Durham.

Hammond, J.L. and B. (1919), *The Skilled Labourer*.

Hammond, J.L. and B. (1928), *The Town Labourer*.

Harazsti, M. (1977), *A Worker in a Worker's State*.

Harris, J. (1972), *Unemployment and Politics*.

Harrison, R. (1965) *Before the Socialists: Studies in Labour History 1861–81*.

Hill, S. (1981), *Competition and Control at Work*.

Hinton, J. (1972), *The First Shop Stewards Movement*.

Hobsbawm, E.J. (1970), *Industry and Empire*.

Hobsbawm, E.J. (1976), *Labouring Men*.

Hobson, J.A. (1909), *The Crisis of Liberalism*. Reprinted 1974.

Hobson, J.A. (1922), *Incentives and the New Industrial Order*.

Holbrook Jones, M.R. (1979), 'Work, Industrialisation and Politics: A Study of the Work Experience of Spinners, Coalminers and Engineering Workers, 1850–1914;, Ph.D., Durham.

Howell, G. (1890), *The Conflicts of Capital and Labour*.

Howkins, A. (1977), 'Edwardian Liberalism and Industrial Unrest', *History Workshop*, No. 4.

Hughes, T. (1860), 'An Account of the Engineers in 1852' in *Trade Societies and Strikes*. Reprinted, New York, 1968.

Hunt, R. (1856), 'Our Coal Trade in 1856', *London Statistical Society*.

Imlah, A. (1958), *Economic Element of the Pax Britannica*, Cambridge, Mass., USA.

Iron Trades Employers' Association (1876), 'The Piecework question and its results in Engineering and other shops in the Iron Trades of the Country'. Available at the LSE, London.

Jeffries, J.B. (1938), 'Trends in Business Organisation in Great Britain since 1856', Ph.D., London.

Jeffries, J.B. (1945), *The Story of the Engineers*.

Jeffries, J.B. and M. (1947), 'The wages, hours and trade customs of the skilled engineer in 1861', *Economic History Review* XVII.

Jevons Stanley H. (1915), *The British Coal Trade*.

Jewkes, J. (1933), 'The localisation of the Cotton Industry', *Economic Journal* II.

Jewkes, J. and Gray, E.M. (1935), *Wages and Labour in the Lancashire Cotton Spinning Industry*.

Johnson, T. (1980), 'Work and Power' in G. Esland (ed.), *The Politics of Work and Occupations*, Colchester.

Jones, G.S. (1975), 'England's First Proletariat' *New Left Review*, 90.

Kenwood, A.G. and Lougheed, A.L. (1975), *The Growth of the International Economy 1820–1960*.

Kingsford, P. (1960), *F.W. Lanchester: a Biography*.

LRD (Labour Research Department) (1922), *Capitalism in the Engineering Industry*.

Landes, D. (1977) *The Unbound Prometheus: Technological Change from 1750 to the Present*, Cambridge.

Lawson, J. (1933), *A Man's Life*.

Lee, C.H. (1968), 'Market Organisation and Policy in the Cotton Trade: McConnel and Kennedy', *Business History*, X.

Lee, C.H. (1972), *A Cotton Enterprise 1795–1840 – A history of McConnel and Kennedy, fine cotton spinners*, Manchester.

Lefebvre, H. (1972), *The Sociology of Marx*.

Leifchild, J.R. (1860), *Our coal and our coal pits*. Reprinted 1967.

Lenin, V.I. (1964), *Collected Works*, Vol. 21, Moscow.

Lenin, V.I. (1969), *British Labour and British Imperialism*.

Lenin, V.I. (1970), *Selected Works*, Vol. I, Moscow.

Levine, A.L. (1954), 'Industrial Change and its effect on Labour 1900–1914', Ph.D., London.

Levy, H. (1927), *Monopolies, Cartels and Trusts in British Industry*. Reprinted 1968.

Lupton, T. (1963), *On the Shop Floor*.

MacDonald, J.R. (1912), *Socialism and Government*.

McKibbon, R. (1974), *Evolution of the Labour Party, 1906–14*.

McLaine, W. (1939), 'The Engineers Union Book I: the Millwrights and the "Old Mechancis" ', Ph.D., London.

Macrosty, H.W. (1907), *Industrial Combination in Britain*.

Mandel, E. (1977), 'The Leninist theory of Organisation' in R. Blackburn (ed.) *Revolution and Class Struggle*.

Marglin, S. (1974), 'What do the Bosses do? Origins and Function of Hierarchy in Capitalist Production', *Review of Radical Economics*, Vol. 6, No. 2, Summer.

Marshall, C. (1976), 'Levels of Industrial Militancy and Political Radicalisation of the Durham Miners', M.A., Durham.

Marx, K. (1968), *Selected Works*, Vol. II.

Marx, K. (1970), *The Communist Manifesto*, Moscow.

Marx, K. (1970a), *The German Ideology*.

Marx, K. *Capital* (1976), Vol. I; (1978), Vol. II; (1972), Vol. III; Moscow.

Marx, K. and Engels, F. (1971), *Articles on Britain*, Moscow.

Mathias, P. (1976), *The First Industrial Nation*.

Mawdsley, J. (1885), 'Labour and Capital' in *Report of the Industrial Remuneration Conference*. Reprinted 1968.

Meacham, S. (1977), *A Life Apart: the English Working Class 1890–1914*.

Melling, J. (1980), 'Non-Commissioned Officers: British Employers and their supervisory workers, 1880–1920', *Social History*.

Miliband, R. (1973), *Parliamentary Socialism*.

Wright Mills, C. (1959), *The Sociological Imagination*.

The Miners Next Step (1911), Cardiff. Reprinted, London, 1973.

Mitchell, K. (1964), 'The Coming of the Railway to the UK', *Journal of Economic History*, XXIV.

Morris, J.H. and Williams, L.J. (1957–8), 'The Discharge Note in the South Wales Coal Industry 1841–1898', *Economic History Review*, 2nd Series X.

Morris, J.H. and Williams, L.J. (1958), *The South Wales Coal Industry*, Cardiff.

Munro, J. (1891), 'The probable effects of an Eight Hour Day on the production and the wages of coal', *Economic Journal*.

Murphy, J.T. (1917), *The Workers' Committee*, Sheffield. Reprinted, London, 1972.

Murphy, J.T. (1941), *New Horizons*.

Musson, A. (1954), *The Typographical Association*, Oxford University Press.

Musson, A. (1972), *British Trade Unions 1800–75*.

Nairn, T. (1966), 'The British Political Elite', *New Left Review*, No. 29.

Nef, J.U. *The Development of the Coal Industry* (1932), Vol. I; (1934), Vol. II.

Neuwirth, A. (1970), 'A Weberian Analysis of the Class Structure,' *British Journal of Sociology* (20) 2, June.

Nichols, T., and Beynon, H. (1977), *Living with Capitalism*.

Parkin, F. (1972) *Class, Inequality and Political Order*.

Parkin, F. (1974), 'Strategies of Social Closure in Class Formation' in F. Parkin (ed.), *The Social Analysis of the Class Structure*.

Parkinson, G. (1912), *True Stories of Durham Pit-life*.

Parks, J. (1975), 'Memories and Recollections', *North East Labour History Society Bulletin*, No. 4.

Pelling, H. (ed.), (1968), *Popular Politics in Late Victorian Society*.

Pelling, H. (1976), *The Origins of the Labour Party*.

Pollard, S. (1964), 'Fixed Capital in the Industrial Revolution in Britain', *Journal of Economic History*, XXIV.

Pollard, S. (1968), *The Genesis of Modern Management*.

Porter, J.H. (1967–8), 'Industrial Peace in the cotton trade 1875–1913', *Yorkshire Bulletin of Economic and Social Research*, 19.

Porter, J.H. (1970), 'Wage Bargaining under Conciliation Agreements, 1860–1914', *Economic History Review*, XXIII.

Poulantzas, N. (1972), *Political Parties and Social Classes*.

Roberts, R. (1976), *A Ragged Schooling*.

Roberts, R. (1978), *The Classic Slum*, Manchester University Press.

Rogers, T. (1866), *A History of Agricultural Prices*, Vol. I.

Rolt, L.T.C. (1965), *Tools for the Job*.

Rolt, L.T.C. (1965), *A Short History of the Machine Tool Industry*, Cambridge, Mass., USA.

Rose, F. (1909), *The Machine Monster: A warning to all skilled workers*.

Rose, M. (1978), *The Quarrybank Mill at Styal, Cheshire*, Wilmslow.

Rowe, J.W.F. (1923), *Wages in the Coal Industry*.

Rowe, J.W.F. (1928), *Wages in the Engineering Industry*.

Rowe, J.W.F. (1928), *Wages in Theory and Practice*.

Roy, D.F. (1952), 'Quota Restriction and goldbricking in a machine shop' *Amercian Journal of Sociology*, 57, March.

Roy, D.F. (1960), 'Banana Time: job satisfaction and informal interaction' *Human Organisation*, 18.

Roy, D.F. (1961), 'Efficiency and "the fix": informal intergroup relations in a piecework machine shop', in S.M. Lipset and N.J. Smelser (eds.), *Sociology: the progress of a decade*, Cambridge, Mass., USA.

Samuel, R. (1977) 'Workshop of the World: Steam power and Hand Technology in Mid-Victorian Britain', *History Workshop*, No.3.

Samuel, R. (ed.) (1981), *People's History and Socialist Theory*.

Sandberg, L. (1974), *Lancashire in Decline*, Cambridge, Mass., USA.

Saul, S.B. (1967), 'The Market and the Development of the Mechanical Engineering Industries in Britain 1860–1914', *Economic History Review*, 2nd Series, XX.

Saul, S.B. (1968), 'The Engineering Industry' in D.H. Aldcroft (ed.), *The Development of British Industry and Foreign Competition, 1875–1914*.

Saul, S.B. (ed.) (1970), *Technological Change: the USA and GB in the Nineteenth Century*.

Saville, J. (1956), 'Sleeping Partners and Limited Liability 1850–6', *Economic History Review*, 2nd Series, VIII.

Saville, J. (1969), 'Primitive accumulation and early industrialisation in Britain', *Socialist Register*.

Saville, J. (1973), 'The Ideology of Labourism' in R. Benewick (ed.), *Knowledge and Belief in Politics*.

Schloss, D. (1907), *Methods of Industrial Remuneration*.

Schorske, C.E. (1970), *German Social Democracy 1880–1914*.

Schumpeter, J. (1939), *Business Cycles*, New York.

Semmel, B. (1960), *Imperialism and Social Reform 1895–1914*.

Shannon, R. (1976), *The Crisis of Imperialism 1865–1914*.

Singer, C. *et al.* (1958), *A History of Technology*, Oxford.

Skelley, J. (ed.) (1976), *The General Strike 1926*.

Smellie, R. (1924), *My Life for Labour*.

Smiles, S. (1883), *James Nasmyth, Engineer: an Autobiography*.

Smiles, S. (1908), *Lives of Engineers*.

Smith, R. (1954), 'A History of the Lancashire Cotton Industry between the years 1873 and 1896', Ph.D., Birmingham.

Snowden, P. (1912), *Syndicalism and Socialism*.

Steeds, W. (1969), *The History of Machine Tools, 1700–1910*, Oxford.

Sweezy, P. (1938), *Monopoly and Competition in the English Coal Trade 1550–1850*, Cambridge, Mass., USA.

Tariff Commission (1909), *Report on the Engineering Trades*, Vol. IV.

Taylor, A.J. (1948–9), 'Concentration and Specialisation in the Lancashire Cotton Industry, 1825–50', *Economic History Review*, 2nd Series, I.

Taylor, A.J. (1960), 'The sub-contract system in the British Coal Industry' in L.S. Pressnell, *Studies in the Industrial Revolution*.

Taylor, A.J. (1961–2), 'Labour Productivity and Technological Innovation in the British Coal Industry, 1850–1914', *Economic History Review*, 2nd Series, XIV.

Taylor, A.J. (1968), 'The Coal Industry' in D.H. Aldcroft, *British Industry and Foreign Competition 1875–1915*.

Taylor, P. (1903), *Autobiography of Peter Taylor*, Paisley.

Terkel, S. (1975), *Working*.

Thompson, E.P. (1967), 'Time, Work-Discipline and Industrial Capitalism', *Past and Present*, No. 38.

Thompson, E.P. (1968), *The Making of the English Working Class*.

Thompson, E.P. (1977), *William Morris*.

Thorpe, (1969), 'Industrial Relations and the social structure: a case study of Bolton cotton mule spinners, 1884–1910', M.Sc., Salford.

Trist, E.A. *et al.* (1963), *Organisational Choice*.

Turner, H.A. (1962), *Trade Union Growth, Structure and Policy: A comparative study of the Cotton Unions*.

Ure, A. (1834), *The Philosophy of the Manufacturers*. Reprinted 1967.

Walters, R. (1975), 'Labour Productivity in the South Wales Steam-Coal Industry, 1870–1914', *Economic History Review*, Vol. XXVIII.

Watson, W.F. (1935), *Machines and Men*.

Webb, S. (1912), *The Story of the Durham Miners*.

Webb, S. (1917), *The Works Manager Today*.

Webb, S. and B. (1920), *Industrial Democracy*.

Webb, S. and B. (1950), *History of Trade Unionism*.

Weber, M. (1929), *General Economic History*.

Weekes, B.C.M. (1970), 'The Amalgamated Society of Engineers 1880–1914: A Study of Trade Union Government, Politics and Industrial Policy', Ph. D., Warwick.

Welbourne, E. (1923), *The Miners of Northumberland and Durham*, Cambridge.

Williams, A. (1915), *Life in a Railway Factory*. Reprinted, Newton Abbot, 1969.

Williams, D.J. (1924), *Capitalist Combination in the Coal Industry*.

Williams, J.E. (1962), *The Derbyshire Miners; a study in Industrial and Social History*.

Williams, R. (1972), 'Base and Superstructure', *New Left Review*, April-May.

Wilson, J. (1907), *A History of the Durham Miners' Association 1870–1904*, Durham.

Wolpe, H. (1970), 'Some Problems of Revolutionary Consciousness', *Socialist Register*.

Wood, G.H. (1901), 'Stationary Wage Rates', *Economic Journal*, June.

Wood, G.H. (1910), *A History of Wages in the Cotton Trade during the Past Hundred Years*.

Wood, G.H. (1910), 'The Cotton Trade over the Past Hundred Years', *Journal of the Royal Statistical Society*, LXXIII, June.

Woodbury, I. (1961), *The History of the Lathe to 1850*, Cambridge, Mass., USA.

Woodhouse, M. (1970), 'Rank and File Movements among the Miners of South Wales 1910–26', D.Phil., Oxford.

Wright, T. (1867), *Some Habits and Customs of the Working Classes*. Reprinted, New York, 1967.

Yates, M.L. (1937), *Wages and Labour Conditions in British Engineering*.

Index